The Politics of International Shipping

The Politics of International Shipping

Conflict and Interaction in a
Transnational Issue-Area
1946-1968

Olav Knudsen
Institute of Political Science,
University of Oslo

Lexington Books
D.C. Heath and Company
Lexington, Massachusetts
Toronto   London

Library of Congress Cataloging in Publication data

Knudsen, Olav.
    The politics of international shipping.

    Originally issued as the author's thesis, University of Denver, 1971.
    Bibliography: p.
    1. Shipping. I. Title.
HE581.K59 1973   387.5'44   72-11506
ISBN 0-669-85290-2

International Standard Book Number: 0-669-85290-2

Library of Congress Catalog Card Number: 72-11506

To Ragnhild

Contents

List of Figures

List of Tables

Preface

The following study seeks to illuminate certain aspects of two rather broad questions. One has to do with the interrelationships between economics and politics in shipping; the other concerns the processes of nonviolent international conflict.

As to the first question, students of shipping economics have often pointed out how acts of national policy affect the international maritime transport market. The approach taken here, on the other hand, is whether and to what extent national shipping policies are functions of economic conditions in international maritime transport, and to what extent they are reflections of patterns of world politics.

The second question has its main relevance in a narrower context: the study of international politics. It implies a view rejecting the focus on "dramatic" conflict—the kind of conflict which touches the very existence and survival of nation-states. Nonviolent, low-intensity conflict is a daily occurrence in intergovernmental affairs, but it appears to be somewhat neglected as a topic of serious study in itself. The present study is intended to remedy some of this neglect by inquiring into some characteristic features of shipping conflict. It must necessarily deal with a set of considerably more restricted and clearly defined problems. Therefore, keeping the broader questions in mind might provide the reader with a sense of direction as he proceeds.

The study is concerned with the political aspects of shipping. The technical and economic aspects of shipping are examined only to the extent that they are found to throw light on the central political questions involved. Nor is the following intended as a complete study of political aspects. Its emphasis on the general rather than the unique must necessarily give nuances a secondary place. To those who look for specific answers to specific questions, therefore, this study may fall short of the ideals. Still, it is hoped that it may both stimulate thinking on shipping in a nontraditional perspective and be of interest to students of international politics in other functional areas.

Acknowledgments

This work was the author's doctoral dissertation for the Graduate School of International Studies, University of Denver. Its completion puts me in overlapping debts of gratitude: to people who stimulated a special way of thinking, to people who conveyed ideas, and to people who provided crucial assistance. My three dissertation advisors, Professors Edward Miles, Maurice A. East, and Bernhard Abrahamsson were especially helpful. I would like to thank them for their thoroughgoing and detailed criticism of the original draft. Their comments played an important part in shaping the final version.

For insight and ideas regarding international shipping, I want especially to thank Rear Admiral John D. Hayes, who took two entire days of his time to discuss a broad range of shipping problems with me in Texas City. In Norway, at perhaps the most difficult stage of my work, I was also fortunate to get incisive criticism from Dina Zinnes (of Indiana University), which has been a valuable corrective.

My thanks for financial assistance go first of all to the Woodrow Wilson National Fellowship Foundation, whose dissertation research grant sustained me during most of my full-time research. The Graduate School of International Studies kindly financed a trip to Texas, and the Institute of Political Science at the University of Oslo allowed me free computer time and assisted in many other ways. Special thanks in this regard to Henry Valen and Ulf Torgersen.

In collecting the data I received kind advice and assistance from Mr. Reinholdt Eriksen of the United Nations Information Service in New York. The patient cooperation of the 34 delegates to UNCTAD's Committee on Shipping, whom I interviewed in 1969, gave me a closer look at the politics of shipping than I would otherwise have had. Both the Norwegian Shipowners' Association and Det Norske Veritas provided data not available elsewhere.

Several tasks could not have been completed without the help of family and friends. Thanks go to Mrs. Elin Grethe Andresen for punching assistance and to Miss Vibeke Knudsen for checking punching errors. My wife Ragnhild also helped with punching and managed to retain her sanity throughout the confusing job of typing the first draft, in addition to working a full day at the office and being a mother and housewife. Mrs. Riborg M.K. Knudsen typed a perfect final version and would not even let a broken right arm keep her from completing the last sixty pages. I am sure neither of them would want to go through it again.

Last, but not least, I owe a special debt of gratitude to Nils Ørvik of the Institute of Political Science (Oslo), who at a crucial moment lent me a spacious and convenient office where I could work undisturbed. I also want to thank him for his cheerful company, and for the many other occasions—ever since we met in 1965—on which he has given me assistance in many ways.

Oslo, September 1972   **Olav Knudsen**

The Politics of International Shipping

1

Introduction

The Significance of International Shipping Services

The 20th century has seen revolutionary changes in the speed, volume, and quality of international communications. A person celebrating his seventieth birthday at the time of this writing will have marveled at the advent of the automobile, the wireless, the telephone, the airplane, the teletype and telephoto, the television, the guided missile, the communications satellite, and flights to the moon. But steamships, to many people, are still steamships, the "pedestrians" in an age of high-speed travel. Today's septuagenarian was probably told in grammar school that he lived in the age of the steamship and might protest vigorously against the suggestion that he still does. Yet that is, in a sense, precisely what is suggested here.

In the international transportation of goods, shipping still holds a commanding position for the world as a whole. In 1969, air freight amounted to only .04 percent of total international freights by volume, after having expanded from 1960 to 1968 by an average annual increase of 25 percent.[1] Land-based transport by road or rail is of major significance only in intra-European trade and in the U.S.-Canada trade. For the rest, world trade is carried on chiefly by ships. According to the UNCTAD Secretariat, "the major mode of transport used in international trade is sea transport in cases where the trading partners are noncontiguous."[2]

A comparison of the growth of world trade and world seaborne trade shows total world trade increasing from 1948 to 1968 by an annual average of slightly less than 6 percent,[3] while the volume of world seaborne trade in the same period increased by 16.3 percent per year.[4] In the postwar period, in other words, the seaborne transportation of goods has expanded more than twice as fast as the volume of world trade as a whole. By comparison, the volume of world railway traffic in the 1948-1968 period increased at an average annual rate of 3.6 percent.[5] On the whole, the expansion of world seaborne trade since 1945 is vastly greater than at any other time in recent history (the highest annual growth rate in volume of seaborne cargoes between 1909 and 1939 was less than 2.5 percent).[6] From a long-term perspective, Charles P. Kindleberger observes: "What the railroad was to do for increased specialization and the development of national markets in England and France, or for transcontinental trade in North America, the development of cheap ocean shipping has done for world trade."[7]

1

Shipping, in short, is as important to world trade as it has ever been. Whether this trend will keep up during the next 50 years or so is open to question, however. In terms of technology, it is theoretically possible that shipping will find its importance considerably reduced by such innovations as pipelines—which may also be used for the movement of certain bulky dry goods such as ores and minerals—and by the continued development of air freight. But in practice, the competitive position of each of these means of transportation will depend on a host of additional factors. International political upheavals, major changes in international trade patterns, and the speed with which innovations are put to use are only a few examples. To attempt prediction on this basis would be somewhat hazardous. All that can be noted with reasonable confidence is that the present predominant position of maritime transport seems to make gradual change more likely than abrupt change. Moreover, the likely *direction* of change would seem to be a decline in the relative, if not the absolute, importance of shipping.

Main Types of International Shipping Services

Numerous criteria may be employed to distinguish between different types of shipping services.[8] Normally, however, these criteria will roughly coincide to yield a few main categories. Here, services will be distinguished by type of freight contract into three main groups, namely *liner services, open market tramping*, and *contractual tramping*. In effect, these categories differ in the kinds of service offered to the customer (shipper), the general types of goods carried, the kinds of market in which freight rates are determined and, to some extent at least, the kinds of ship employed.

Liner services operate on fixed routes by relatively fixed time schedules. A cargo-liner usually has some passenger accommodations, normally for 12 persons, but the emphasis is on freight. Its cargo space is shared by many shippers—if a shipper has a full shipload of cargo, he will not normally use a liner for carriage. Hence, liner cargoes are highly heterogeneous, mostly non-liquid. Specifically, liners may be said to carry two general classes of cargo: (1) manufactured and semi-finished products; (2) other goods that require careful handling and stowing or that are not commonly shipped in bulk form, as for example coffee, fruits, live cattle, vegetables, etc.

Liner freight rates are fixed by the shipowner according to his estimate of "what the traffic will bear." Most liner freight rate determination is done jointly, however, by shipowners associated in liner conferences, which are international cartels organized to restrain cutthroat competition.[9]

A liner is ordinarily a ship of about 5,000-15,000 deadweight tons,[10] adapted to carry a great variety of goods. The modern cargo liner will often have at least three different types of cargo space: (1) refrigerated space for perishable commodities, (2) deep tanks for smaller liquid cargoes, and (3) space for the great assortment of general cargo that usually makes up most of the load.

Open market tramping is undertaken by vessels hired to carry a full load of cargo for one shipper between any two ports. A tramp cargo normally is a homogeneous cargo, i.e., a full load of one specific commodity. Hence, tramp service may already be distinguished from liner service by the absence of fixed routes and time schedules, and by the fact that it usually carries a full load exclusively for one shipper at a time.[11] Tramp cargoes are often of the kind that lend themselves to bulk shipment, that is, without any kind of packaging. Typical examples are grain, coal, metals and scrap, non-ferrous ores, timber, etc. Tramps also frequently carry commodities with unstable trade patterns (e.g., seasonal fluctuations in volume, frequently changing destinations), including such things as sugar, manufactured fertilizers, copra, and cement. (Unpredictable trade patterns, of course, also apply to some of the bulk commodities listed above.)

The term "open market tramping" refers first of all to how the ships are hired and the freight rates determined. Liner operators charge fixed rates for each type of commodity on a unilateral basis, i.e., with no bargaining between shipper and shipowner involved, while rates for tramping in the open market are arrived at through bargaining between representatives (brokers) for shippers and ship-owners respectively—for each voyage to be undertaken (*voyage charter*), for a limited number of *consecutive voyages*, or for a short-term (one year or less) *time charter*. The characteristics of this market are aptly described in a 1968 report of the UNCTAD Secretariate:

The open market embraces the aggregate at any given time of tramp shipowners seeking employment for their vessels and shippers requiring the services of tramp ships for a limited period. The keynote of the open freight market is the quick and easy communication of information. The basis is an international network of shipowners, shipbrokers and charterers closely and continuously linked by telecommunication. Thus, any charterer needing a ship of a certain size and type available at a specific port on or about a specified date can be assured that his needs will be made known to shipowners in all countries which possess merchant fleets. In the reverse direction, by circulating through the same network the positions of his fleet and the cargoes most actively sought by individual vessels the shipowner informs all potential hirers/charterers of the shipping space he can offer, its nature and when and where it will be free and available for service.[12]

The traditional world center of this activity is the Baltic Shipping Exchange in London. Here, bargaining between brokers takes place in ways that in many respects resemble those on the commodity exchanges.[13] Two other major centers exist in New York and Hong Kong, and there is also some activity in West European countries and in the East European socialist countries. The latter use their state freighting organizations for all their external chartering needs. London is still, however, the most important center of activity in the open market.

Freight rates in the open market fluctuate considerably, while liner rates may remain relatively stable over several years.[14] A fact that may reinforce freight rate fluctuation is that more and more bulky commodities are gravitating into the market of negotiated long-term fixtures, leaving a smaller number of commodities for the open market and thereby reducing the probability that the effects of different world market conditions for different commodities will cancel each other out in the open tramping market.[15]

The open market encompasses both dry cargo and oil, although the latter is only a small share of the petroleum transport market. Petroleum carriage is mostly undertaken under long-term negotiated fixtures or by tankers owned by the oil companies themselves.[16] Hence, at least three common types of ships are found in open market tramping: (1) tankers, ranging from 20,000 to 300,000 tons deadweight (most of these in the open market are probably under 100,000 deadweight tons); (2) bulk carriers defined by Lloyd's Register as "a single-decked ship over 400 feet in length with engine room aft,"[17] usually used for heavier dry cargo such as ores and minerals and ranging from about 10,000 to about 150,000 deadweight tons; (3) the conventional tramp, a ship resembling the cargo liner, although usually slower and less elaborately fitted and normally without specialized cargo space such as deep tank or refrigerated space. The conventional tramp is the more common ship in the open market.

Negotiated fixtures or contractual tramping; the essential character of this service is above all that it is a long-term contract between charterer and shipowner covering periods of three to twenty years, as opposed to the short-term time charter of one year or less, typical of the open market. It is the aspect of time, in other words, which makes the difference in terms of the kind of service offered in contractual tramping.

The typical kinds of commodities carried under such contracts are crude and refined petroleum. Oil dominates this market—as, in terms of volume, it dominates the entire business of international seaborne trade. But other goods, such as ores and minerals, have been gaining in importance, especially in the last decade. What makes a commodity suitable for long-term contracts appears to be stable trading patterns and a large volume of trade. Hence, it does not necessarily have to be a product like oil or iron ore, although these remain typical and dominate the business. The Economist Intelligence Unit singles out seven commodity types, in addition to oil, "for which long-term freighting is basically attractive":[18]

Iron, manganese and chrome ores:	worldwide
Bauxite:	worldwide
Coals:	certain routes only
Phosphate rock:	basically worldwide
Sulfur (dry):	basically worldwide
Sulfur (molten):	basically worldwide
Lumber:	one route only

As the list indicates, these are all raw materials widely used in industry. Hence, a long-term charter offers the industry concerned a secure flow of the raw materials it uses regularly and in large quantities. Often, shipper and consignee will be the same firm.

As implied in the term "negotiated fixtures," freight rates are determined through bargaining, but what distinguishes negotiated fixtures is that the bargaining takes place directly between shipowner and charterer, and not through shipping exchanges like "the Baltic." The bargaining situation may often be less formal, and the importance of personal acquaintances and contacts considerably greater than in the open market.[19] Another common trait of negotiated fixtures is that they are often concluded before the ship itself has been built, as Mr. Høegh's story shows.[20] In such cases, construction is frequently financed by a loan on the security of the charter party.

The ships typically engaged in contractual tramping are highly specialized vessels of large size, including most of the larger tankers of from 100,000 to over 300,000 tons deadweight, and the upper limit is steadily being pushed higher. Many of the world's biggest shipyards are now theoretically able to expand their facilities to build tankers of up to one million deadweight tons.

The large specialized bulk carriers are not found in the same size ranges as tankers. Today they normally stay below 200,000 deadweight tons. These ships are in general considerably more complicated and expensive to build than tankers. Some of them (e.g., liquid methane tankers, molten sulfur tankers) are so specialized that they can only carry the type of commodity for which they were designed and must sail in ballast on the back-haul.[21]

For the chartering company there is always the alternative of acquiring its own ships to take care of such long-term transport needs, and this is what many of them do. The word "alternative" may, however, not be altogether appropriate in this connection, since many of them have found that to rely entirely on their own ships may have disastrous consequences, as when production cut-backs greatly reduce the need for shipping tonnage.[22] Hence, the more common pattern has been that developed by the oil companies, whereby their own tankers cover 30 to 40 percent of their needs, tankers owned by independent shipowners and chartered on long-term contracts another 30 to 40 percent, with the remaining shipping being secured through open-market contracts on a voyage basis or for a limited number of consecutive voyages.[23] The world tanker ownership pattern seems a reflection of this: about 40 percent of the world's commercial tankers are owned by the oil companies and their subsidiaries, with independent shipowners and governments owning the rest.[24] In 1962, over 500 million of the 615 million tons of oil shipped internationally was carried by integrated fleets or tankers on long-term charter.[25] Other industries appear to be following the oil companies' example. They can thus guard themselves against over-tonnage and at the same time have established procedures for securing additional tonnage if their shipping requirements were to rise abruptly.

The Questions: Focus of the Study

The activities just described have traditionally been studied by economists, and in the perspective of economics. Governmental policies are typically analyzed for their effects on the micro- and macroeconomics of shipping. This has a rather important consequence: the activities of governments are viewed as significant forces shaping economic processes, whereas the ways in which economic processes contribute to shaping state policy are either neglected or treated in a simplistic fashion.

This author sees a challenge in reversing the questions normally asked in this area: What are the determinants of governmental behavior in shipping affairs—the economics of world maritime trade, world political conditions, or both? Under what economic or political conditions are governments more likely to engage in conflict concerning maritime transport?

Notes

1. Egil Budde, "From Dakotas to Jumbo Jets in the Service of Air Freight," NORWEGIAN SHIPPING NEWS, no. 10 c, 1970, p. 295.

2. UNCTAD, Trade and Development Board, Committee on Shipping, INTERNATIONAL TRANSOCEANIC TRANSPORT AND ECONOMIC DEVELOPMENT. REPORT BY THE UNCTAD SECRETARIAT IN CON-NEXION WITH ECONOMIC AND SOCIAL COUNCIL RESOLUTION 1372 (XLV) CONCERNING ACTIVITIES OF THE UNITED NATIONS SYSTEM OF ORGANIZATIONS IN THE TRANSPORT FIELD (TD/B/C.4/46), January 6, 1969, p. 3.

3. UN quantum index of world trade, UNITED NATIONS STATISTICAL YEARBOOK, 1969 (New York: Statistical Office of the United Nations, Department of Economic and Social Affairs, 1970).

4. Percentage computed from UN figures on world seaborne trade quoted in Kaare Petersen, "Trends in Shipping 1945-1970," NORWEGIAN SHIPPING NEWS, no. 10 c, 1970, p. 29.

5. UN STATISTICAL YEARBOOK, 1969.

6. Arnljot Strømme Svendsen, "Trends in World Seaborne Trade," NOR-WEGIAN SHIPPING NEWS, June 1967.

7. Charles P. Kindleberger, FOREIGN TRADE AND THE NATIONAL ECONOMY(New Haven: Yale University Press, 1962), p. 24.

8. S.G. Sturmey, BRITISH SHIPPING AND WORLD COMPETITION (London: The Athlone Press, 1962), pp. 235 ff.

9. Liner conferences are more fully discussed below, Chapter 3.

10. Sturmey warns against using deadweight tons in measuring the carrying capacity of liners, op. cit., p. 8. Deadweight tonnage indicates the "actual weight

in tons of cargo and fuel that a ship can carry when down to her load line." This is an appropriate measure for ships carrying a homogeneous cargo in full load, but is misleading in the case of liners which carry heterogeneous cargoes, often including bulky but lightweight commodities such as cotton. Deadweight is nevertheless used here, for three reasons:

a) What is desired is to convey a general notion of size, not an accurate estimate of cargo space (this would require a *net tonnage* measurement or a *cubic feet* measurement).

b) Tankers, bulk carriers, and traditional type tramps are conventionally measured in deadweight tons. Doing the same for liners enhances comparability, it is hoped, for the reader unfamiliar with matters of shipping.

c) Sturmey's rule is frequently violated by writers on the subject, such as the contributors to *Norwegian Shipping News* and similar publications.

11. Note that tramps may also be part-chartered. Homogeneous cargoes seem to be the rule, however.

12. UNCTAD, Trade and Development Board, Committee on Shipping, FREIGHT MARKETS AND THE LEVEL AND STRUCTURE OF FREIGHT RATES. REPORT BY THE UNCTAD SECRETARIAT (TD/B/C. 4/38), December 16, 1968, p. 32.

13. A report by the Economist Intelligence Unit for UNCTAD has a good brief discussion on the day-to-day functioning of "the Baltic." See OCEAN SHIPPING AND FREIGHT RATES, AND DEVELOPING COUNTRIES (E/CONF. 46/27), January 28, 1964, pp. 2 ff.

14. Ibid., p. 167.

15. The Economist Intelligence Unit suggests this point in its report, op. cit., p. 199.

16. Also known as *proprietary* or *industrial* carriers, or *integrated fleets*.

17. Report by the UNCTAD Secretariat, December 16, 1968, op. cit., p. 26.

18. Economist Intelligence Unit Report, op. cit., p. 26.

19. As an example, though possibly not totally representative, of how such contracts can come about, Norwegian shipowner Leif Høegh relates the story of his "golf negotiations" in the early 1930s: "Mr. Chambers of the Pan-American Petroleum Co. [later absorbed by Standard Oil] did not have time to stay long in Norway, but the main features were drawn up sufficiently to allow me to contact the shipbuilders. It turned out, however, that Mr. Chambers was also vacationing in Europe at the same time he was to negotiate these charter parties. This created no problems, as he was a passionate golfer, and I traveled around with him in Germany, Northern Ireland and England playing golf, which also was my favorite pastime. We talked charter-party clauses in the evenings. He was a total abstainer, in which I joined him without much sacrifice. In the course of about one week we set up some very satisfactory charter parties, and the signing

took place in London." The following year Høegh and Chambers arranged two more charter parties in the same manner, "this time in Northern Ireland, where he was from originally, and where the golf courses were first rate." These contracts were for a duration of ten years.

Leif Høegh, I SKIPSFARTENS TJENESTE (Oslo: Gyldendal, 1970), pp. 19-20.

20. Sturmey, op. cit., p. 184.
21. Economist Intelligence Unit, op. cit., p. 30.
22. For a good example, see ibid, pp. 26-27.
23. Sturmey, op. cit., p. 75 and p. 262; Economist Intelligence Unit, op. cit., p. 21.
24. Sturmey, op. cit., p. 262.
25. Economist Intelligence Unit, op. cit., p. 199.

2

Theoretical Foundations

The Problem

The argument that the political aspects of international shipping are worthy of attention implies a conception of international politics broader than the traditional one. Clearly, shipping is not a field for violence between governments. But to argue that shipping and other international problem-areas removed from questions of war and peace or "high politics" are therefore irrelevant to the student of international politics, would be to overlook a rather crucial point. Merely because interaction is rarely, if ever, violent over shipping matters does not mean that conflict is absent. It is the phenomenon of nonviolent international conflict, therefore, that is the main point of this study.

The idea that international politics as a field of study should also encompass less spectacular processes and events is not new. It counters a traditional emphasis, yet has been promoted by several scholars in the field for some time. The definition of international politics employed by Sprout and Sprout does open the way for such an interpretation: they regard the field as covering "all transactions and relationships between or among organized independent national communities which exhibit some significant conflict of purpose or interest, regardless of whether military or non-military forms of action are involved."[1]

More explicit arguments began appearing in the early 1960s. Thus, in a 1963 article, Rosenau criticizes users of the systems concept in international politics for overlooking nonviolent systemic processes and confining their analysis to processes involving the use and restraint of force.[2] To put the phenomena of crises and wars in a more comprehensive cognitive perspective, therefore, we need to study the less dramatic interaction between states. Only then can the really dramatic events of international relations reveal the extent of their significance as part of a larger whole.

Even more to the point in the present context is McClelland's statement: "We need to know what is normal in the short run in the relations of all pairs of nations."[3] This is the central concern of the present study. Its focus is on how governments go about managing that sector of their foreign affairs not directly linked to national survival. That is, it centers on the kind of everyday business consuming most of the time and much of the resources of almost any foreign ministry.

Some important work is now being done in this area, notably three rather large projects in the United States: the pioneering World Event/Interaction

Survey (WEIS) undertaken by the University of Southern California under the direction of Charles A. McClelland,[4] the COPDAB project at the University of North Carolina led by Edward Azar,[5] and the CREON project at Ohio State University headed by Charles F. Hermann.[6]

The present study attempts to take up a problem pointed out by McClelland on an earlier occasion. In a discussion of interaction studies, McClelland suggests that international interaction be viewed as two basic global networks. One encompasses "administered and routinized activities," being "substantially self-organizing and self-directing."[7] The other network "is created and perpetuated by out-of-the ordinary, non-routine sequences of occurrences that require active intervention and guidance by national governments."[8] The important subject for further investigation is, according to McClelland, the nature of the linkages between the two networks,[9] of the relationships between predominantly non-governmental international *trans*actions and governmental *inter*action. (Operational criteria for this distinction will be introduced below.)

If the normal, everyday activities of shipping as such are regarded as a network of transactions of the former kind, and if the interaction between governments over shipping matters corresponds to the second type, then it can be said that a vital concern of this study is precisely the nature of the relationships between these two networks.[10]

To summarize: At this stage, two major points for investigation can be identified: (1) What factors determine the frequency of conflict in shipping? (2) In what ways are government interaction and non-governmental transactions related in the field of shipping?

A Focus on Events and Interaction

With the central concerns of the study thus defined, it should be clear that the following efforts will concentrate heavily on the processes of intergovernmental interaction in shipping.

Interaction analysis has become increasingly popular in the field in recent years. Yet, to single this out as a specific mode of analysis requires drawing some fine distinctions. Many approaches to the study of international politics center on the interaction of states without falling clearly under the heading of "interaction analysis" as the term is used here.[11] The present usage of the term connotes no single easily definable set of operations. Still, what is common to all varieties of interaction analysis is that the events and relations between governments are broken down into specific, discrete items of *action*—each of which is classified according to some relevant typology and then "reassembled" into aggregates by criteria of the typology. After this, the different versions branch off in different directions according to the specific interests of the researchers. The key is therefore the emphasis on governmental actions, and the practice of including all kinds of actions, no matter how insignificant they might appear in other research contexts.

The important consideration in interaction analysis is not whether and to what extent an action is significant or momentous, but what kind of an action it is, who the actor is, against (or toward) whom the action is directed, and so forth. The reason for this inclusiveness is that interaction analysis works with aggregates of action, which obscures the matter of "what actually happens" in the historical sense and illuminates the abstract and theoretical aspects of action in the international system. An early example of interaction analysis is afforded by Robert Bales (1950),[12] who develops a framework for recording interaction in small groups by direct observation. Actions are broken down into 12 types relevant to Bales' specific theoretical interest:

The key assumption which provides this articulation [i.e., the set of categories] is the notion that all organized and at least partially cooperative systems of human interaction, from the smallest to the most inclusive, and of whatever concrete variety, may be approached for scientific analysis by abstracting from the events which go on within them in such a way as to relate the consequences of these events to a set of concepts formulating what are hypothetically called 'functional problems of interaction systems.'

For purposes of the present set of categories we postulate six interlocking functional problems which are logically applicable to any concrete type of interaction system. . . . these are in one-word terms: problems of orientation, evaluation, control, decision, tension-management, and integration. These terms are all related to a hypothetical conception of an overarching problem-solving sequence of interaction between two or more persons.[13]

The first part of the quotation is in itself an excellent exposition of the rationale behind interaction analysis.

In the field of international politics, two American scholars have made particularly useful early contributions in applying interaction analysis to specific research problems: Chadwick Alger and Charles McClelland.

Chadwick Alger has employed interaction analysis in several studies of United Nations organs.[14] Inspired by anthropological field methods, he has based his analysis on directly observed interaction among delegates in the setting of formal meetings.

Alger's work is remarkable for its efficient utilization of rather basic interaction characteristics. Being unable to establish what is actually happening in the interaction he observes, Alger selects for analysis the variables of *direction* (who interacts with whom), *time* of occurrence, *duration*, and *frequency*. Two of these—direction and frequency—are important variables also in this project. But in addition we want to know more about the *content* of interaction, about the kinds of actions exchanged between the participants, and it is here that McClelland's work is of special interest.

Charles McClelland makes the non-organizational setting his focus. Through a series of articles over at least a decade, McClelland has developed his own special brand of interaction analysis in an intellectual process that led to the start of the World Event/Interaction Survey several years ago. His point of departure in this work seems to have been the phenomenon of acute international crisis.[15] In the article so entitled, which appeared in *World Politics* in 1961, McClelland took issue with Quincy Wright's suggestion that a succession of crises between two states will increase the probability of eventual war. According to McClelland, the world after World War II, at any rate, is different, and a succession of crises is more likely to be a learning process for the participants, so that the probability of war will decrease—rather than increase—with each succeeding crisis. The learning process, he suggests, will take the form of increasingly routinized crisis management. Handling crises becomes "bureaucratized," in other words.

With this general hypothesis in mind, McClelland and his associates set out to study a series of international crises, in particular the several Berlin crises and Formosa straits crises. They adopt interaction analysis as the way of getting at the crisis phenomenon, dissecting these critical events into their smallest components—the stream of discrete actions flowing from the participants. In one of the earlier studies, published in 1964,[16] McClelland limits his attention to non-diplomatic, physical acts or "moves," and arranges these in chronological order on charts to establish the characteristic ordered sequences of action—or "structures of action"—of two crises: the Berlin crisis of 1948-49 and the Quemoy crisis of 1958.

A central idea here was the proposition that "action talks"—emphasized earlier by Schelling[17] in conjunction with the notion of "tacit bargaining." In examining how the two crises moved through successive stages, McClelland found that while the Berlin crisis was "demobilized" through direct verbal negotiation, the Quemoy crisis tapered off by a process which fit Schelling's description of tacit bargaining very well.

Although the actions in this study were classified as one of three types,[18] the emphasis was on the "structure" of the interaction *sequences*—a sort of stylized diplomatic history. McClelland's final study of interaction processes in the Berlin setting contrasts rather sharply with this emphasis in its heavy reliance on quantitative techniques and in its focus on a more elaborate typology of actions.[19]

Here, the earlier hypothesis on the routinization of crisis management is taken up again, along with an interest in an empirically derived definition of "crisis threshold." At the core of the analysis stands an 18-item typology of international governmental actions, differentiated according to the "essence" of the action. Some examples with synonyms: "accede" (agree, give consent, praise etc.), "propose" (suggest, urge), "accuse" (censure, indict, "score"), "force" (seize, arrest, take territory), "attack" (exert force violently against resistance of the other, employ military or police force against active resistance, etc.).[20] Actions were coded from *The New York Times*.

McClelland's typology of actions in the Berlin study formed the skeleton of the vastly more elaborate WEIS classification system (reproduced below). The latter consists of 63 discrete types of actions, grouped into 22 broader clusters, ultimately reducible to the following five major classes: cooperative action, verbal cooperation, participation,[21] verbal conflict, and conflict action.

The WEIS project itself is first of all a huge mapping operation. Beginning in 1966, it records the totality of "event/interactions" reported in *the New York Times* for the world as a whole. The items included are restricted to actions by carefully defined official decisionmakers acting in behalf of their governments.

The main strengths of this analytical apparatus are first, its comprehensiveness, and second, its flexibility in application. All conceivable actions by one government *vis-à-vis* another (or directed at the external environment) will fit into (ideally) one and only one specific action category. A well worked-out coding guide accompanies the classification system, which has been revised in the light of experience time and time again since 1959 until the categories were "frozen" as they were in 1967.[22]

The WEIS category system will be used here to operationalize the general concept of intergovernmental interaction, as well as the more specific concept of international conflict. The various types of conflict actions in the WEIS typology constitute the basic elements of such conflicts as considered here. (Table 2-1, p. 14).

It would be wrong, however, to leave the reader with the impression that the WEIS system rules the field of events studies alone. Other events projects, such as those headed by Azar and Hermann (respectively) were also initiated in the late 1960s. The earlier and probably the larger of the two, Azar's Conflict and Peace Data Bank (COPDAB), grew out of a previous project at Stanford headed by Robert North. Azar uses (op. cit. passim) a more flexible procedure for coding events than does McClelland, so that COPDAB events may be recoded, if desired, into most other events classification systems. COPDAB covers events in the Western hemisphere, the Middle East, Western Europe, and parts of Southeast Asia for the period since 1945.

Hermann's category scheme (pp. 15ff) is more elaborate and specifically geared to a number of research questions in the comparative study of foreign policy. The CREON project covers a worldwide sample of 30 nations for the 1958-1968 period.

"Issue-Area" as an Analytical Perspective

By now, the central questions of the study have been raised in general form, a mode of analysis and a specific technique have been selected as a potentially useful road towards answering those questions. It still remains, however, to put it all into a coherent theoretical framework. As a first important step, it will be

Table 2-1
Weis Coding System as of 5/67[2][3]

Cooperative Action	011 Surrender, submit
	012 Yield position; retreat
	013 Retract statement
	061 Express regret; apologize
	062 Give state invitation
	063 Grant asylum
	064 Grant privilege
	065 Suspend sanctions
	066 Return persons or property
	071 Extend economic aid
	072 Military assistance
	073 Other assistance
Verbal Cooperation	041 Praise, hail
	042 Give verbal support
	051 Promise policy support
	052 Promise material support
	053 Promise other future support
	054 Assure; reassure
	081 Make substantive agreement
	082 Agree to future action
	091 Request information
	092 Request policy assistance
	093 Request material assistance
	094 Request action
	095 Entreat; plead for; appeal to
	101 Offer proposal
	102 Urge action or policy
Participation	021 Decline to comment
	022 Pessimistic comment
	023 Neutral comment
	024 Optimistic comment
	025 Explain policy position
	030 Meet with; confer with
Verbal Conflict/Defensive	111 Reject proposal, demand etc.
	112 Refuse, oppose
	131 Make complaint (not formal)
	132 Make formal complaint or protest
	141 Deny accusation
	142 Deny an attributed policy, action, role, or position
Verbal Conflict/Offensive	121 Criticize; charge; blame
	122 Denounce; denigrate; abuse
	150 Demand; issue order or command
	160 Give warning

Table 2-1 (cont.)

	171 Threat—not specific
	172 Threat—nonmilitary
	173 Threat—force specified
	174 Ultimatum
Conflict Action	181 Nonmilitary demonstration
	182 Armed force mobilization, exercise and/or display
	191 Cancel planned event
	192 Reduce international activity, recall officials etc.
	193 Suspend aid
	194 Halt negotiations
	195 Break relations
	201 Expel personnel
	202 Expel organization
	211 Seize position or possessions
	212 Arrest or detain persons
	221 Destructive act
	222 Nonmilitary injury
	223 Military engagement

necessary to give a theoretical justification for looking only at shipping. International shipping will here be studied from the perspective of an *issue-area*, as the concept has been developed by James Rosenau.[24]

Rosenau's use of the concept seems to have been inspired first of all by Robert Dahl's study of local politics in New Haven,[25] but also by other analysts of domestic politics. The term "issue-area" itself appears to be traceable to Robert Dahl, whose use of it is unselfconscious and suggestive. Thus, he has no straightforward definition of the term. Dahl's main point is that influence and political behavior are different in the different issue-areas he studied—he is not interested in constructing any systematic typology of issue-areas. Indeed, Rosenau criticizes Dahl for neglecting the concept in his later work.[26]

Three issue-areas were selected for study in the New Haven project: urban development, public education, and political nominations.[27] The expressed reason for picking out these three issue-areas was their "importance" in the city's political life. But wherein lay this importance? What Dahl and his associates seem to say is that the issue-areas were important in the sense of directly and vitally affecting the lives of New Haven's citizens. However, if one takes a closer look at them, one will find another common trait that bears on their importance: they are not clear-cut issues, but rather a multiplicity of specific issues. Both urban redevelopment and public education have many different aspects affecting different groups in different ways, while political nominations clearly affect all issues.

An issue-area in this early conception can therefore be characterized as a cluster of problems and the attitudes of groups toward them. In fact, as will be seen, the idea of the multifaceted character of issue-areas is constant from one author to the next among those who use the concept or any of its equivalents.

The next steps in the development of the issue-area concept after Dahl were taken by Rosenau,[28] and Alker and Russett.[29]

One of Rosenau's arguments was that another dimension—that of time—should be added to the concept. In his conception, an issue-area can span a considerable time period and become dormant and reactivated at different points during this period.[30] The element of duration remains central in more recent conceptualizations.

Alker and Russett take a more operational approach to issue-areas ("super issues" in their terminology). By using factor analysis to study voting behavior in the UN General Assembly, the two authors can point to a few dimensions of disagreement and conflict underlying the large number of specific issues voted upon. The dominant super-issues at the UN between 1947 and 1961 were found to be five factors, labeled by the authors as follows: "cold war issues," "self-determination," "Palestine questions," "UN supranationalism," and "anti-interventionism (Africa)."[31] It was found, in other words, that groups of specific issues tended to cluster together in terms of the typical voting behavior they brought about.

More importantly, however, the voting behavior on the five super-issues is fundamentally different from one super-issue to the next. In the words of the authors:

To recapitulate, these findings suggest that at least five distinct, interpretable, and relatively frequent voting alignments have regularly appeared in Assembly voting. . . . The fact that the voting alignments on these issues in any particular year are largely uncorrelated among themselves means that knowing an unidentified state has a particular score on any one of these super-issues (say, the cold war) does not help to predict its position on self-determination and supra-nationalism issues. All five super-issues need to be accounted for . . . .[32]

This is again consonant with the characterization given earlier of Robert Dahl's three issue-areas, namely that they are composed of clusters of specific issues, and that behavior varies from cluster to cluster.

Finally, the relevance of the duration aspect was clearly reflected in the data. According to Alker and Russett, "the most arresting and least expected finding of this study is the continuity of the main super-issues revealed in Assembly voting."[33]

Both theoretical discussions and empirical analyses, then, emphasize some key aspects of issue-areas which can be summarized as follows:

1. Issue-areas are not single, overwhelmingly important issues, but rather groups or clusters of related, specific issues.

2. Issue-areas span considerable time periods.
3. Issue-areas are distinct from each other, giving rise to different political behaviors in each area.[34]

In 1966, James Rosenau again came forth with a valuable addition to the theoretical discussion of issue-areas.[35] In this case, however, he embedded the concept in a broad "pretheoretical"[36] effort, seeking to give comparative foreign policy studies an inspirational push. For this reason, much of the discussion is only marginally relevant here, and I shall consequently focus only on his definition of issue-areas. The question of operationalization was left essentially unsolved by this article.[37] As will be seen below, this problem is ignored here. The present study is not concerned with developing a systematic typology of issue-areas, but rather with the analysis of politics in *one* such area fitting Rosenau's definition.

In short, I have chosen to use the following definition of issue-areas by Rosenau as basis for the present study:

Stated formally, an issue-area is conceived to consist of (1) *a cluster of values, the allocation or potential allocation of which (2) leads the affected or potentially affected actors to differ so greatly over (a) the way in which the values should be allocated or (b) the horizontal levels at which the allocations should be authorized that (3) they engage in distinctive behavior designed to mobilize support for the attainment of their particular values.*[38] [Rosenau's emphasis.]

How does this fit in with the three central aspects of issue-areas just outlined above? First of all, the clustering aspect is here: many specific issues concerning the allocation of specific values cluster together in an issue-area. Secondly, the duration aspect is brought out again in Rosenau's comments on the definition where he uses the distinction between a *dormant* and an *activated* issue-area, as in the previous article.[39] Thirdly, of course, the distinctiveness of issue-areas is the main rationale for using the concept. In Rosenau's words there is now

. . . mounting evidence that the functioning of any type of political system can vary significantly from one issue-area to another. Data descriptive of local, party, legislative, national, and international systems are converging around the findings that different types of issue-areas elicit different sets of motives on the part of different actors in a political system, that different system members are thus activated in different issue-areas, and that the different interaction patterns which result from these variations produce different degrees of stability and coherence for each of the issue-areas in which systemic processes are operative.[40]

Whether this holds true for international shipping is still a question for empirical analysis. For the moment, intergovernmental interaction over shipping will be regarded from the *perspective* of an issue-area—a difference of nuance only—which should be taken to mean that shipping is tentatively regarded as a field of interaction that may be studied in comparative isolation, and that this field can be fairly accurately delimited for the purposes of analysis. In other words: I shall first make the analytical assumption that shipping *can* fruitfully be singled out for separate study; then I shall go back and see to what extent the assumption holds up, i.e., whether shipping interaction differs in key respects from world politics generally.

A first requirement is therefore to specify what is covered by the term "shipping," so that the subject matter at hand comes more clearly into focus: *By "shipping" is meant the commercial, oceangoing engagement of cargo-carrying ships between two or more countries, as well as certain activities involving physical or other immediate contact with the vessels or their cargoes.* To explain a bit more fully: only merchant ships carrying cargo for payment are included. This means that activities pertaining to such vessels as naval vessels, pleasure craft, passenger vessels that do not carry cargo, tugs, ice-breakers, coast guard vessels, etc., are all excluded.

The requirement that carriage be between two fixed points in different countries excludes not only coastal trade, but also fishing vessels, sealing vessels, whaling vessels, fish-meal or whale-oil factories of the floating variety, and similar vessels.[41] Also excluded is all inland waterborne trade. This means that the activities of ocean-going vessels in places such as the Great Lakes and St. Lawrence Seaway, Switzerland, and other inland points of direct contact with open sea, are excluded from this study.

The additional activities cover the following: shipbuilding, governments seeking or extending credit for ship purchase,[42] matters directly pertaining to cargo handling in port, shipwrecks, collisions, rescue services, navigational matters, welfare of crews, bunkering, provision of ship's stores, etc.[43] It is required that these activities be related to cargo vessels, and that they involve two or more countries in each case.

Since the international affairs of shipping are regarded as a potential issue-area, it is essential also to specify just what values are being allocated. Basically, the values accruing to a country from shipping and shipping-related activities are assumed to be reducible to the following: a) the *transport function* of ships, i.e., the benefit of having goods transported between two points at the right time and price; b) the *earnings of ships*; c) the *national registry* of ships, and implications of registry.

The categories are considered to be exhaustive but not completely mutually exclusive. Category c), for instance, may have certain elements in common with both category a) and category b). Yet the important point is that it has significant implications *beyond* these common elements, as will be seen presently.

A number of secondary values derive from the three listed above. The most important ones can be summarized as follows:

1. the earnings of land-based facilities for ships, such as ports, shipyards, canals, bunker and supply facilities;
2. the implications and impact of earnings under points b) and 1. (above) on the national economies, especially on balances-of-payments;
3. the military defense advantages of having a national-flag merchant fleet (implication of point c) above);
4. the national prestige presumably deriving from the national registry of a merchant fleet (implication of point c) above).

With this, the stage is set for an expansion of and elaboration upon the ideas implicit in Rosenau's definition of issue-areas. This leads, first of all, to a more explicit conceptualization of international politics and the link between shipping and politics.

International politics is defined as *the processes of interaction (1) taking place between the national governments of the world (2) in which each government seeks for itself what it regards as a satisfactory share of the international allocation of values.* The international allocation of values is defined as *the process whereby valued objects or conditions become accessible to the inhabitants of different nation-states in amounts varying between one nation-state and another at any given point in time, and varying over time for any one nation-state.*

The values concerned may be any concrete object or abstract state of affairs sought by inhabitants of more than one state and international in character. Access to this value, therefore, involves relationships with inhabitants of states, whether these are officials or private citizens.

Hence, the processes referred to as the international allocation of values may be regarded as the substance of the totality of international relations in its broadest sense,[44] or "transnational activities" as Sprout and Sprout prefer to call them,[45] covering everything from correspondence between private citizens through tourism and trade to the waging of war.

The definition of international politics rests in part on the concept of "processes of interaction" between governments. It is important to note that this is not meant to cover all external activities undertaken by governments. Rather, following the usage of McClelland and Hoggard, interaction and transactions are considered to be analytically distinct.[46] The basis for the distinction is that

... transactions are defined as items of action that have at some point in time become so numerous, so commonplace, and so normal to their situation that they are accounted for conventionally in an aggregated form, usually by some unit other than item frequency (i.e., dollar values of trade, number of troops in the field etc). Interactions are, by our definition, single action items of a nonroutine, extraordinary, or newsworthy character that in some clear sense are directed across a national boundary, and have, in most instances, a specific foreign target.[47]

The term "international politics" is therefore synonymous with the term "intergovernmental interaction," as defined here. "Intergovernmental transactions," on the other hand, are conceived to be part of the great volume of everyday routine exchanges across national borders, which in this study is assigned the label "international transactions." It will be noted that this distinction is merely the logical extension of McClelland's two international networks discussed earlier.[48]

The question as to how the two networks are related—how transactions and interaction are linked—was singled out as an important research question. In the following section, this question will first be discussed at the theoretical level.

International Shipping and
International Politics

International shipping is here regarded as one aspect of the international allocation of values, that is, as one of the many processes whereby certain valued objects or conditions—those specifically related to shipping activities—become accessible to the inhabitants of different nation-states.

The actual everyday operations of transporting goods between ports in different countries, of obtaining, loading and unloading cargoes, and of determining freight rates and other conditions of carriage fall entirely within the category labeled *international transactions*. Most of these are nongovernmental transactions, but increasingly governments are also taking part on a routine basis.

It will be seen that the definitions used involve an attempt to separate operationally the politics and economics of international shipping. Other aspects of shipping, such as regular contacts with port authorities, documentation of cargo for customs officers, etc., are also part of international transactions. This, of course, involves many routine governmental transactions.

It is only when shipping becomes a matter of interaction between governments that it enters the realm of international politics. The question of how this occurs will, for the moment, be regarded from a purely theoretical point of view.[49]

As was just pointed out, whether a matter of interaction or transactions, shipping is regarded as always involving the international allocation of the values connected with it, such as freight income, the benefits of service, etc. At the transaction level, the manner in which these values become allocated internationally is predominantly a result of economic processes. That is to say, no decisions are taken by anyone as to how the values should devolve upon each different country. This just happens, as it were, being determined by traditional trading patterns, by the supply and demand for the various commodities in world trade, by the consequent supply and demand for shipping services, and by international movements of capital and labor. Over time, the resulting transactions assume certain patterns of relative stability by being repeated and becoming habitual. Normally, they will tend to change only gradually. But some of these transaction patterns may also be subject to abrupt, violent, and erratic changes stemming from breakdowns in commodity markets, from problems in ocean-transport markets, or from large-scale international disasters like general war.

At the level of governmental interaction, on the other hand, the international allocation of values becomes a matter of concrete governmental efforts to affect the way the values are distributed. In most cases, top level decision-makers will have some kind of mental picture of a situation with regard to a specific value allocation that would be, if not ideal, at least satisfactory from their point of view. It is now more than fifteen years since Herbert Simon pointed out that it is probably more accurate to say that decision-makers tend to settle for a *satisfactory* alternative rather than the *best possible* alternative in situations of choice.[50] What is referred to here, of course, is goal images—not alternatives for action—but the lesson may be the same. Thus, it is assumed here that decision-makers are relatively pragmatic human beings who seek to put their country in what they regard as a satisfactory or adequate position with respect to the international allocation of values.

Matters of shipping, then, may be said to become matters of international politics when governments take specific action in order to improve their country's situation with regard to shipping values. In terms of the international allocation of shipping values and the resulting patterns of transaction, a government can improve its position only by (a) trying to change existing patterns, or (b) trying to forestall changes in such patterns.

It has already been noted that some transaction patterns in shipping are relatively stable and slow-changing, while others are highly volatile and unpredictable. Both have important political implications—the first because a government that thinks its country is at a disadvantage is not likely to accept the long-run implications of a stable situation, and the second because no government is likely to take such shifts as a matter of fact if shipping is important to the country. Any specific aspect of shipping, in other words, is liable to political interpretations to the extent that it (1) occurs in highly stable patterns, or (2) occurs in highly unpredictable patterns; in terms of which nations derive more and which derive less of the values from that specific aspect. A closer description of trends and conditions of the international allocation of values in shipping is provided in Chapter 3.

The political aspects of shipping, in short, are closely connected with the efforts of governments to influence the allocation of values in shipping *between nation-states* rather than between *individual economic operators* regardless of their nationality. From the perspective of economics, nationality is an irrelevant criterion in allocation processes. From the perspective of governments, nationality is a paramount criterion in allocation processes.

It is necessary to be more specific, however, to get to the core of the problem of how the two networks are related. This will be done by way of the second main research question identified earlier in this chapter, namely the question pertaining to the determinants of conflict frequency.

To pull the threads of the discussion together, the issue-area perspective implies that interaction between states takes the form of a continuous contest over the allocation of values. In other words, interaction, and hence conflict, arise from demands for change in an existing distribution of values and from efforts to resist such change.

The main focus of this dissertation, then, can be summarized in the following question: To what extent is the frequency of conflict interaction in shipping matters explainable in terms of the characteristics of a particular distribution of shipping values?

There are three important aspects of any distribution of values expected to have particular relevance for the frequency of conflict among interaction participants: a) the existence or nonexistence of *skew* in the distribution; b) the *amount* of skew if it exists; and c) the *duration* of skew.

If the existence of skew can be established, then two relationships may be hypothesized:

1. *The greater the amount of skew over a certain minimum period of time, the higher the frequency of conflict;*
2. *Given a certain amount of skew, the longer it persists over time, the higher the frequency of conflict.*

These are not novel ideas. The hypotheses reflect a familiar theme in political theory—the link between social inequality and conflict.

Note that these hypotheses suggest the presence of an interaction effect between the variable of skew and the variable of time. A large skew is not expected to be related to the frequency of conflict unless it persists for a certain minimum length of time. Furthermore, as the possible duration of skew is extended in time the frequency of conflict is expected to increase, even if there is no increase in skew.

The present study will not seek to distinguish between the effects of amount of skew and duration of skew. It seeks, rather, to study the relationship between value distribution and conflict, as compared to *other* possible correlates of conflict. Therefore, the two hypotheses just stated will be combined into one for the purpose of this study:

If a skewed distribution of values persists or is reinforced over time, then the frequency of conflict in the respective interaction system will increase.

The hypothesis is expected to hold up, minimally, in a period of increasing international communication and proliferation of egalitarian ideals among the states of the world.

In testing it, the procedure will be as follows. Beginning the analysis at the systemic level, the distribution of values in shipping must be described on the basis of some indicator to be selected.[51] The extent of skew in the distribution must then be measured. Secondly, variation in skew over time and the possibility of a persistent skew must be considered. Thirdly, the trends in conflict frequency over the years must be ascertained and compared with the measurement of degree and duration of skew. The results must then be controlled for by introduction of variables describing non-shipping international conflict. At the systemic level, the frequency of conflict is to be considered as an aggregate, i.e., the total number of conflict actions over shipping matters by all states, relative to the total volume of interaction by all states.

So far, however, only *systemic* shipping conflict will have been considered. There remains the important question of how the aggregate behavior patterns of the system are reflected in the behavior of the states which are its component parts. For example, if the distribution of values in the system as a whole is—or is not—related to the systemic frequency of conflict, then how is a particular state's share of this value distribution related to its output of conflict actions? The analysis at the nation-state level is undertaken in recognition of the fact that inference carried over directly from one level of analysis to another may easily be fallacious.[52] Whether or not the main hypothesis is confirmed at the systemic level, very little may be inferred directly about behavior at the state level.

In this connection, the distinction between a value distribution among states on the one hand, and a given state's share of that distribution on the other hand, must be kept clear. The value *distribution* is a characteristic of the *system*, while the value share is a characteristic of each *unit* of the system. *Either one* (distribution or share), or *both combined*, may conceivably affect the behavior of the single state. Furthermore, any number of additional variables may intervene to make the relationships considerably more complex.

The analysis of behavior at the level of the nation-state will therefore begin by examining the relationship between a state's propensity to conflict behavior and its share of the distribution of values. To the extent that the results may prove to be unsatisfactory at this point, additional variables will be drawn into the analysis. The dependent variable will, at this level of analysis, be defined as the proportion of conflict acts out of all acts committed by the state in a given period of time.

Definition of the System

In the following, the term "the international system" will refer to all of the nation-states existing in the world at any particular time, and to the relationships between them. International shipping—as seen from the issue-area perspective—is conceived of as forming an *international subsystem* of intergovernmental interaction pertaining only to shipping issues as defined above.

The members of this subsystem are those states, intergovernmental organizations, and liner conferences which participate regularly in shipping interaction in a specific period of time. The boundaries of the interaction subsystem are defined in terms of the subject matter of shipping. In membership terms, therefore, the system boundaries are not fixed, but must rather be expected to expand and contract over time. The interaction subsystem of shipping is, in short, an analytic system in the sense that only certain aspects of the concrete entities (e.g., states) are subjected to analysis, namely those aspects pertaining to shipping.

Procedure to be Followed in the Empirical Part of the Study

The main steps in the analysis that follows can now be briefly summarized. First, Chapter 3 will provide a description of transaction patterns in shipping in the 1946-68 period, while Chapter 4 gives an overview of the issues that have been important in international shipping politics. Next, in Chapter 5, the main hypothesis will be tested, and the relationship between shipping conflict and non-shipping conflict will be analyzed. In Chapter 6, the correlates of the individual state's propensity to engage in conflict behavior will be analyzed. Finally, Chapter 7 gives a summary of findings and formulates the main conclusions of the study. For a complete discussion of methodology the reader is referred to Appendix A.

The Data

Data used in Chapters 3 and 4 are gathered from official published statistics such as the *UN Statistical Yearbooks*; from nonofficial published statistics; and from the general literature of international shipping. Statistics on liner operators have been compiled by the author.

Data for Chapters 5 and 6 are in the main gathered from two newspapers, *the New York Times* (Index version), and the *Norges Handels og Sjøfartstidende* by means of the WEIS coding procedure, which is described in Appendix A.

Notes

1. Harold Sprout and Margaret Sprout, FOUNDATIONS OF INTERNATIONAL POLITICS (Princeton: Van Nostrand, 1962), p. 76.

2. James N. Rosenau, "The Functioning of International Systems," BACK-GROUND, November 1963.

3. Charles A. McClelland, THEORY AND THE INTERNATIONAL SYSTEM (New York: Macmillan, 1966), p. 106.

4. See for example, McClelland and Hoggard, "Conflict Patterns in the Interactions among Nations," in James N. Rosenau, ed., INTERNATIONAL POLITICS AND FOREIGN POLICY, 2nd ed. (New York: Collier-Macmillan Free Press, 1969), (referred to in the following as "Rosenau II"), pp. 711 ff.

5. Edward Azar et al., "Making and Measuring the International Event as a Unit of Analysis," STUDIES OF CONFLICT AND PEACE REPORT NO. 3 (Department of Political Science, University of North Carolina, Chapel Hill, January 1972). Forthcoming in SAGE PROFESSIONAL PAPERS IN INTER-NATIONAL STUDIES, 1972.

6. Charles F. Hermann, "Comparing the Foreign Policy Actions of Nations," (paper presented at the 66th Annual Meeting of the American Political Science Association, Los Angeles, California, September 9-12, 1970).

7. McClelland, THEORY AND THE INTERNATIONAL SYSTEM, pp. 104-105.

8. Ibid., p. 105.

9. Ibid.

10. A further discussion of this research question will be found on pp. 19-20.

11. In the most recent usage, the kind of interaction analysis referred to here is denoted as "events analysis" or "events studies."

12. Robert F. Bales, "A Set of Categories for the Analysis of Small Group Interaction." AMERICAN SOCIOLOGICAL REVIEW, 1950, pp. 257-63, reprinted in J.D. Singer, ed., HUMAN BEHAVIOR AND INTERNATIONAL POLITICS (Chicago: Rand McNally, 1965), pp. 349-58.

13. Ibid., in Singer, p. 352.

14. See, for example, his "Interaction in a Committee of the UN General Assembly," in Singer, ed., QUANTITATIVE INTERNATIONAL POLITICS (New York: Free Press, 1968), pp. 51-84. Also "Interaction and Negotiation in a Committee of the UN General Assembly," in Rosenau II, pp. 483-97.

15. Charles A. McClelland, "The Acute International Crisis," WORLD POLITICS, vol. 14, no. 1.

16. "Action Structures and Communication in Two International Crises," reprinted in Rosenau II, pp. 473-82.

17. Thomas C. Schelling, THE STRATEGY OF CONFLICT (Cambridge: Harvard University Press, 1960), pp. 1-83.

18. "(1) Threats or direct attacks on 'the temporary status quo,' (2) defense or manipulation of 'the temporary status quo,' (3) yielding acts or withdrawing from the position of 'the temporary status quo.'" ("Action Structures," Rosenau II, p. 474.)

19. "Access to Berlin: The Quantity and Variety of Events," in Singer, ed., op. cit., pp. 159-86.

20. Ibid., p. 168.

21. Participation includes such things as comments on world situation, state visits, unspecified consultations, etc.

22. "World Event/Interaction Survey Handbook and Codebook," Technical Report no. 1, World Event/Interaction Survey, Dept. of International Relations, University of Sourthern California, January 1969, pp. 10-11.

23. Wayne R. Martin and Robert A. Young, "World Events/Interaction Survey (WEIS) Program Rules and Instructions," Department of International Relations, University of Southern California, January 1968, p. 14.

24. James N. Rosenau, "The Functioning of International Systems," BACK-GROUND, November 1963; "Pre-theories and Theories of Foreign Policy," in R. Barry Farrell, ed., APPROACHES TO COMPARATIVE AND INTERNATIONAL POLITICS (Evanston: Northwestern University Press, 1966), pp. 27-92; "Foreign Policy as an Issue-Area," in Rosenau, ed., DOMESTIC SOURCES OF FOREIGN POLICY (New York: Collier-Macmillan, 1967), pp. 11-50.

25. Robert A. Dahl, WHO GOVERNS? (New Haven: Yale University Press, 1961).

26. Rosenau, "Pre-theories," op. cit., p. 74.

27. Nelson W. Polsby, COMMUNITY POWER AND POLITICAL THEORY (New Haven: Yale University Press, 1963), pp. 70-79 ff.

28. Rosenau, "The Functioning of International Systems," op. cit.

29. Hayward R. Alker and Bruce M. Russett, WORLD POLITICS IN THE GENERAL ASSEMBLY (New Haven: Yale University Press, 1965).

30. Rosenau, "Functioning of Systems," op. cit.

31. Alker and Russett, op. cit., pp. 302-07, also pp. 126 ff.

32. Ibid., p. 134.

33. Ibid., p. 126.

34. For a different way of thinking systematically about issues and politics, see Herbert J. Spiro, WORLD POLITICS: THE GLOBAL SYSTEM (Homewood, Ill.: The Dorsey Press, 1966), especially pp. 50 ff.

35. Rosenau, "Pre-theories . . . ," op. cit.

36. See Ibid., p. 41 (note).

37. Ibid., pp. 82-88.

38. Ibid., p. 81.

39. Ibid.

40. Rosenau, "Pre-theories," op. cit., p. 71.

41. Strictly speaking, the exclusion of fishing vessels may not follow logically from this criterion, since fishing vessels from one country may often sell their catch in other countries. For the sake of the homogeneity of the cases under study, however, it was decided to exclude this category here.

42. But not the sale or purchase of cargo vessels by governments. This decision may seem somewhat arbitrary, but is based on the distinction made below between interaction and transactions.

43. A more complete specification is found in the list of specific shipping issues included, in Appendix E.

44. I.e., as suggested by Fred Sonderman, "The Linkage Between Foreign Policy and International Politics," in Rosenau ed., INTERNATIONAL POLITICS AND FOREIGN POLICY, lst ed., (referred to in the following as "Rosenau I"), p. 9 (note).

45. Sprout and Sprout, op. cit., p. 74.

46. Charles A. McClelland and Gary Hoggard, "Conflict Patterns in the Interactions Among Nations," in Rosenau II, p. 713.

47. Ibid. The term "interaction" (in the singular) is preferred here.

48. See p. 14. Keohane and Nye assign the term "transnational relations" to these phenomena. See Keohane and Nye, "Transnational Relations and World Politics: An Introduction," in Keohane and Nye (eds.) TRANSNATIONAL RELATIONS AND WORLD POLITICS (Cambridge, Mass.: Harvard University Press, 1972), pp. IX-XXIX.

49. A broader theoretical approach geared to the study of transnational politics in general is found in Karl Kaiser, "Transnational Politics: Toward a Theory of Multinational Politics," INTERNATIONAL ORGANIZATION, vol. 25, no. 4, Autumn 1971, pp. 790-817. See also, by the same author, "Transnational Relations as a Threat to the Democratic Process," in Keohane and Nye, op. cit., pp. 356-370.

50. Herbert A. Simon, "Recent Advances in Organization Theory," in Stephen K. Bailey et al., RESEARCH FRONTIERS IN POLITICS AND GOVERNMENT (Washington, D.C.: Brookings Lectures, 1955).

51. On the question of levels of analysis, see in particular J. David Singer, "The Level-of-Analysis Problem in International Relations," in Knorr and Verba, eds., THE INTERNATIONAL SYSTEM (Princeton: Princeton University Press, 1961), pp. 77-92, and Johan Galtung, THEORY AND METHODS OF SOCIAL RESEARCH (Oslo: Universitetsforlaget, rev. ed. 1969), pp. 37-48.

52. See especially Galtung, op. cit., pp. 45-48.

3 Transaction Patterns in International Shipping

Politics is an aspect of everyday relations between human individuals and groups. It is not something apart from these relations but is, rather, solidly rooted in them. In line with this general outlook, shipping politics is considered to be closely connected with the routine activities of maritime transport. To fully grasp some of the essential traits of shipping politics, therefore, it is necessary to examine more closely the *transactions* typical of shipping. The present chapter will give a description of patterns and trends in international shipping transactions over time. Special attention will be given to the possibility that conflict in international shipping is inherent in maritime transaction patterns. In general, political implications will be pointed out and discussed wherever appropriate.

The description of the transactions can be summed up in the question "whose ships carry whose goods where?" The attempted answers will be given in terms of the nationality of ships (by registry) and the geographical origin and destination of goods.

Note that the term "whose ships" refers not to ownership, but to registry. Owners are not necessarily nationals of the country of registry, although with a few important exceptions they tend to be. (The main exceptions, of course, are Liberia and Panama and the shipowners of US and Greek nationality—in particular—who are attracted to these flags.)

The crucial question, however, is this: Are governments likely to take no interest in the fate and wellbeing of ships that carry their flags abroad? Our answer would be *no*: the great majority of governments do care what happens to national-flag ships abroad, and—provided they have the necessary resources—will act to defend or even promote the interests of national-flag shipping. Thus, the community of interests between a government and the nationally registered shipowners are the key to understanding the politics of shipping.

General Transaction Patterns

Transaction patterns will first be described in general terms under the headings of *registry* and *seaborne trade*. Later, liner transactions and bulk transactions will be considered separately.

Patterns of National Registry

The trends in registry patterns in shipping concern the first part of the question: "*whose* ships" and are shown in Table 3-1, by main region.[1]

A note of explanation is in order on the definition of regions. I have attempted to make each region as homogeneous as possible in terms of national economies (more developed/less developed), political systems, and (to some extent) shipping background.

Some countries are conspicuously different from the other countries in the respective geographic regions with these criteria. That applies in particular to Japan, South Africa, Israel, and also Yugoslavia, which are therefore included in the Western Europe group in this study.

It also seemed most natural to restrict a region of socialist states to the Soviet Union and Eastern Europe. These countries are closely coordinated in their foreign policy, while the Far Eastern states of China, North Korea and North Vietnam fall outside this general pattern and are therefore included in Asia. There are two other exceptions: Cuba is included with Central America and the Caribbean, and Albania is included with Eastern Europe.

Table 3-1
Shipping Registry by Main Region 1947-67 in Percent of World Tonnage[a]

	1947	1952	1957	1962	1967
Western Europe	45.9	52.6	54.4	59.4	57.2
Eastern Europe	—[b]	3.1	2.8	4.2	6.9
Asia	1.8	2.3	2.3	3.2	4.1
Africa	0.0	1.0	6.8	7.6	12.2
Arab states	0.1	0.1	0.1	0.7	0.5
South America	1.9	2.6	2.3	2.3	2.1
Central America	2.7	4.8	4.7	3.0	3.0
North America	43.6	32.1	24.9	17.8	12.4
Oceania	1.1	0.8	0.8	0.6	0.6
Total	97.1	99.1	99.1	98.8	99.0

[a]Source: UNITED NATIONS STATISTICAL YEARBOOKS.
[b]Incomplete data.

Table 3-1 shows first of all the marked and increasing concentration of shipping tonnage in Western Europe. At the same time, there is a drastic decline in the shipowning status of the USA and Canada. In the Western Europe category, the two strongest growth units have been Japan and Norway.

Africa also shows a strong increase over the years, but here the figures may be somewhat misleading. Although many African states have recently established their own merchant marines, the overwhelming bulk of African tonnage shown here is the Liberian flag-of-convenience fleet whose owners are in large part US and Greek nationals. In 1967, the Liberian fleet amounted to 12.0 percent of the world total—leaving only 0.2 percent for other African merchant fleets.

Similar conditions obtain in Central America, where three other flag-of-convenience fleets are found: Panama, Honduras, and Costa Rica. Panama benefited from the early rush to the "convenient" flags of registry after World War II, but was soon overtaken by its African competitor. Still, even today Panama has one of the world's larger merchant fleets. Honduras and Costa Rica, on the other hand, never achieved the large fleets which Panama and Liberia have, and Costa Rica has in recent years practically eliminated itself from the group of "run-away flags" by tightening up registry procedures and requirements.

Central and South America show parallel trends of growth and decline of fleets. For both regions, the post-war peak was reached in the early 1950s, after which there has been a gradual decline. Asia, in contrast, is the only less-developed region where steady and significant growth is found in the period covered. The Eastern European region has experienced a similar pattern of growth.

In short, growth in merchant fleets is confined to Eastern Europe, Western Europe and Asia, and to one flag of convenience, Liberia. That is: in these regions merchant fleets increase faster than the world average. In the entire Western hemisphere, on the other hand, there is a noticeable decline.

Patterns of Seaborne Trade

The origin of goods in seaborne trade is more widely dispersed than tonnage registry (Tables 3-2a and b). Five of the nine regions are rather large shippers of goods, and only two are persistently small (Central America and Oceania).

In 1948 it was North America, Western Europe, and South America that predominated. The strong showing of Western Europe so soon after the war is noteworthy, but it should be observed that the the figures for each region also cover *intra*regional trade. Thus, while a large part of the goods shipped from North and South America probably were destined for other regions, the West European shipments in all likelihood were short-haul affairs at that time.

Later on, however, all three of these regions declined in relative importance. The growth region *par excellence* in terms of goods loaded is the Arab world, and this is due almost exclusively to the growing shipments of crude oil and petroleum products, as will be seen below.

Asia, after an initial drop,[2] is also gaining on the rest of the world, as are Eastern Europe and Africa. As for Africa, Dag Tressvelt has pointed out in his excellent study of the West African shipping range that:

It is natural that, when a geographical area is at an early stage of development, the important commodity flow tends to be larger than the export flow. West Africa is now [1967] beyond that stage, and its current problem is how to transform the positive physical balance of trade into a monetary surplus.[3]

Eastern Europe, similarly, gives evidence of a rather slow growth, although this is not in itself an accurate reflection of real growth in foreign trade, but rather an

Table 3-2a

Goods Loaded in Seaborne Trade, by Region (Million Metric Tons)[a]

	1948	1952	1957	1962	1967
Western Europe[cd]	95.2	148.6	184.8	225.2	299.5
Eastern Europe[cd]	13.5	11.5	32.0	80.6	128.0
Asia[bcd]	57.5	48.1	86.3	128.1	215.4
Africa[bcd]	15.6	21.1	34.8	45.3	88.3
Arab states[bcd]	11.9[f]	20.5[f]	60.3	258.0	450.0
South America[bcd]	91.3	113.7	184.9	224.9	262.9
Central America[bcde]	9.9	12.8	22.8	32.9	45.2
North America	98.7	128.0	199.5	178.1	243.8
Oceania[bc]	7.3	8.4	14.8	24.8	38.4
Total	400.9	512.7	820.2	1197.9	1771.5

[a]Source: UN STATISTICAL YEARBOOKS.

[b]Including all colonies and non-self-governing territories.

[c]No data for the following:

Western Europe—1948: Greece; 1952: Malta; 1967: Gibraltar; throughout: Ireland.

Eastern Europe—1948, 1952: Albania, Bulgaria, East Germany, Romania, USSR; 1957: Albania, Romania.

Asia—1948: North Borneo; 1967: South Vietnam; throughout: China, North Korea, North Vietnam.

Africa—1948: Kenya, Liberia, Somalia, Tanganyika, Zanzibar; 1952: Kenya, Liberia, Tanganyika; 1962: Ifni; 1967: Canary Islands, Cape Verde Islands, Ceuta, Equatorial Guinea, Afars and Issas, Melilla, Zanzibar.

Arab states—1948: Aden, Jordan, Libya; 1952: Aden, Jordan; 1957: Jordan.

South America—1948: (Brit.) Guyana, Surinam; 1952, 1957: Surinam.

Central America—1948: Honduras, Panama; 1952: Panama; 1967: Brit. Honduras, Grenada, St. Lucia.

Oceania—1967: French Polynesia, Guam, Nauru, New Caledonia, New Guinea, Papua.

Note that, generally, countries reported with "no data" are countries that have been reporting statistics on seaborne trade to the UN for other years. Thus, very small territories that have not been reporting data regularly may also have been omitted above.

[d]Estimates for the following:

Western Europe—1948: France.

Eastern Europe—1952: Poland, 1957: Poland, USSR; 1967: Albania.

Asia—1948: Malaya, Pakistan, Philippines, Thailand, Turkey; 1952: Malaya, Turkey; 1967: India.

Africa—1967:Guinea.

Arab states—1962: Algeria; 1967: Algeria, Iraq, South Yemen.

South America—1967: Chile, Colombia, Surinam.

Central America—1962: Panama; 1967: Honduras, Jamaica, Nicaragua, Trinidad and Tobago.

[e]Excluding Netherlands Antilles.

[f]Excluding oil from Iraq and Lebanon.

Table 3-2b
Goods Loaded in Seaborne Trade, by Region (Percent)[a]

	1948	1952	1957	1962	1967
Western Europe	23.7	29.0	22.5	18.8	16.9
Eastern Europe	3.4	2.2	3.9	6.7	7.2
Asia	14.3	9.4	10.5	10.7	12.1
Africa	3.9	4.1	4.2	3.8	5.0
Arab states	3.0	4.0	7.4	21.5	25.4
South America	22.8	22.2	22.5	18.8	14.8
Central America	2.5	2.5	2.8	2.7	2.6
North America	24.6	25.0	24.3	14.9	13.8
Oceania	1.8	1.6	1.8	2.1	2.2
Total	100.0	100.0	99.9	100.0	100.0

[a]All notes for Table 3-2a apply here as well. Percentages computed by the author.

understatement of it. The reason for this is that overland transport predominates *within* the region, which actually includes, in addition to the USSR, only East Germany, Poland, Bulgaria, and Romania as significant coastal states. According to Alexandersson and Nordstrøm, sea transport within Eastern Europe is economically attractive only between East Germany and the Soviet Union.[4] For the rest railways, river transport, and pipelines are the really important means of transportation.

Hence, the figures for Eastern Europe in Table 3-2 reflect the trends in *inter*regional trade, or—more specifically—they reflect mainly the amount of cargo loaded for destinations *outside* Eastern Europe.

The amount of cargo loaded in Western Europe, on the other hand, reflects intraregional as well as interregional trade movements. Here, shipping is for geographical reasons just as important as land-based transport. The gradual decline in these figures may be traced to several developments, of which the most important probably are: (1) the shift in composition of commodities exported towards greater amounts of lightweight general cargo (i.e., finished and semifinished goods), and (2) the expansion of intraregional trade in the EEC-area, where much of the cargo moves by rail, road, or river.

Intraregional trade in Asia is even more dependent on maritime transport, due to the lack of railways and highways. Africa is in a similar situation, as—to some extent—is South America. Hence, the volume of goods loaded in these regions is probably close to the total volume of their exports.

The loading of goods in seaborne trade occurs mainly in the major production centers of the world. It should be kept in mind that the composition of trade in terms of commodity types is obscured by the figures reported. Two general facts are relevant here: (1) when cargo is measured by weight, as in the UN data, raw materials and non-processed goods such as crude oil, iron ore, or wheat are emphasized, and finished or semifinished goods are de-emphasized; (2) the share of nonprocessed goods is generally much larger in the exports of developing countries than in the exports of developed countries.

In volume terms, then, production is fairly evenly spread among world regions, although this production is largely extractive in the less-developed regions and industrial in the more developed regions.

With this in mind, the patterns of goods unloaded should now be considered. Table 3-3 sums up the destinations of the cargo moving in seaborne trade.

Note the heavy concentration of goods unloaded in Western Europe. In fact, the two European regions are the only regions having a steadily increasing share of seaborne international trade since 1948. All other regional shares have stagnated or declined throughout the period.

Seaborne transport therefore reflects the major trends in post-war international trade and illustrates the influence of important economic factors. Basically, the movement of goods in international trade follows three key economic processes: production, consumption, and investment. Raw materials move to areas where industrial production is concentrated; finished goods move to areas where consumption is high and to areas where investments are especially heavy. In an economically developed region these three factors will overlap to a great extent. We will find a large inflow of (mostly) lower-valued raw materials as inputs in industrial production. In addition, there will be a large intraregional trade, a somewhat smaller interregional outflow to other developed regions, and a very small outflow to underdeveloped regions.

Correspondingly, the less developed regions will have a large outflow of goods in volume terms—mainly raw materials of various kinds—while the inflow-volume will be of a more modest magnitude, not only because consumption and investment are smaller, but also because the composition of commodities in the inflow consists largely of lower-weight consumer and investment goods. Table 3-4 illustrates this rather well.

This, however, has not always been so. The transport of low-valued goods of great weight or volume was insignificant until technological improvements made it a more reasonably priced undertaking. Indeed, in the nineteenth century high transport costs usually protected a developing economy from cheaper imports from the more industrialized countries, thus serving the same function as a protectionist tariff.[5] Today, transport costs are low enough to make it more profitable to bring unprocessed raw materials from developing countries to the industrialized countries rather than process them in the country of origin.[6] After processing, the "same" goods are re-exported to the developing countries. This, in fact, is not a phenomenon restricted to developing countries. As is pointed out by Kindleberger, it actually pays for Australia to ship *wool* 14,000 miles to have it made into cloth in Britain, and then bring it the 14,000 miles back again, rather than have it processed on the spot.[7]

Table 3-3a
Goods Unloaded in Seaborne Trade, by Region (Million Metric Tons)[a]

	1948	1952	1957	1962	1967
Western Europe[ce]	210.6	314.5	488.1	709.5	1147.4
Eastern Europe[ce]	3.1	2.5	10.0	26.7	37.8
Asia[bce]	36.0	45.8	67.7	85.9	131.7
Africa[bce]	13.4	19.4	28.8	34.0	40.9
Arab states[bce]	10.2	11.4	19.7	26.7	33.5
South America[bce]	26.8	28.7	36.9	33.9	42.2
Central America[bcde]	6.9	11.0	14.7	19.6	27.2
North America	94.6	140.4	202.9	240.0	294.7
Oceania[b]	9.7	18.5	21.5	26.3	38.6
Total	411.3	592.2	890.3	1202.6	1794.0

[a]Source: UN STATISTICAL YEARBOOKS.
[b]Including all colonies and non-self-governing territories.
[c]No data for the following:
Western Europe – 1948: Malta; throughout: Ireland.
Eastern Europe – 1948, 1952: Albania, Bulgaria, East Germany, Romania, USSR.
Asia – 1948: North Borneo; 1952: Sarawak; throughout: China, North Korea, North Vietnam.
Africa – 1948: Kenya, Liberia, Somalia, Tanganyika, Zanzibar; 1952: Kenya, Liberia, Tanganyika; 1962: Ifni; 1967: Cape Verde Islands, Ceuta, Equatorial Guinea, Guinea, Melilla, Zanzibar.
Arab states – 1948: Aden, Libya; 1952: Aden; 1962: Bahrain.
South America – 1948: (Brit.) Guyana, Surinam; 1952, 1957, 1967: Surinam.
Central America – 1948, 1952: Honduras, Panama; 1957: Panama; 1967: Brit. Honduras, Grenada, Honduras, Nicaragua, St. Lucia.
[d]Excluding Netherlands Antilles.
[e]Estimates for the following:
Western Europe – 1948: France; 1967: South Africa.
Eastern Europe – 1957: Poland, USSR; 1967: Albania.
Asia – 1948: Malaya, Iran, Pakistan, Philippines, Thailand, Turkey; 1952: Malaya, Turkey; 1967: India.
Africa – 1967: Afars and Issas, Canary Islands.
Arab states – 1962: Algeria; 1967: Algeria, Iraq, South Yemen.
South America – 1967: Chile, Colombia.
Central America – 1962: Panama; 1967: Jamaica, Trinidad and Tobago.

After World War II, therefore, two primary patterns can be discerned in international seaborne trade: (1) the carriage of bulky and/or unprocessed raw materials and foodstuffs from the less to the more developed regions; (2) the carriage of all kinds of goods—though mainly of the finished and semifinished varieties—between the major industrialized areas of the world (Western Europe, North America, and Japan). Secondary patterns are the movement of

Table 3-3b
Goods Unloaded in Seaborne Trade, by Region (Percent)[a]

	1948	1952	1957	1962	1967
Western Europe	51.2	53.1	54.8	59.0	64.0
Eastern Europe	0.7	0.4	1.1	2.2	2.1
Asia	8.7	7.7	7.6	7.2	7.3
Africa	3.3	3.3	3.2	2.8	2.3
Arab states	2.5	1.9	2.2	2.2	1.9
South America	6.5	4.8	4.2	2.8	2.4
Central America	1.7	1.9	1.7	1.6	1.5
North America	23.0	23.7	22.8	20.0	16.4
Oceania	2.4	3.1	2.4	2.2	2.1
Total	100.0	99.9	100.0	100.0	100.0

[a]Source and notes as in Table 3-3a.

finished goods from industrialized to developing regions and the movement of all kinds of goods between the less developed regions.

Who carries the goods? It has already been shown that the registry of merchant tonnage is heavily concentrated in the industrialized part of the world, supplemented by the two major flags of convenience, Liberia and Panama.

Table 3-4
Goods Loaded and Unloaded in Seaborne Trade, by Region, in 1948 and 1967 (Million Metric Tons)[a]

	1948		1967	
	Loaded	Unloaded	Loaded	Unloaded
Western Europe	95.2	210.6	299.5	1147.4
Eastern Europe	13.5	3.1	128.0	37.8
Asia	57.5	36.0	215.4	131.7
Africa	15.6	13.4	88.3	40.9
Arab states	11.9	10.2	450.0	33.5
South America	91.3	26.8	262.9	42.2
Central America	9.9	6.9	45.2	27.2
North America	98.7	94.6	243.8	294.7
Oceania	7.3	9.7	38.4	38.6
Total	400.9	411.3	1771.5	1794.0

[a]Source: As in Table 3-2a.

Some Political Implications

The main political implications of these patterns are the following: (1) the concentration of tonnage registry in the developed world raises the *image* of "imperialist" or "neo-colonialist" exploitation—regardless of whether this is in fact the case; (2) the influence of freight costs on the *market price* of the commodity is greater for the low-value, bulky or high-weight commodities exported by developing countries to the industrialized world, than for the high-value, light-weight commodities exported by industrialized countries to the "third world." Both points require some clarification.

As for the first, "neo-colonialism" is above all a matter of perception guiding action. Is this really a relevant fact today? Dag Tresselt may indicate the direction of a general answer with his observation on a specific region:

The countries of West Africa are . . . currently debating whether the severing of the ties with the old colonial firms is merely a prelude to new and conceivably stronger ties with interests investing in the region's geological resources. This anxiety with regard to "neo-colonialism" is today a stern reality for businessmen of foreign origin in West Africa, and a factor of importance in the development of the psychological environment . . . [8]

Tresselt also points out that not only are West African trading patterns dominated by former colonial ties for the exports as well as the imports of the region, but the goods are in large part shipped in vessels flying the flag of the European importing country.[9] Furthermore, "even in West Africa, with its tradition of indigenous small-scale trading, the export and import business done by firms of foreign origin amounts to perhaps 90 percent of the total. The largest firms are, without exception, of foreign origin."[10] Thus, the image of colonialism is not a mere product of lively imaginations; it has several foundations in solid facts.[11]

The second point made above turned on the composition of commodities in the trade of developing countries. It was argued that the cost of transport relative to commodity value is higher for the exports than for the imports of developing countries, since the former are generally low-value, heavy or bulky goods, while the latter tend to be high-value, light, and less bulky.

The argument, at the moment, does not concern the question of who pays the freight—or the more complex question of who actually bears the cost.[12] The present argument is, rather, that on many of the typical exports of developing countries the cost of shipment is high enough to affect the market price of the product and hence its competitive position *vis-à-vis* the same product shipped from other parts of the world, or *vis-à-vis* possible substitutes.

The fact that freight costs on heavy, low-value raw materials, such as ores, are higher in proportion to commodity price than lighter-weight, high-value commodities seems to be well established.[13]

Other typical non-processed goods such as jute, which is actually a light-weight commodity, also have problems. At the third session of UNCTAD's Committee on Shipping in April 1969, the delegate of Pakistan claimed that jute—an export product of crucial importance for Pakistan—was in danger of being priced right out of the market due to "prohibitive" freight rates.[14] And in a general reference to goods (excluding oil) typically exported by developing countries, the Economist Intelligence Unit points out the contrast between "the long term decline in world commodity prices over the last decade, on the one hand, and . . . [the] stable and often rising shipping and insurance costs and port charges, on the other."[15]

A second implication of the typical trading patterns between developed and developing areas involves the terms of shipment. The terms of shipment refer to the conditions under which cargo-handling-costs, insurance, and freight charges are paid either by the seller or the buyer, or arranged some other way. The most common terms of shipment are *CIF* (cost, insurance, freight), and *FOB* (free on board). Under CIF terms, cost, insurance, and freight are included in the agreed price, so that the buyer pays the seller for the goods as well as the costs of insurance and freight, and the seller then makes the necessary payments to shipping company, insurance company, etc. Under FOB terms, on the other hand, the seller delivers the goods free on board and the buyer settles insurance and freight costs directly with the companies concerned upon receiving the goods without involving the seller.

On the face of it, then, this is merely the question of who—buyer or seller—should run errands to the shipping and insurance companies. The important point is, however, that *whoever makes the freight payment will be able to choose the shipping company and the ship to carry the goods.*[16] The choice of a national-flag ship would then come rather naturally.

Ordinarily, the terms of shipment are a matter of negotiation, and ideally traders would like to buy imports on FOB terms and sell exports on CIF terms. The choice of ship, of course, should not be assumed to be primarily a matter of nationalistic emotion. Many practical considerations are involved. Choosing the ship means first of all choosing the right ship at the right time, at the right price. and in the best possible location. The ship should be suitably equipped for the carriage of the particular commodity in question, and a company with a reputation for carefulness and responsibility in cargo handling will have an edge on its competitors. Indeed, the shipowners themselves also engage in this process. According to Sturmey:

In practice, shipowners try to ensure that goods shipped from their own country are carried CIF, that is, the exporter pays the freight and insures the goods before departure. There are administrative reasons for this preference in that it saves the shipowner having to collect his freight from the foreign importer and arranging himself to insure the goods in transit. It also protects the shipowners from the risks of variations in foreign exchange rates. With imports to their own country, shipowners are generally willing to accept FOB shipments, for, although they leave the insurance question open, the payment of freight in the home currency is secured. In the case of indirect trades, the shipowner will usually be indifferent between CIF and FOB shipment, unless it is markedly easier to collect freight payments from one country than from the other.[17]

In determining the terms of shipment, the party (buyer or seller) currently favored by the market situation will normally win out. For the commodities usually exported from developing countries, however, there has long been a buyer's market, and the situation does not appear to be about to change in the near future.[18] And in the several cases where large shipowning countries in the developed world are also big in seaborne trade, additional pressure on exporters in developing countries is probably applied by the Western shipowners, if Sturmey's description just quoted is correct.

This all points to the conclusion that the developing countries are in a consistently unfavorable position with respect to terms of shipment. So far, however, there is only circumstantial evidence, and the conclusions of the report of the UNCTAD Secretariat in its study of terms of shipment may therefore be a valuable addition.

First of all, the Secretariat points out that

There is little in the way of a consistent pattern except in the trade of the socialist countries, which usually try to import FOB and export CIF. *However, on balance it appears that, by and large, FOB is more important than CIF in the export trades of developing countries, while CIF is more important than FOB in the import trades.*[19] (Italics mine.)

The Secretariat also explicitly observed that

No evidence emerged that traders in the traditional maritime countries consistently used the terms of shipment as a means of favoring their national-flag shipping, although the studies revealed that a certain amount of nomination, for various reasons, does occur.[20]

It seems unlikely, however, that a West European trader would nominate a ship registered in a developing country, when ships from either his own or a neighboring country are available. Moreover, the distribution of shipping tonnage in the world as it is means that West European ships will normally be available most of the time in any ports of significance around the world.

Hence, the entire structure of shipping relations between developed and developing countries favors the payment of freight to ships registered in the industrialized countries. Both the overwhelming concentration of tonnage in the developed world and the terms-of-shipment factor, combined with the composition of commodities in trade between developed and developing areas, contribute to this state of affairs.

The question of who derives the freight income should therefore be clear. Where balances of payments are concerned, however, the question of who makes freight payments to whom also becomes important. This again is a matter of nationality: if a trader makes payment to a shipowner in his own country, there is no "drain" of money from the national economy; if he makes payment abroad, this is an element of "drain."

As has been shown above, it is more usual for payment to be made by the trader in a developed country to his own country's ships or to the ships of neighboring countries, than to ships of developing countries. If the developed country in question has both a large merchant fleet and a large seaborne trade, chances are that payments will be made to shipowners in the same country. In any case, the foreign exchange involved is likely to remain within the developed region.

Even though it is less usual for traders in the developing countries to arrange for freight payments, these are still likely to be made to shipowners of the developed countries, simply because there are so few ships available that are registered in the less developed countries. There can be no obscuring the fact, therefore, that developing countries in general suffer a considerable drain on their already slim foreign exchange reserves due to payments of freight and insurance on their seaborne trade. The following table, compiled by Bela A. Balassa and reproduced in Dag Tresselt's study of West Africa, amply illustrates this point:

Table 3-5

Developing Countries: Receipts and Payments on Account of Freight and Insurance, 1960 (Billions of Dollars)[a]

	Latin America	Africa	Middle East	Asia
Receipts	0.13	0.10	0.02	0.11
Payments	0.79	0.53	0.25	9.64

[a]Source: Bela A. Balassa, TRADE PROSPECTS FOR DEVELOPING COUNTRIES (Homewood, Ill.: Richard D. Irwin, Inc., 1964), as found in Tresselt, op. cit., p. 48.

Tresselt makes the same point, if possible more forcefully, in a study of Latin America,[21] and even the cautious report of the Economist Intelligence Unit makes the same observation in no uncertain terms.[22]

Patterns of Shipping Transactions in the Bulk Trades

For convenience, the shipping business will in this chapter be considered under two main headings: (a) liner trades; and (b) bulk trades. The latter actually lumps together the two kinds of service referred to in Chapter 1 as *open market tramping*, and *contractual tramping* (negotiated fixtures), although the emphasis here will be somewhat more on contractual tramping.

Available statistics are not conveniently ordered for this kind of analysis. In terms of shipping tonnage, statistical sources distinguish between "dry cargo vessels" and "tankers." There is no distinction between ships engaged in liner services and ships in the open market or contractual tramping business in the dry-cargo category. Some data are available on (dry-cargo) bulk-carriers, but this creates a residual category out of tramps not built as bulk-carriers, and therefore does not solve any problems. For this reason, the following examination of tonnage registry trends will have to be restricted to tankers in the carriage of crude oil and other petroleum products. Dry-cargo tramp tonnage will not be considered; instead, the focus will be on the cargo carried by such ships. For liners, a particular substitute for the consideration of tonnage registry will be introduced.

Patterns of Tonnage Registry in Petroleum Transport

In volume terms, which is the only way seaborne trade is considered in this chapter, crude oil and petroleum products are the most important commodity types in seaborne trade, in later years accounting for more than half of the total volume.[23]

Table 3-6 shows the distribution of tanker registry among main world regions in selected postwar years. The table shows clearly a drastic decline in the importance of US tanker tonnage, an equally dramatic increase in the African share—all of which is accounted for by Liberia(!)—and the increasing concentration of tanker registry in the industrialized West European countries, including Japan. Another noteworthy development is the expansion of the East European tanker fleet. The Panamanian tankers, which make up the bulk of the Central American registry, have a declining share of the total as the vogue in "convenient" registry shifts from Panama to Liberia.

The break in Liberia's growth pattern in 1962 was a transitory phenomenon, due mainly to the transfer of considerable tonnage from Liberian to Greek registry as a result of changes in Greek taxation laws some years earlier. A large share of Liberia's tanker tonnage is now made up of vessels belonging to the world's major oil companies.

In other countries, the independent tankship owners have a more prominent position. Some of these countries deserve a bit closer attention, since the regional figures obscure certain trends. Thus, within the West European group the British, Japanese, and Norwegian fleets are the more important ones, yet give evidence of rather divergent growth patterns. The British tanker fleet actually shows strong marks of stagnation, declining from 23 percent of the world total in 1948 to only about 13 percent in 1966. The Norwegian fleet, on the other

Table 3-6

Oil Tankers by Region of Registry (Millions of Gross Register Tons, and Percent)[a]

	1948		1959		1962		1967	
	Mill. G.R.T.	Percent	Mill. G.R.T.	Percent	Mill. G.R.T.	Percent	Mill. G.R.T.	Percent
W. Europe	7.1	46	20.9	55	27.9	62	35.2	59
E. Europe	–	–	0.9	2	1.3	3	2.8	5
Asia	–	–	–	–	0.3	1	0.6	1
Africa	–	–	7.1	19	6.8	15	12.1	20
Arab st.	–	–	–	–	0.1	0	0.2	0
S. America	–	–	–	–	1.3	3	1.4	2
C. America	1.4	9	2.6	7	2.3	5	2.9	5
N. America	5.5	36	4.3	11	5.0	11	4.6	8
Oceania	–	–	–	–	–	–	0.1	0
Others[b]	1.4	9	2.1	6	0.4	1	0.3	0
Total	15.4	100	37.9	100	45.4	101	60.2	100

[a]Source: UN STATISTICAL YEARBOOKS.

[b]Covers data missing from certain regions.

hand, has increased its share from 12 to 15 percent in the same period, while Japan has jumped from practically nothing in 1948 to more than 8 percent of the total in 1966, and its pace of increase has been even more rapid in the years after 1966.[24]

Hence, among the world's five largest tanker fleets two—the American and the British—are stagnating or declining, while three—the Liberian, Japanese and Norwegian—are growing rapidly.

The developing countries are even less involved in tanker ownership, using other vessel types. This fact is probably due to the general nature of their shipping policies, which stress the participation of national-flag shipping in each country's foreign trade. Oil consumption is low in the less developed countries, and indeed the petroleum transport business in general is in large part a matter of third-flag carriage, all of which makes it less interesting from the point of view of developing countries.[25]

It seems a bit curious, however, that the several developing countries in the Middle East and the Caribbean area, accounting for most of the world's oil exports, have not developed their tanker fleets. In 1966, according to UN statistics, the tanker fleets of the oil-exporting countries amounted to only 379,000 gross register tons taken together.[26]

Over the years, a few attempts at development have been made, but with rather limited results. Thus, Lebanon—a major shipper of petroleum arriving via pipeline from Iraq and Saudi Arabia—has established itself as a flag of convenience, but without managing to attract significant amounts of tonnage. A different ploy was attempted by Saudi Arabia, which in 1954 made an agreement with Aristotle Onassis whereby Onassis' tankers would be registered under the Saudi Arabian flag and receive preferential treatment in carrying the nation's petroleum exports. Predictably, West European shipping interests and governments reacted strongly,[27] and their pressures—probably supplemented by the influence of important oil companies—succeeded in killing the plan, which apparently was quietly dropped in 1956.

Lately, there has been some talk of a common effort by Arab states to develop a regional tanker fleet, although no concrete measures appear to have been taken so far.

A likely reason—if one may be allowed some speculation—for the lack of tanker fleets in oil-exporting countries could be opposition from the major oil companies. Ultimately, the oil-exporting countries control the wells, and they also control a considerable mileage of pipelines, especially in the Middle East. Beyond that, however, they seem to have had little or no influence over petroleum transport, and the oil companies would stand to lose both the savings they normally make by having their own tankers, and the efficient and flexible transport apparatus which they now have in conjunction with the independent tankship owners, if the transport of oil were to come more closely under the guidance of the foreign policy-making bodies of the oil-exporting countries. In the current world situation, this issue is more touchy in the Middle East than anywhere else, and it is not inconceivable that the oil companies for these reasons have exerted themselves to keep the Arab states out of tanker shipping.

Tanker registry patterns can be briefly summed up in two statements: (1) Industrial ownership is prominent, accounting for about 40 percent of the world's tanker fleet, with independent, private tankship owners accounting for almost all the remainder. (2) Tanker registry is regionally confined to the Western, industrialized countries and two flags of convenience.

Patterns of Petroleum Carriage

The maritime transport of oil occurs in relatively simple patterns. (See Table 3-7 and 3-8.)

In Table 3-7, South America (confined mainly to Venezuela) and the Arab states stand out as the major exporting areas. Their relative importance, however, has shifted: while in 1959 the two regions were roughly equal in volume loaded, in 1966 the Arab states exported more than twice the amount of South America. Earlier, the "Caribbean" area[28] was more prominently in the picture even than in 1959. In the first postwar years, pipelines in the Middle East were not so well developed. Although some oil from Iraq was brought in pipelines to the Eastern Mediterranean coast and loaded for Europe there, most

Table 3-7

Petroleum (Crude and Products) Loaded in Seaborne Trade (Million Metric Tons, and Percent)[a]

	1959		1966	
	Million Tons	Percent	Million Tons	Percent
Western Europe	30.8	6.9	61.5	6.7
Eastern Europe	19.5	4.4	55.4	6.0
Asia	61.7	13.8	125.7	13.7
Africa	1.8	0.4	44.5	4.8
Arab states	174.4	39.0	433.6	47.1
South America	142.0	31.7	173.6	18.9
Central America[b]	10.6	2.4	21.7	2.4
North America	5.6	1.3	3.2	0.3
Oceania	1.2	0.3	1.4	0.1
Total	447.6	100.2	920.6	100.0

[a]Source: UN STATISTICAL YEARBOOKS, 1967 and 1969.

[b]The Netherlands Antilles have been excluded from these tables, since the refining business on the islands has only a transit function and is unrelated to local oil consumption. Inclusion would simply imply a double count of much of Venezuela's oil exports.

Table 3-8

Petroleum (Crude and Products) Unloaded in Seaborne Trade (Million Metric Tons, and Percent)[a]

	1959		1966	
	Million Tons	Percent	Million Tons	Percent
Western Europe	219.5	51.5	570.0	64.6
Eastern Europe	1.2	0.3	5.9	0.7
Asia	26.5	6.2	52.3	5.9
Africa	13.8	3.2	21.8	2.5
Arab states	12.3	2.9	14.9	1.7
South America	21.2	5.0	22.0	2.5
Central America[b]	13.4	3.1	30.5	3.4
North America	104.9	24.6	142.0	16.1
Oceania	13.4	3.1	23.3	2.6
Total	426.2	99.9	882.7	100.0

[a]Source: As in Table 3-7.

[b]Excluding Netherlands Antilles. (See note to Table 3-7.)

Middle East shipments were at first made in the Persian Gulf and taken through the Suez Canal to Western Europe. In these early years, substantial amounts of oil moved from the Caribbean to Western Europe, though the United States and Canada have been and still are the main markets for Venezuelan oil.

Over the years, several developments combined to change these patterns:

1. New production areas closer to Europe were found. Libya is the major one, but Saharan oil (shipped from Algeria and Tunisia) and Nigerian oil are also important.
2. New pipelines have been built from Iraq and Saudi Arabia to the Eastern Mediterranean (Lebanon and Syria).
3. Japan has emerged as a major market.
4. Passage through the Suez Canal was disrupted for about six months in 1956-57, and the Canal has remained entirely closed since the 1967 Middle East War. Another result of this war was the blowing-up of Aramco's "Tap-Line" to the Eastern Mediterranean.[29]

The consequent shifts in petroleum transport patterns have been as follows: Western Europe has been supplied by shipments from Lebanon, Syria, and Libya, and by direct shipments from the Persian Gulf. Since 1967, the latter flow has been diverted around the Cape of Good Hope, a voyage that can be made economically if the tanker is large enough (preferably about 200,000 dwt. or more).[30] At the same time, many Persian Gulf shipments now go to Japan, which also receives most of the oil exported by Indonesia.

The third main consumption area, the US and Canada, is supplied mainly by Venezuela, whose importance as supplier to Europe has declined, as mentioned above.

Political Implications of Petroleum Carriage

It is a special characteristic of petroleum carriage that so much of it takes place in industrial carriers or in tankers on long-term charter to the main oil companies. This gives the business a rather closed, private character. The Economist Intelligence Unit puts this very succinctly in a discussion of Liberia's seaborne trade, though the description is probably to the point for a great many other countries as well: "... in most cases, the shipowners are also the oil producers, exporters, refiners, importers and distributors ... "[31] This may be the reason why "oil cargoes ... are substantially less affected by discrimination than dry cargoes ... "[32] Sturmey also claims that, "In their chartering the [oil] companies are internationally minded and, apart from the entry of some Cold War tensions, will normally charter the most suitable tankers, irrespective of nationality."[33]

Still the highly integrated character of the whole business may create visions of the ultimate "monopolistic capitalists," of a worldwide network of control over a strategically and economically important commodity. But the single fact subsuming the most important political implication of the oil tanker business is this: From 1946 to 1968, the major oil producing areas were physically remote from the major consumption areas, and to this geographical distance may be added a corresponding *political* distance, especially as concerns the Middle East. To the Western consumer countries, oil is (1) business, and (2) strategy. To the Middle East producer countries oil, to be sure, is business, but it is also tainted by the "imperialist" dimension, in turn linked with an increasing nationalism and a growing political self-consciousness, as well as with the entire Palestine complex of issues.

The strategic significance of oil is a source of leverage for the Arab states, as it would be for any state or coalition of states with the capacity to shut off the supplies to a consuming country through an embargo or a blockade. For example, the Arab states closed the tap on oil to Western countries for a period in 1967, and the UK has tried since 1965 to enforce a UN embargo on petroleum shipments to Rhodesia. Both examples show the limits of the leverage: the Arab states needed the oil income too badly to maintain their policy, and the UN was unable to secure South African compliance with the Rhodesia embargo.[34] Thus, in the strategic dimension, the subjective factor of what statesmen *think* about the importance of oil may be more politically relevant than the actual, "objective" importance of oil.

Transaction Patterns in Other Bulk Commodities

Non-petroleum bulk commodities include, among the more important ones, grains, ores, and coal. Table 3-9 gives a rough picture of the shares of the total dry cargo market accounted for by different types of carriers in 1962. Note that slightly less than half the total dry-cargo volume is estimated to belong to the

Table 3-9
Total Volume of Dry-Cargo Carried in 1962, by Type of Carrier (Estimates)[a]

Carried by:	
Liners	300 mill. tons
Integrated fleets and contractual tramps	165 mill. tons
Open market tramps	120 mill. tons
Total dry-cargo	585 mill. tons

[a]Source: Economist Intelligence Unit, op. cit., p. 199.

category being discussed here—non-petroleum bulk commodities. Vessels in the long-term charter market or owned by the extracting and/or producing industries carry a larger share of these cargoes than the traditional tramps, although the difference is moderate.

As mentioned earlier, sources do not distinguish readily between different types of dry-cargo vessels. Some informed guesswork could, however, give an indication of what countries' fleets are engaged in the business.

An initial clue is found in the category "integrated fleets." These vessels are in all likelihood mostly registered under flags of convenience (Panama and Liberia). Industries that are not primarily concerned with shipping are likely to place a high premium on tax benefits and opportunities for saving labor costs, typical advantages of PANHOLIB registry.[35] More concretely, however, large corporations and their integrated fleets have played a crucial role in the development of the flag-of-convenience fleets, as they were the initiators of this practice on a large scale in the late 1930s and the earlier post-war years. Thus, the impetus to Panama's growth came initially from Standard Oil, whose Esso Shipping Company had 25 ships, originally German-registered, transferred at first to the flag of the Free City of Danzig (in 1935).[36] Liberia, similarily, became a flag of convenience after World War II, when the Stettinius Associates of New York founded the Liberia Company to develop Liberian mineral resources and "arranged the formalities for granting Liberian registration on terms still more liberal than those of Panama."[37] One may assume that the ships concerned were ore carriers. The Honduras experience, finally, had its origin in the transfer of the United Fruit Company's fleet to Honduran registry.[38]

From what we know about the chartering practices of companies that have large bulk-transport requirements, it seems reasonable to conclude that the above category of dry cargo carried by "integrated fleets and contractual tramps" is shared about fifty/fifty by the integrated fleets on the one hand and the contractual tramps on the other. Some 82.5 million tons of bulk dry cargo may thus be attributed to integrated carriers registered mostly in Panama and Liberia. An almost equal volume of bulk dry cargo correspondingly falls on the contractual tramps, where registry is concentrated under flags of convenience, Greece, Norway, and (in later years) Japan, but with significant participation also by most of the traditional European maritime countries' fleets. (The development of specialized ore carriers as they are today can be credited largely to the Swedish mining company Grängesbergsbolaget, which today possesses one of the world's largest integrated ore-carrier fleets. Grängesberg is also one of the more active companies in the exploitation of Liberia's mineral resources.)

Because of the unpredictable movements of grains in world trade, dependent on harvests as well as the shifting of political winds,[39] grains are carried by tramps on short-term charters rather than by integrated or contractual carriers. Ores and coal are therefore the most important commodities on the latter kinds of vessels.

Table 3-10 shows the main movements of iron ore in 1960:

Table 3-10
International Seaborne Iron Ore Trade over Major Trade Routes 1960 (Million Tons)[a]

	Importing Countries			
Exporting Countries	EEC	UK	US	Japan
Sweden and Norway	13.6	5.1	0.1	–
Spain and Portugal	1.5	1.1	–	–
North Africa	2.5	3.7	–	–
West Africa	3.0	1.7	1.0	–
India and Goa	3.0	0.0	0.1	4.5
Malaya	0.1	–	–	5.3
Philippines	–	–	–	1.2
Canada	1.8	3.3	10.6	1.1
United States	–	–	–	0.8
Venezuela	2.7	1.6	14.6	0.0
Brazil	1.8	0.6	1.5	0.4
Chile	0.5	–	3.9	0.3
Peru	1.5	–	2.8	0.6

[a]Quoted in full from Alexandersson and Nordström, op. cit., p. 81.

Before World War II, the UK and Northwestern Europe got most of their iron ore from Sweden, Spain, and North Africa.[40] Table 3-10 reveals how the patterns have changed, in particular for the EEC-area. Though Swedish iron ore (considerable amounts of it shipped through Narvik in Norway) retains its leading position as supplier to the West European steel industry, Spain and Portugal and North Africa have declined in importance as suppliers. In their place have come mining areas in West Africa, India, and South America, which implies much longer hauls made increasingly economical by huge, specialized bulk carriers. The change in pattern is more noticeable for the EEC six than for the UK, whose traders may be more reluctant to give up long established economic relationships, and whose shipowners have been slow getting into the bulk carrier business.

The two other major importing countries, the US and Japan, give evidence of distinctly regional trading patterns in iron ore.[41]

Coal represents different patterns. Formerly, coal was a commodity of tremendous importance in international seaborne trade and, although large quantities are transported even today, its importance is greatly reduced. The most obvious reason for this decline is the competition from other energy sources, mainly oil. Still, coal shipments have been substantial on certain routes throughout the period covered in this study. More than three-quarters of all coal shipped moves under long-term freighting arrangements.[42]

Major trade routes in the carriage of coal on long-term contracts are US East Coast to Japan, US East Coast to Italy and to North West Europe, Australia to Japan, and US East Coast to East Coast South America.[43] Thus, long-term coal carriage is primarily an "in-group" activity among the industrialized countries, and with the United States in a crucial position as shipper.

Next to iron ore, bauxite and manganese are the major commodities in the maritime transport of ores. Bauxite, used in aluminum production, is exported predominantly from Jamaica, Guyana, and Surinam. The major destinations are US Gulf ports, Canada, and to some extent Norway and Germany.[44] Trinidad plays a role for bauxite analogous to the role of the Netherlands Antilles for oil: in both cases mainland ports cannot accommodate more than very shallow-draft vessels and the product concerned goes to islands just off the coast for transshipment.[45] Other bauxite trade routes are intra-European (with France in a pivotal position as both importer and exporter), and South-East Asian, moving from Malaya, Sarawak, and India to Japan and Australia.[46]

Manganese is used in steel production, and is commonly found in association with iron ore in varying concentrations.[47] "The largest exporters [of manganese ores] are India, (including Goa), the Soviet Union, Brazil, Ghana, the Congo, and South Africa,"[48] while the major importers are found in the US and Western Europe.[49]

In sum, in the carriage of bulky dry cargo by integrated fleets or under long-term charter, ores and coal predominate—the latter moving mainly among the developed countries, the former moving mainly from the less developed to the more developed countries.

Turning now to the open tramp market, we find that grain is by far the most important commodity. In 1964, it accounted for 54.2 percent by weight of the cargo carried under voyage charter; in 1965 the figure was 60.1 percent; in 1967 it was down again to 53.5 percent.[50] Other important commodities are ores and coal (i.e., the shares not covered by integrated fleets or contractual tramps), metals and scrap, and sugar.[51]

Some of the vessels engaged in this market are specialized, but the majority tend to be all-purpose tramps. In the grain trade, tankers were used to a considerable extent in the late 1950s and early 1960s.

Tramping appears to be distinctly popular only among a few national shipowner groups. The British and Greek fleets stand out in this respect, while the two major flags of convenience probably cover at least an equally significant number of these vessels.[52] But in this special area the smaller flags of convenience, such as Honduras, Costa Rica, and Lebanon, also seem to be of more consequence.[53]

Among the reasons why a particular commodity is not suitable for long-term freighting arrangements are usually unstable production and unstable demand in the various importing areas. Such conditions are found typically in the grain trade.

Wheat tops the list of grains in seaborne trade by volume. The US, Canada, Australia, and Argentina are by far the largest and most stable exporters employing oceangoing tonnage. The directions of the wheat trade are unstable, but some patterns may be distinguished: The US ships mainly to Western Europe, excluding the United Kingdom, and to certain Asian countries, especially India and Japan. Canada ships wheat above all to the British Isles, but also to the Philippines and Ceylon, and in smaller quantities worldwide. Argentina ships wheat mainly to Europe and Brazil, while Australian wheat goes in large part to the UK and to East and South-East Asian countries.[54]

Exceptional patterns have occurred from time to time since the late 1950s because of crop failures in the communist countries, requiring them to buy wheat from (especially) Canada, Australia, and the United States. For political reasons Canada and Australia were the more popular suppliers in the late 1960s. By 1972, however, the US-Soviet detente returned the US to its former role as a politically acceptable wheat supplier. As noted earlier, what marks these transactions is above all their lack of predictability, which is probably in part intentional (for tactical reasons in bargaining), and partly unintentional (due to a natural reluctance to admit failures in agricultural policies and then turn to the citadels of capitalism for help).

The wheat trade employs a fleet about six times as large as that engaged in the carriage of the second most important grain type: barley.[55] The barley trade is partly an intra-European matter, partly transoceanic carriage from the United States and Canada, as well as from Australia, Argentina, and the Soviet Union.[56] Other grain types of some consequence are corn and rice. The points of origin of corn are concentrated in the US and Argentina. Europe is the main importing area. Rice is carried mostly on intra-regional Asian trade routes, with Burma and Thailand as the largest exporters.[57]

It is evident that the greater volume of grain carried in seaborne trade moves from a few (mostly) highly developed countries to both developed and underdeveloped areas. The significance of the latter should not go unnoticed: grain is the only kind of bulky commodity moving in large quantities from the more to the less developed countries of the world. Another typical characteristic of the grain trades is that *governments* frequently appear in the roles of shippers as well as consignees. Not surprisingly, therefore, grain carriage is a bulk transaction pattern where flag discrimination is hardly an exception any more. The US government has shown the way here with its well-known cargo-preference policy. (See below.)

Of the other commodity types in the voyage charter market, ores and coal are "residuals" of the more substantial carriage of these goods under long-term charter, though it should be noted that this has not been so for the entire postwar period. Long-term charter in the dry-cargo business is a relatively recent development. It reflects a cautious attitude on the part of shipowners, and a confidently optimistic outlook on the part of charterers. It also reflects technological developments in shipbuilding, in the direction of larger, more specialized vessels that are at the same time more expensive to build and more economical to operate. The earlier postwar years concealed these changes as they were in the making. Government regulation of the market hung over from the war, and reconstruction needs in Europe and elsewhere meant exceptional transport requirements. In this period, coal was especially important, "with European industry to a high degree dependent on coal from USA for its reconstruction efforts."[58] After a brief downturn in the transatlantic coal trade in 1948-49, the Korean War prompted a tremendous increase in this trade in 1950, and it remained a most active section of the dry cargo market until the general post-Suez decline of 1957, from which it never really recovered.

During this period, however, another significant trade route for coal was developing, the Hampton Roads (US)-Japan trade. From the late 1950s this trade grew into the world's dominant one for coal, while another coal trade in the Pacific began to grow in the 1960s on the East Australian-Japan run. In short, the major destination for coal has shifted decisively in the postwar period from Europe to Japan, while the US has remained the major supplier.[59]

The iron ore section of this market has not been comparable to coal in importance. More than coal, open-market iron ore carriages is a characteristic "leftover" from the long-term charter market. Steelmakers engage long-term tonnage on the larger-volume stable runs from their closer supply areas, with open-market contracts apparently being reserved for the longer hauls from more distant supply areas when marginal requirements turn up. Thus, during the 1950s the India-Europe trade is the one most frequently quoted on iron ore by the Platou report.[60] In the 1960s, however, Japan has been the major destination—chiefly for ore from Australia, Canada, and several South American countries—but also from supply points as far away as West Africa.[61]

In contradistinction to the grain market, the open-market carriage of coal and iron ore rarely involves governments as parties to transactions. Consequently, there is less room for governmental interference in the form of cargo reservation. The potential political significance of this market lies in the strategic importance of the commodities. Open-market tramps become crucial in the coal and iron ore trades mainly when exceptional demand for these commodities arises (again, due to the habits of charterers), and such exceptional demand has a way of showing up particularly in times of serious and protracted international crisis, as illustrated, *inter alia*, by the Korean War.

Transaction Patterns in the Liner Trades

As mentioned earlier, shipping statistics do not distinguish between liners and tramps, but report shipping tonnage for these two categories (and including also bulk carriers) in a lump "dry cargo" category. In the following, an untraditional approach has been adopted to estimate the sizes of the various national liner fleets.

Table 3-11 shows the approximate relative sizes of the liner fleets of the world, based on a *size index*. This index refers only to liner conferences, covering a total of 447 shipowners. The index value itself gives the number of regularly scheduled calls abroad made by the liner companies of each country. A "call" is here defined as *one* shipowner maintaining regular service at *one or more* ports in *one* country (other than his country of registry) through membership in a liner conference. Thus, a British company which serves three different French ports through membership in three different liner conferences would still only be counted as one call, whereas two British companies serving French ports via membership in any number of liner conferences would count as two "British" calls. In other words, neither the number of ports served *within* another country, nor the number of liner conferences through which the service is maintained, makes any difference to the number of calls. All that counts is the number of shipowners in a given country and the number of other countries they serve.

It is therefore assumed that the larger the number of calls made by any one shipowner, the greater is his service capability—and, by implication, the larger his fleet must be. Hence the index shows the size of a given liner fleet relative to other fleets with greater or smaller numbers of calls.

Table 3-11 also gives an idea of the geographical coverage of each country's liner fleet by showing the number of other countries served by each country's liner fleet. (The total number of countries is 106. The maximum number of "other countries" is therefore 105.)

Table 3-11 reflects a clear predominance by developed countries in the world's liner services; the eleven highest-ranking countries all belong to this group.[62] Among the less-developed countries, the Philippines, Indonesia, and India, at ranks 12, 13, and 14, form sort of an elite group in liner services, placing considerably higher than the next group of developing countries, which begins at rank 20.

These facts should also be viewed in a wider perspective, however, by comparing the registry of cargo liners in developing countries with the registry of tankers, tramps, and bulk carriers in the same countries: whereas the less-developed countries (excepting flags of convenience) possess only minimal amounts of tonnage in the latter categories, their share of liner registry is by comparison considerable.[63]

If geographical coverage is added to the number of calls as an indicator of size, the ten (rather than eleven) first countries seem to be in a class by themselves—all of them serving 100 or more countries. An intermediate group is found approximately in the range between 11 and 32, consisting of a mixture of more- and less-developed countries, followed by an intermediate-low group

Table 3-11

Size Index and Geographical Coverage of Liner Fleets with Liner Conference Membership in June 1968, in Rank Order by Country of Registry[a]

Rank	Country	Size Index (Number of Calls)	Geographical Coverage (Number of Countries Served)
1	UK	1848	105
2	USA	960	105
3	Norway	655	104
4	Netherlands	566	105
5	France	518	104
6	West Germany	517	104
7	Japan	487	104
8	Italy	426	101
9	Sweden	354	103
10	Denmark	264	100
11	Canada	218	72
12	Philippines	171	42
13	Indonesia	168	68
14	India	161	71
15	Yugoslavia	133	60
16	Belgium	127	83
17	Spain	122	57
18	South Africa	99	34
19	Greece	98	43
20.5	Brazil	83	53
20.5	Pakistan	83	50
22	Israel	82	54
23	Finland	81	53
24	Portugal	80	31
25	Argentina	56	56
26	Colombia	54	48
27	Taiwan	53	47
28	Burma	49	49
29.5	Kenya	47	30
29.5	Poland	47	47
31	Malagasy	46	46
32	Monaco	34	34
33	Mexico	32	32
34.5	Ghana	30	30
34.5	Nigeria	30	30
36	UAR[b]	29	29
37.5	Nicaragua	28	28

Table 3-11 (cont.)

Rank	Country	Size Index (Number of Calls)	Geographical Coverage (Number of Countries Served)
37.5	Venezuela	28	28
39	Switzerland	27	23
41	Australia	25	20
41	Guatemala	25	25
41	Liberia	25	25
43	Turkey	24	16
44	Peru	22	19
45.5	Chile	21	21
45.5	Iran	21	21
47	Ethiopia	20	20
48.5	Sudan	19	19
48.5	Thailand	19	15
50	Iraq	17	17
51	Ivory Coast	15	15
52	Singapore	9	4
53	Malaysia	8	2
54	New Zealand	7	6
55	Hong Kong	6	6
56	South Korea	6	6
57	Morocco	5	4
58.5	Ireland	3	3
58.5	Panama	3	3
60	Algeria	2	2
61	Tunisia	1	1

[a]Source: CRONER'S WORLD DIRECTORY OF FREIGHT CONFERENCES, 4th ed. (New Malden (England): Croner Publications Ltd.), June 1968 version.
[b]For convenience, Egypt has been designated UAR in all tables.

(ranks 32 through 51), consisting primarily of developing countries. Finally, there is a low group of ten countries, again a composite of more- and less-developed states.

Of these groups, the top one may be described as maintaining a truly global service, and the low group as maintaining only local service with contiguous countries, assuming that the number of calls will increase with the distance of sailing. Such a classification, however, has further implications in the context of this study, because it is related to the phenomenon of *third-flag carriage.*

Third-flag carriage refers to a ship carrying goods between two countries, neither of which is its country of registry (also called "cross trade"). In the controversial practice of flag discrimination by cargo preference, the discriminating country often makes exceptions from the preference of national-flag ships to the benefit of the ships of the country (or countries) with which it trades. This habit is often formalized in bilateral cargo-reservation agreements, in which two countries agree to split the cargo volume of their mutual seaborne trade by a fifty/fifty formula, to the exclusion of other carriers.[64]

The implication for the present discussion is clear: it is countries whose fleets engage predominantly in third-flag carriage that are hit the hardest by cargo reservation. These countries may therefore be expected to form the core of any anti-discrimination coalition, and indeed they do: the OECD's Maritime Transport Committee, which has been crusading against discrimination since 1954, includes nine of these ten states as its most active members.[65]

Most of the discriminating countries may, on the other hand, be expected to belong to the intermediate groups, since the rationale of a cargo-reservation policy obviously is to have a liner fleet that is too small to make money in extensive third-flag carriage, yet large enough to benefit from the reservation of cargo. Of 25 countries identified by the Economist Intelligence Unit as practicing cargo reservation by unilateral legislation, bilateral treaties, and/or administrative pressures in the early 1960s,[66] 17 belong to the intermediate groups, one belongs to the low group, and none to the high group, as expected. (It should be noted that some countries, especially among the less-developed ones, have liner fleets which are not represented in the liner conferences. It is likely that the remaining seven countries belong to this category, though existing data cannot pinpoint this clearly.)

So far it has been established *who* tends to do most of the liner carriage. The next question is where the goods originate and where they are carried. The present data cannot link origins and destinations,[67] but focus on points of call (defined by nation). Table 3-12 shows which countries' ships tend to call at which countries (other than their own), grouped by region.

The main pattern in Table 3-12 is very clear: the ships of any region in the world call (a) on the other countries in the same region, and (b) on the countries of Western Europe. Furthermore, Western Europe and North America are the only regions in the world that rather consistently (i.e., country by country) maintain global services.

Indeed, the developed countries dominate not only in liner shipping in Western Europe and North America, but in every other region in the world, with the possible exception of Eastern Europe. The liner services of the developing countries focus on carriage between the home region and the developed countries, but occupy obvious "number two"-positions across the board.

The political implications of such a pattern of international transactions in 1968 should be equally clear: it conforms to the less developed countries' general image of the world—an image that is none to good.

The United Nations Conference on Trade and Development was created in an

Table 3-12
Regular Scheduled Calls of Liner Shipowners, by Country of Registry and Region of Destination, June 1968[a]

To From	Africa	Arab States	Asia	East Europe	Latin America	North America	Oceania	West Europe	Total
Ethiopia	1	3	–	3	–	–	–	13	20
Ghana	14	–	–	3	–	2	–	11	30
Ivory Coast	14	–	–	–	–	–	–	1	15
Kenya	7	7	2	4	–	–	–	27	47
Liberia	1	10	5	3	–	1	–	5	25
Malagasy	17	9	2	1	–	–	–	17	46
Morocco	–	–	–	–	–	–	–	5	5
Nigeria	14	–	–	3	–	2	–	11	30
Sudan	1	3	–	3	–	–	–	12	19
Algeria	–	–	–	–	–	–	–	2	2
Iraq	1	1	1	2	–	–	–	12	17
Tunisia	–	–	–	–	–	–	–	1	1
UAR	4	9	4	3	–	–	–	9	29
Burma	3	9	14	5	–	–	–	18	49
Taiwan	4	10	8	5	–	1	–	25	53
Hong Kong	–	–	5	–	–	1	–	–	6
India	27	33	40	7	–	3	1	50	161
Indonesia	5	24	20	20	23	2	–	74	168
Iran	1	5	–	2	–	–	–	13	21
S. Korea	–	–	5	–	–	–	–	1	6
Malaysia	–	–	8	–	–	–	–	–	8
Pakistan	8	22	18	1	–	1	–	33	83
Philippines	–	–	104	2	46	7	–	12	171
Singapore	–	–	7	–	–	–	2	–	9
Thailand	–	–	14	1	–	2	–	2	19
Turkey	–	6	2	5	–	–	–	11	24
Poland	4	10	9	4	–	–	–	20	47
Argentina	2	6	12	–	18	–	–	18	56
Brazil	2	12	7	2	26	2	–	32	83
Chile	–	–	–	3	4	2	–	12	21
Colombia	–	–	7	3	26	4	–	14	54
Guatemala	–	–	–	–	12	–	–	13	25
Mexico	–	–	3	–	14	1	–	14	32
Nicaragua	–	–	–	–	14	1	–	13	28
Panama	–	–	–	–	1	2	–	–	3
Peru	–	–	–	3	6	1	–	12	22
Venezuela	–	–	–	–	14	1	–	13	28

Table 3-12 (cont.)

To From	Africa	Arab States	Asia	East Europe	Latin America	North America	Oceania	West Europe	Total
Canada	24	36	12	16	35	7	–	88	218
USA	80	91	226	51	269	21	4	218	960
Australia	2	–	15	–	–	1	2	5	25
New Zealand	–	–	3	–	–	2	2	–	7
Belgium	23	20	10	9	23	3	–	39	127
Denmark	37	35	41	18	49	8	1	75	264
Finland	3	8	2	10	19	3	–	36	81
France	174	82	45	33	51	6	2	125	518
W. Germany	67	63	63	35	75	13	4	197	517
Greece	5	32	15	12	6	2	–	26	98
Ireland	–	–	–	–	–	2	–	1	3
Israel	16	14	11	5	1	2	–	33	82
Italy	43	79	43	36	86	9	1	129	426
Japan	57	37	202	14	115	12	8	42	487
Monaco	1	6	2	5	1	2	–	17	34
Netherlands	64	73	87	40	113	12	5	172	566
Norway	133	79	113	37	121	24	5	143	655
Portugal	9	16	12	1	–	–	–	42	80
Spain	6	27	10	6	19	4	–	50	122
Sweden	25	40	44	34	69	18	4	120	354
Switzerland	17	2	–	–	1	2	–	5	27
S. Africa	9	28	25	–	–	1	–	36	99
UK	161	256	298	120	229	50	38	696	1848
Yugoslavia	11	25	23	13	5	5	–	51	133
Total	1097	1228	1599	583	1491	245	79	2872	9194

[a]Source: As in Table 3-11.

effort to change—or to prepare the way for change in—exactly the kind of dominance pattern found here. The point is not really its cause, or how it works, but rather the simple fact that phenomena controlled from abroad are not distinctly popular in any country. Proximity may not exactly guarantee effective influence, but distance certainly makes it less probable.

But this is far from the whole story on this point. In addition to the patterns of carriage in the liner trades, this sector of the shipping industry is also politically important due to other distinctive characteristics, which may be summarized under the following headings:

1. Rate-making in liner conferences.
2. Liners as "common carriers."
3. The special interest of the less-developed countries in liner services.

Rate-making in Liner Conferences. Liner rates are, as mentioned in Chapter 1, fixed without bargaining taking place between shipper and shipowner, according to the latter's estimate of "what the traffic will bear." This much-used and rather suggestive phrase should not be allowed to stand without further explanation. What it conveys is an impression that liner rates are made in an arbitrary fashion. This in a sense, is true, but one should *not* necessarily jump to the conclusion that liner rates are therefore made in an *irresponsible* fashion.

Clarification is needed here on two main points. First: how are liner freight rates usually arrived at? Secondly: why is this process the source of so much political controversy? I have already intimated that misunderstanding is part of the answer to the second question. A fuller answer requires further probing of the factual conditions of liner rate-making, in answer also to the first question.

What appears to be inadequately understood is this: Liner rates are to some extent arbitrarily fixed *because the cost of carriage cannot be linked directly to any particular item of cargo.* This important point is well brought out by Sturmey, who emphasizes "the higher proportion of costs which are independent of the volume of cargo carried."[68] What exactly are these costs, then?

First of all, a cargo-liner service requires an extensive network of agents and regional offices along the routes served to handle cargo procurement. This organizational apparatus is peculiar to the liner business. Next, by definition there must be ships *maintaining regular service*, regardless of the volume of cargo awaiting carriage at any particular time. Cargo volume governs only the marginal decisions (apart from minor route adjustments)—namely whether to get out of the business on this particular route, and whether to get into it in the first place. Thus, once a liner company is established in service on a particular run, "practically all costs become overhead costs and the additional cost of carrying an extra ton of cargo is only the cost of loading and discharging that cargo."[69]

A further quote from Sturmey will serve to illustrate this even more clearly:

Taking a modern cargo liner with only 'normal' repair costs of general maintenance and repairing damage, the following division is suggested:

Organizational overheads	35-40 percent
Voyage overheads	45-50 percent
Variable costs	10-20 percent[70]

To some extent, this is true also for tramps, as is pointed out by Daniel Marx.[71] The liner operator, however, in many respects finds his hands tied when trying to cope with this situation.

Every now and then, the ships of regular operators are liable to voyage half empty, when the demand for a particular voyage is low or when trade is poor. In a normal competitive market entrepreneurs would react by reducing the frequency or the quality of the service, by transferring some of their ships to the tramp trades (where rates might be higher), or by changing freight rates in line with the level of demand. However, these responses to short term fluctuations in demand conflict with the provision of a regular common carrier liner service. In the short run the supply curve is inelastic and consequently during a bad season or in a bad year unit costs of regular line operators will be high and total revenue reduced. The return on capital will compare unfavorably with the average real rate of interest. The maintenance of a regular service at unchanged freight rates in bad years is, therefore, to be regarded as a form of investment in future years when it is hoped demand will be higher and the return on capital above average to recoup the operators.[72]

The liner operator's problem should be clear by now: he has no way of systematically relating his costs to the act of physically moving a particular item of cargo from one place to another. Yet the cargo is his only source of income, and so he has to find some way of apportioning his costs on different types of cargo according to certain criteria. These "arbitrary" considerations normally boil down to rate making on the basis of loadability, bulk in relation to weight, and—most importantly—the value of each particular type of cargo.[73] Other factors also taken into account are "the volume of cargo from the port [in question], the cargo handling facilities available, the balance of the inward and the outward trade, and the distance to be steamed with the cargo."[74]

There appears to be general agreement that most conceivable schemes for revising the system of rate determination in the liner business would lead to increased rates for *cheap* commodities, such as the typical exports of developing countries, while correspondingly reduced rates for *high-value* goods would scarcely bring more of them into seaborne trade.[75] Indeed, the Economist Intelligence Unit comes to the conclusion that "It is . . . doubtful if a rational structure of [liner] freight rates can be devised, i.e., one which would be reasonably self-consistent and one which would appear just and make economic sense to all the parties concerned . . ."[76]

Controversy over rate-making is not fully explained by this, however. Part of the explanation lies with the organizational context of most liner-rate determination: the liner conferences. To the uninitiated, the term "liner conference" may raise all sorts of associations, and a more precise description may therefore be fitting:

A conference is an association of competing liner owners engaged in a particular trade who have agreed to limit the competition existing among themselves. As a minimum, they will have agreed to charge freight rates or passenger fares for each class of traffic according to an agreed schedule of charges and to show no discrimination between shippers. To the agreement forswearing all forms of price competition may be, and usually is, added an agreement to regulate sailings according to a predetermined pattern and to recognize the berth rights of other members. A further step may be to add a full pooling agreement under which profits and losses on the trade covered by the conferences are shared between the member lines. When this stage is reached competition between the conference lines has ceased completely.[77]

Liner rates are, in other words, normally determined in a setting of limited competition. The question then becomes: how limited? Are conferences actually monopolies?

Sturmey outlines some of the limits to the monopolistic tendencies of liner conferences.[78] First, there is competition from tramps—though conferences do have fairly effective means for countering this. Second, big shippers may retaliate against conferences by establishing their own lines—still a remote and rather drastic measure for most shippers. Third, there is often competition involving the same commodity carried over different trades even when the distance of carriage is comparable. This means that shippers may be forced to abandon a higher-priced conference to be able to compete with shippers in other countries who are shipping to the same third country. Fourth, and probably most important, the liner conferences face competition from non-conference lines.

Daniel Marx, in a similar vein, characterizes the liner market with conferences as "a limited monopoly," i.e., a market structure with more limited competition than is found in oligopolistic market structures, yet falling short of a complete monopoly.[79]

It should be clear by now that a combination of circumstances makes the liner industry open to attacks that are not always justified: (1) the basis for rate-making is rather arbitrary, and (2) this rate-making takes place in a setting of limited monopoly. It is not particularly difficult to draw the conclusion that the second condition is a cause of the first, but the opposite would probably be closer to the truth. Rate-making is by necessity arbitrary, due to the cost structure of liner operations. But this in turn was part of the reason for the emergence of the conference system. To put a previous quote from Sturmey[80] into its full context:

The need for a conference system arises from the economics of liner operations. Once a ship has been put on berth in a trade practically all costs become overhead costs and the additional cost of carrying an extra ton of cargo is only the cost of loading and discharging that cargo. This means that if a liner operator can secure a rate of freight above the costs of handling the cargo, . . . it is worth taking the extra cargo [rather than sail with empty space]. Clearly, if all the cargo is at that rate the liner operator cannot survive, but as long as he is free to vary rates it will always pay him to accept such a rate rather than refuse cargo. *With free competition, all rates would be forced to this level whenever any surplus of shipping space appeared and operations would become unprofitable for all concerned.*[81]

Thus, the conference system may be said to be a consequence of the cost structure of liner operations and the way rates are determined. But once the conference has been established, a new dimension has been added to the process of rate-making: a setting of limited competition. In this setting, where ship-owners get together to determine rates to be charged by all, what were initially worthy and reasonable motives may easily degenerate into monopolistic abuses. First, the initial goal of the members is usually to *minimize* the *losses*—but, once this has been achieved, the chief goal has a tendency to become *maximized gains.*[82]

At this stage, moreover, there are two main ways for members to increase their profits, "namely, by lowering costs or by raising freight rates . . . It is always administratively easier to raise prices than to lower costs, so that high-cost liner owners operating within tightly-knit conferences and lacking non-conference competition have a considerable incentive to think of profits in terms of the level of rates rather than the level of costs and to lose the cost consciousness which is essential to a vigorous and expanding enterprise."[83]

Thus, the setting of limited competition reinforces the arbitrary character of rate-making in the liner industry, leading to a vicious circle of sorts. From this, further negative consequences follow. Above all, these pertain to the necessity of maintaining the limited-monopoly situation, to which end several means are employed, of which the most important are (a) tying arrangements, and (b) the practice of closed membership.

Tying arrangements are agreements between individual shippers of goods on the one hand, and liner conferences on the other, by which the shipper promises to confine his shipments exclusively to conference ships and is granted reduced rates in return. To the conference this is an important instrument in fighting competition from non-conference lines, while the shipper is assured fairly reasonable rates and a stable arrangement for continuous shipments.

There are several kinds of tying arrangements. The most widely discussed (and criticized) of these is the *deferred rebate* system. A somewhat complex arrangement, this system is based on *loyalty periods*, normally of twelve months.[84] During such periods, the shipper pays the full rate for all his shipments, but receives a refund at the end of the period, usually 10 percent of the payments he has made in the *first half* (i.e., normally six months) of the loyalty period, provided he has confined himself to the use of conference ships. The conference is, in other words, always six months (or half the loyalty period) in arrears in its payment of refunds to the shipper. Should the shipper violate the contract, however, he loses not only the rebate he has earned in the current half year, but also the entire refund due to him from the previous half year.[85]

The strength of this kind of tying arrangement is not difficult to imagine. It also has serious ethical implications. In the words of the Economist Intelligence Unit, "This is a doubtful practice. It amounts to an attempt at tying a customer by owing money to him."[86]

Not surprisingly, the deferred rebate system has been outlawed in the United States trades since 1916,[87] though it is "still fairly widely used on ocean routes not touching United States shores."[88]

A less forceful kind of tying arrangement is found in the *contract* or *dual rate* system. Here the shipper is granted an immediate reduction of rates for his pledge of loyalty. Should the shipper break his pledge, all benefits are immediately cancelled for a specified period of time or indefinitely. In some cases he will also have to pay a fine.[89]

Tying arrangements cover the customer side of conferences' attempts to cope with competition from non-conference lines. A supplementary instrument is the practice of *closed membership* in the conferences. Outside lines are, in other words, not only fought by keeping customers away from them, but also by denying them the possibility of sharing in the spoils of limited competition.[90] Institutional arrangements for exclusion are rather simple: first, existing members decide by vote whether to admit outsiders;[91] second, membership is often conditional on payment of a substantial admission fee, sometimes in the form of a deposit or bond to cover the possibility of a later breach of contract by the new member.[92] Writing in 1953, Daniel Marx, Jr., gives a 25,000 dollar bond as an example.[93]

In practice, closed conferences do not constitute a universal phenomenon. In US trades, for instance, open membership is required by law,[94] and in other trades, such as most of West Africa, the conferences have followed an open-door policy *vis-à-vis* the local, national lines.[95] Indeed, there have even been cases where outside lines have competed so effectively with conferences that they have been requested to join![96] Such cases are probably rare, however.

The chief international political implication of closed membership is that it is especially effective against the limited resources of shipping lines in the developing countries. Not surprisingly, closed conferences have been a problem particularly in trades covering those less-developed countries that have been seeking to expand their liner fleets—such as India and several Latin American countries.[97] As is hinted by Sturmey,[98] one cannot overlook the possibility of a link between such practices on the part of conferences and the propensity of some countries to institute flag-discriminatory measures. This question is explored further below.[99]

Liners as "Common Carriers"

Liner operators are able to strengthen their position considerably by joining together in conferences. A major source of weakness, however, that cuts through most of their protectionist efforts is their formal status as "common carriers":

Whereas the tramp owner is only bound to carry a cargo from one place to another after he has engaged himself by charterparty to do so, the liner is legally defined as a 'Common Carrier' in all countries. This means that having advertised a sailing from 'A' to 'B' the liner has a legal obligation to accept all cargo offering on that route, provided he has suitable space in his ship, save for certain dangerous or obnoxious goods which he has specially excluded in his advertisements. In essence the tramp owner can pick and choose what cargo he carries and the liner operator cannot.[100]

Unlike other kinds of cargo-carrying ships, in other words, the liner is a *public means of transport*, and as such it is liable to governmental regulation and control of various kinds. When such measures of regulation and control are applied only to foreign liner operators and not to domestic operators, they are commonly referred to as *flag discrimination* or preferential treatment of national-flag ships. The most common forms of flag discrimination are cargo reservation (a specified percentage of cargoes leaving and/or entering the country by sea must be carried in national-flag vessels), preferential treatment of national-flag vessels in ports (regarding wharfage, port charges, pilotage, berthing rights, etc.), withholding import or export licenses from foreign-carried cargoes, and manipulating foreign exchange transactions.[101]

Of these, cargo reservation is probably the most widespread practice. Despite the famous example of the British *Navigation Acts*, it is particularly United States policy that has been of interest in the present century. Reserving government-financed cargoes to US-flag vessles on a minimum basis of 50 percent,[102] US legislation has been charged with inspiring the considerable proliferation of such practices among the less-developed countries in recent years. The extent to which the charge is justified is not altogether clear. It should be noted that although the desire to protect a national-flag fleet is present in all cases, the motives behind this desire are probably different in the United States from what they are in other countries, in view of the heavy American emphasis on the national defense argument.

The heart of the matter appears to be not so much governmental regulation and control in itself, but rather the fact that it is applied to *foreign* liner operators alone. A slightly different aspect of the same conflict is the unilateral attempts of a number of governments to regulate the activities of liner conferences that (by definition) have only half or less of their activities focused on any one country. The conferences have used this as an argument in their resistance to unilateral control, but they are protected from the logical alternatives of bilateral or multilateral control because the countries at the other end of the trade (i.e., usually in Western Europe) are quite often more interested in protecting than in regulating the position of liner operators.

As a result, liner conferences have acquired a rather diffuse type of international (or non-national) status that substantially enhances their freedom of action. They are "public carriers," but the public in question has no authoritative representative to defend its interest except those governments that are prepared to regulate unilaterally.[103]

The main point, then, is that the status of liners as "common carriers," combined with the strongly international character of their activities, makes such vessels particularly inviting objects of governmental regulation and—consequently—highly probable sources of intergovernmental conflict.

The Special Interest of Less-Developed
Countries in Liner Services

In addition to the sources of intergovernmental conflict already described, developing countries quite often take a very special interest in liner services, a fact which further intensifies this entire pattern of conflict. The reasons for this interest are several, but may be summed up as follows:

1. The types of commodities typically found in the trade of developing countries often make liners the "natural" kind of carrier.
2. If a developing country wants, for whatever reason, to establish a merchant marine, the liner sector seems the most logical place to start.

Regarding the first proposition, one could point above all to the import side of the developing countries' trade, which in the majority of cases is dominated by manufactured goods.[104] These are obvious liner cargoes.

Secondly, although the export side is normally dominated by non-processed goods that may be suitable for conventional or contractual tramp services, the volume of cargo is frequently not large enough to make such services appropriate.[105] The obvious and important exceptions to this are, of course, such goods as petroleum, iron ore, bauxite, etc., but only rarely does a developing country export more than one of these bulky commodities at a time. For the remainder of its trade it will be dependent on the services of liners.

As to the second proposition, part of it is already explained in my comments to the first. It should be remembered that although shipping in general is a capital intensive industry, less capital is required for the acquisition of liner vessels and conventional tramps than for the various kinds of specialized vessels, including modern bulk carriers, especially if the ships are bought secondhand. According to Sturmey, ". . . labor is the most important element in determining the international competitiveness of ships owned in different countries."[106] In countries with high labor costs, shipowners may be expected to concentrate increasingly on ship types where manpower can be reduced by technological improvements. This is most possible in the cases of tankers and bulk carriers. And insofar as liners are the preferred type of ship, emphasis will be on elaborately-fitted vessels.

In a developing country, however, "The use of aged ships involving the outlay of little capital, but the use of a considerable amount of labor in repair and maintenance work is . . . an economic proposition."[107] This goes for the regular crew as well.

Secondly, liners will easily be preferred to conventional tramps because efficient operation of tramps requires use of (and good connections at) the main shipping exchanges such as the Baltic in London. On old tramps, repairs will also be more frequent and their costs unpredictable, because breakdowns are likely to occur anywhere in the world.

Nor can it be discounted that developing countries are chiefly interested in getting into the liner business because this is the sector of shipping causing most of their troubles in maritime transport. If their desire is to substitute their own shipping services for those of the industrialized countries, the logical place to start would seem to be liner services, where the industrialized countries are least successful.

The crucial fact, at any rate, is that developing countries have almost without exception been starting their shipping ventures with liner operations.

Summary

In this chapter the main transaction patterns of shipping since World War II have been described for *open market tramping, contractual tramping*, and *liner services*. Possible political implications of the transaction pattern have been indicated in each case. Theoretically, the service categories that seemed most susceptible to politicization were contractual tramping and liner services. In practice, however, controversial issues turned out to be heavily concentrated in the liner sector. In retrospect it is not difficult to see why this should be so, since liner services (as distinct from the other service categories) are politically relevant for a large number of different reasons:

1. Carriage patterns all over the world are heavily dominated by the developed countries.
2. The cost structure of liners makes it extremely difficult to employ any completely fair and rational way of determining freight rates.
3. Rate-making in the liner sector takes place in a setting of limited competition provided by the liner conferences.
4. The liner conferences are marked by a number of questionable practices such as the deferred rebate system and the custom of closed membership (neither of which is found in all conferences).
5. Cargo liners are generally defined as "common carriers," which makes them a natural object of governmental regulation everywhere.
6. Countries with little experience in shipping tend, for several reasons, to take a particular interest in liner services.

As will be seen, these factors probably reinforce each other, and the result is that liner services are at the center of both the flag discrimination disputes and the liner conference and freight rate disputes.

Notes

1. The regions are defined as follows:

Western Europe: Austria, Belgium, Denmark, Finland, France, Greece, Iceland, Ireland, Israel, Italy, Japan, Luxembourg, Malta, Netherlands, Norway, Portugal, South Africa, Spain, Sweden, Switzerland, West Germany, United Kingdom, Yugoslavia.

Eastern Europe: Albania, Bulgaria, Czechoslovakia, East Germany, Hungary, Poland, Romania, USSR.

Asia: Afghanistan, Burma, Cambodia, China, Cyprus, Hong Kong, India, Indonesia, Iran, Laos, Malaysia, Nepal, North Korea, North Vietnam, Outer Mongolia, Pakistan, Philippines, Singapore, South Korea, South Vietnam, Taiwan, Thailand, Turkey.

Africa: All states on the African continent, plus Malagasy, but excepting South Africa, Algeria, Tunisia, Libya, UAR.

Arab states: Algeria, Bahrain, Iraq, Jordan, Kuwait, Lebanon, Libya, Muscat and Oman, Qatar, Saudi Arabia, South Yemen, Syria, Trucial Oman, Tunisia, Yemen.

South America: All states on the South American mainland south of Panama.

Central America: All states on the American mainland from Panama to Mexico (inclusive), and all island states in the Caribbean area.

North America: Canada, USA.

Oceania: Australia, New Zealand.

2. The drop was due to the nationalization dispute between the Anglo-Iranian Oil Company and the Government of Iran in 1951. In June of that year, Iranian oil exports (26.8 million tons in 1948) ceased altogether, and the 1948 export level was not regained until 1956. S.H. Steinberg, ed., THE STATESMAN'S YEARBOOK. STATISTICAL AND HISTORICAL ANNUAL OF THE STATES OF THE WORLD FOR THE YEAR 1965-1966 (London: Macmillan, 1965).

3. Dag Tresselt, THE WEST AFRICAN SHIPPING RANGE (New York: United Nations, 1967), p. 10.

4. Gunnar Alexandersson and Gøran Nordstrøm, WORLD SHIPPING: AN ECONOMIC GEOGRAPHY OF PORTS AND SEABORNE TRADE (Stockholm: Almquist and Wiksell, 1963), pp. 140-49, pp. 230-33.

5. Erik Nord. "Ytre og indre hindringer for utvikling," INTERNASJONAL POLITIKK, no. 3, 1967, pp. 259-60.

6. Ibid. See also Daniel Marx, Jr., INTERNATIONAL SHIPPING CARTELS (Princeton: Princeton University Press, 1953), p. 28.

7. Charles P. Kindleberger, op. cit., pp. 14-15.

8. Tresselt, op. cit., p. 33.

9. Ibid., pp. 6, 7, and 23.

10. Ibid., p. 31.

11. The possibility should be granted, however, that such relationships are somewhat more common in Africa than in other developing areas.

12. For a thorough theoretical analysis of these questions, see FREIGHT MARKETS AND THE LEVEL AND STRUCTURE OF FREIGHT RATES. REPORT BY THE UNCTAD SECRETARIAT (TD/B/C.4/38), December 16, 1968, Chapter 7.

13. See, for example, Economist Intelligence Unit, op. cit., appendix A, p. 49; Delbert A. Snider, INTRODUCTION TO INTERNATIONAL ECONOMICS (Homewood, Ill.: Richard D. Irwin, Inc., 1963), p. 36.

14. UNCTAD, Trade and Development Board, Committee on Shipping, Third Session, SUMMARY RECORD OF THE FORTY-THIRD MEETING, (TD/B/C.4/SR.43), April 16, 1969.

15. Economist Intelligence Unit, op. cit., p. 187.

16. See Sturmey, op. cit., p. 34; and TERMS OF SHIPMENT. REPORT BY THE UNCTAD SECRETARIAT, (TD/B/C.4/36), December 13, 1968, passim. As will be seen below, terms of shipment are often less relevant in the carriage of petroleum and certain other bulk goods.

17. Sturmey, op. cit., p. 281.

18. Ibid., p. 200.

19. TERMS OF SHIPMENT. REPORT BY THE UNCTAD SECRETARIAT, op. cit., p. 139.

20. Ibid.

21. Dag Tresselt, "Shipping and Shipping Policy in Latin America," Bergen: Skipsfartsøkonomisk Institutt: SMÅSKRIFTER, no. 21, 1967, p. 7. This is in general an excellent study of balance of payments problems in relation to shipping.

22. Economist Intelligence Unit, op. cit., pp. 58-63.

23. See Alexandersson and Nordstrøm, op. cit., pp. 55-57; also Kaare Petersen, "Trends in Shipping 1945-1970," op. cit., p. 29.

24. Kaare Petersen, op. cit., p. 33.

25. Other factors, such as the large investments and the know-how required, are also part of the explanation.

26. Kuwait 101,000 g.r.t.; UAR 79,000 g.r.t.; Venezuela 199,000 g.r.t. (UN STATISTICAL YEARBOOK, 1969).

27. See Organization for European Economic Cooperation, Maritime Transport Committee, MARITIME TRANSPORT (Paris: OEEC, 1954). See also THE NEW YORK TIMES INDEX, 1954, p. 803, columns 2 and 3; NORGES HANDELS OG SJØFARTSTIDENDE, May, June and July 1954.

28. In tanker-market jargon, "Caribbean" refers to Venezuela and the refinery ports on the islands just off the Venezuelan coast.

29. In 1969 and 1970, this event created an unprecedented tanker boom. Fantastic earnings were made; thus shares in the Norwegian company RUTH (nominal N.kr. 1,000) were sold for over N.kr. 400,000. (Ruth is a holding company for WAAGES TANKREDERI.) The coup in Libya reinforced this development.

30. See Sturmey, op. cit., p. 264: and (more recently), Kristen Askvig, "Oljeindustrien og den 'døde kanal'," NORGES HANDELS OG SJØFARTSTI-DENDE, årsnummer 1968, p. 31.

31. Economist Intelligence Unit, op. cit., appendix A, p. 26.

32. Sturmey, op. cit., p. 208.

33. Ibid., p. 263.

34. The recent OPEC successes in bargaining with the oil companies are no proof to the contrary, but testify simply to the expendability of the middlemen.

35. A common abbreviation referring to Panama, Honduras, and Liberia. The Honduras fleet is now insignificant.

36. B.A. Boczek, FLAGS OF CONVENIENCE (Cambridge: Harvard University Press, 1962), p. 10. See also Arnljot Strømme Svendsen, "Sans og usans i skipsfartspolitikken," Skipsfartsøkonomisk Institutt: SMÅSKRIFTER, no. 20 (Bergen: Norges Handelshøyskole, 1967), p. 7. Note that Standard Oil's motive was in large part fear that war would break out, according to Boczek.

37. Boczek, op. cit., p. 13.

38. On chartering practices of oil companies, see Chapter 1. The Economist Intelligence Unit (op. cit.) points out that steelmakers have copied the chartering practices of the oil industry (p. 24).

39. Political uncertainties are introduced by the uneven imports of the communist countries, (especially since their purchases tend to be very large when they occur), and by their practice of keeping their negotiating partners (usually Australia, Canada, and the US) in the dark until the latest possible moment as to who will get the orders and how big they will be.

40. Economist Intelligence Unit, op. cit., p. 23.

41. Two important international trade routes in iron ore go by land rather than by sea. These are the French exports to Belgium, Luxembourg, and Germany; and the Soviet exports to Eastern Europe. (Alexandersson and Nordstrøm, op. cit., p. 81.)

42. FREIGHT MARKETS . . . REPORT BY UNCTAD SECRETARIAT, (op. cit.), p. 28.

43. Economist Intelligence Unit, op. cit., p. 26.

44. Alexandersson and Nordstrøm, op. cit., pp. 84-85.

45. Ibid., p. 85.

46. Ibid.

47. What is referred to as "manganese ores" are actually iron ores containing more than 35 percent manganese.

48. Ibid., pp. 83-84.

49. Ibid.

50. FREIGHT MARKETS . . . REPORT BY UNCTAD SECRETARIAT, (op. cit.), p. 28.

51. Ibid.

52. This assertion is not based on any single source, since all-round tramps are distinguished neither from dry cargo bulk carriers nor from cargo liners in available statistics. My judgment is based (a) on data about liner companies, to be introduced later, and (b) on what is generally known about these fleets. Thus Greece has a large fleet and a very small number of liner operators, and Greek vessels generally tend to be old; all of which points in the direction of a considerable number of tramps. Similarly, the British fleet is very large, but aging; it also has only a rather modest share of tankers and bulk carriers, although the number of liner operators is large. Again, the indication is that British tramps are numerous. R.S. Platou A/S also identifies Japan as a significant tramp-owning country since 1957. (See NORWEGIAN SHIPPING NEWS, no. 10 c, 1970, p. 171.)

53. Both tankers and liner operators are virtually absent from these fleets.

54. Alexandersson and Nordstrøm, op. cit., pp. 86-94.

55. Ibid., pp. 95-96.

56. Ibid.

57. Ibid., pp. 96-101.

58. R.S. Platou A/S, "A Survey of the Dry Cargo Market, 1945-1970," NORWEGIAN SHIPPING NEWS, no. 10 c, p. 161.

59. See ibid., pp. 176 ff.

60. Ibid., pp. 166-76.

61. Ibid., pp. 180-86.

62. Note: only one socialist state (Poland) participates actively in liner conferences. The sizes of the Soviet and other socialist liner fleets are thus not reflected in Table 3-11.

63. Tresselt makes the same observation. See his "Shipping and Shipping Policy in Latin America," SMÅSKRIFTER (Bergen: the Institute of Shipping Economics), no. 21, 1967, p. 4.

64. The Economist Intelligence Unit lists 20 developing countries as parties to discriminatory bilateral treaties at the end of 1960. (Op. cit., p. 90.)

65. The deviant policy of the tenth member state—USA—is paradoxical, to say the least: the United States has been the world's leading discriminator for decades, with the objective of protecting its huge and inefficient fleet for reasons of national defense. Yet, the USA frequently joins in anti-discrimination campaigns against other countries.

66. The Economist Intelligence Unit, op. cit., pp. 90-93.

67. Nor, to the author's knowledge, do worldwide data exist anywhere for liner carriage.

68. Sturmey, op. cit., p. 244.

69. Ibid., p. 323. See also Daniel Marx, op. cit., p. 21; and Leif Nørgård, LINJEFARTEN OG DENS PROBLEMER (Bergen: Norges Handelshøyskole, Skipsfartsøkonomisk Institutt, 1965).

70. Sturmey, op. cit., p. 246, noting that "... on the basis of the limited information available it seems unlikely that for any cargo liner company as a whole the cost distribution will diverge very much from this pattern."

71. Marx, op. cit., p. 21.

72. Economist Intelligence Unit, op. cit., p. 167.

73. Sturmey, op. cit., p. 333.

74. Ibid.

75. Ibid. Also Economist Intelligence Unit, op. cit., p. 185.

76. Economist Intelligence Unit, op. cit., p. 188.

77. Sturmey, op. cit., p. 322.

78. Ibid., p. 327.

79. Daniel Marx, Jr., op. cit., pp. 10-11.

80. See p. 58.

81. Sturmey, op. cit., p. 323. (Emphasis mine.)

82. Marx, op. cit., pp. 3-4.

83. Sturmey, op. cit., pp. 269-70.

84. Ibid., p. 338.

85. Ibid.

86. Economist Intelligence Unit, op. cit., p. 174.

87. Sturmey, op. cit., p. 338.

88. Economist Intelligence Unit, op. cit., p. 174.

89. Ibid.

90. A third instrument in these efforts is the so-called "fighting ships": to combat a non-conference operator, conference members join in financing sailings of single ships to match exactly the sailing time and route of non-conference ships and offering even lower rates. See Sturmey, op. cit., p. 340. Fighting ships have been outlawed in US trades since 1916, and are probably not so commonly found today.

91. Ibid., p. 325.

92. Economist Intelligence Unit, op. cit., p. 171; Marx, op. cit., p. 144.

93. Ibid.

94. Ibid., p. 122.

95. Tresselt, THE WEST AFRICAN SHIPPING RANGE (op. cit.); p. 46.

96. T.K. Sarangan, LINER SHIPPING IN INDIA'S OVERSEAS TRADE (New York: United Nations, 1967), p. 31.

97. Sturmey, op. cit., p. 195. See also Sarangan, op. cit., p. 12.

98. Ibid.

99. See Chapter 6. Note that Arvid Frihagen, in one of the most comprehensive academic studies of the conference system to date (LINJEKONFERANSER OG KARTELL-LOVGIVNING, Oslo, Universitetsforlaget, 1963), claims that

there is "obviously" ("åpenbart") no link between flag discrimination and resentment against conferences (p. 35, footnote). Frihagen does not substantiate his claim in any way.

100. Economist Intelligence Unit, op. cit., p. 14.

101. Ibid., pp. 86-93. For a more thorough discussion, see Sturmey, op. cit., especially pp. 195 ff; also Olof Henell, FLAG DISCRIMINATION: PURPOSES, MOTIVES AND ECONOMIC CONSEQUENCES, Skrifter Utgivna av Svenska Handelhögskolan, no. 3 (Helsinki: Söderström, 1956); MARITIME TRANS-PORT, annual publication of the OECD Maritime Transport Committee, 1954–.

102. For an excellent and thorough study of US shipping policies, see Samuel A. Lawrence, UNITED STATES MERCHANT SHIPPING POLICIES AND POLITICS (Washington, D.C.: The Brookings Institution, 1966).

103. The strength of the conferences' bargaining position can be seen from numerous examples of conflict situations involving the governments of developing countries. For the cases of India, the Philippines, Nigeria, and Chile (among others), see the Economist Intelligence Unit, op. cit., pp. 118-28; Sarangan, op. cit., (passim); Tresselt, THE WEST AFRICAN SHIPPING RANGE, p. 34; Marx, Jr., op. cit., pp. 84 ff.

104. See for example Tresselt, WEST AFRICAN SHIPPING RANGE, p. 23.

105. Economist Intelligence Unit, op. cit., p. 178.

106. Op. cit., p. 271.

107. Ibid., p. 271.

4

Issues in International Shipping, 1946-1968

Governmental Views

So far, the aim has been to indicate at what points international conflict is likely to appear in the field of shipping. Before turning to the actual issues marking the interaction under study, the constellations of governmental views on some of these issues should be considered.

The views of 34 governments, members and observers of the UNCTAD Committee on Shipping, were collected through interviews with delegation members at the third session of the Committee in Geneva in April 1969. The interviews were supplemented by questionnaires.[1] In this presentation of the responses, emphasis will be on the extent to which one of the most basic conflict dimensions in international politics—the split between the industrialized countries and the developing countries—penetrates this field of interaction. The questions relate to liner conference problems and flag discrimination.

Matters pertaining to liner conferences have so far been treated at every session of the Committee on Shipping, and the debates have usually been lively. To a question asking the respondents' opinion on the extent of "unfair or discriminatory business practices" in liner conferences, answers were given as follows:[2]

Table 4-1
"How Common are Unfair or Discriminatory Practices in Liner Conferences?" (Abbreviated Phrasing) Governmental Views, 1969

	Developing Countries	Western Industrialized Countries	Total
Widespread	9	4	13
Found in some conferences	7	7	14
Very rare	0	3	3
Depends, Don't know, etc.	1	2	3
Total	17	16	33[a]

[a]One country was, on request, given an abbreviated schedule of questions. Thus, the total number of respondents will frequently add up only to 33, instead of 34 as was stated above.

The table illustrates a moderate degree of polarization on the issue. A convergence of views is found in the middle category, while a considerable group of developing countries remains convinced that conferences are generally suspect, and even several industrialized countries concede this possibility. It is interesting that only three out of sixteen Western/industrialized countries claim such practices are rare. Still, the main point of the table is the difference—in the category labeled "Widespread"—between the responses of developing countries and industrialized countries.

What conclusions do governments draw from their own opinions on this? Table 4-2 shows governmental views on how conferences should be regulated, if at all, with responses ordered according to view on unfair practice. (See below). It is reassuring to see that there is a certain logic behind governmental views; thus, among those that feel unfair practices are widespread, there is almost unanimous agreement that self-regulation by liner conferences is inadequate. Still, the conclusions of the group that felt unfair practices are found in some conferences are more interesting because of their divergence: on this basis, six out of seven developing countries feel governmental regulation is necessary, while six out of seven Western/industrialized countries feel voluntary self-regulation will do. Again, the North/South dimension makes itself felt. Developing countries tend to view conferences as guilty until proven innocent, while the opposite is the case for the industrialized countries.

Table 4-2
Governmental Views on Desirable Forms of Conference Regulation, by Opinion on Extent of Unfair Conference Practices and Position on the North/South Dimension, 1969

North/South	Developing Countries				Western Industrialized Countries				Total
Unfair practices thought to be	Wide-spread	Some	Rare	Don't Know	Wide-spread	Some	Rare	Don't Know	
International regulation desirable	2	0	0	0	0	0	0	0	2
Unilateral, governmental regulation desirable	6	6	0	0	3	0	0	0	15
Voluntary, self-regulation by conferences desirable	1	1	0	1	1	6	2	2	14
Don't Know	0	0	0	0	0	1	1	0	2
Total	9	7	0	1	4	7	3	2	33

Finally, governmental views on the desirability or necessity of flag discrimination are presented in Table 4-3. The question was whether "preferential treatment of national-flag ships" was considered to be an unnecessary and undesirable policy, an undesirable but necessary policy, or a desirable policy.

Table 4-3
Governmental Views on Preferential Treatment of National-Flag Ships, 1969

Preferential Treatment Is:	Developing Countries	Western Industrialized Countries	Total
Desirable	10	1	11
Undesirable but necessary	1	2	3
Undesirable and unnecessary	3	12	15
Don't know	3	2	5
Total	17	17	34

A remarkable polarization appears. Only three out of fourteen in favor of flag discrimination choose the more diplomatic phrasing "undesirable but necessary." For the rest, a strong majority of developing countries hold flag discrimination unreservedly to be desirable, while an even stronger majority of Western/industrialized countries stick to the opposite view. The table tells the clear story of an issue that brings out strongly held views. It indicates that flag discrimination is not merely a goal in itself, but is actually a general instrument of statecraft in a wider policy context. I base this interpretation on the fact that countries tending to pursue discriminatory policies (i.e., the developing countries) overwhelmingly consider it to be not only necessary, but also *desirable*.[3]

If this is true, it tears away the foundations of the most widely held assumption among (Western) analysts of this question, namely that developing countries pursue discriminatory policies in the hope of improving their own shipping situation. What Table 4-3 indicates is, rather, that developing countries pursue such policies in the hope and conviction that it will *hurt* the shipping of the traditional maritime countries—regardless of the short-run consequences to their own shipping. Thus, flag discrimination on the part of the developing countries must be seen as an attempt to break up existing transaction patterns in shipping, and more than an attempt to facilitate the immediate growth of their own fleets. I do not claim that these two policy goals are necessarily mutually exclusive—to the contrary, the former may often subsume the latter.[4] But as a basis for analysis the latter interpretation leads first to the (probably correct) conclusion that flag discrimination will not contribute to the growth of developing countries' fleets, and from there to the mistaken conclusion that flag discrimination is a policy based on stubborn ignorance on the part of policy-makers in developing countries. It is mistaken, in short, because it assumes a policy goal that does not appear to be held by real-life policy-makers.

This further substantiates the suspicion that the conference system is one of the targets of flag-discriminatory policies.

Chronological Review of Main Issues 1946-1968

The most important issues that have commanded the attention and energies of governmental officials in the fields of shipping and foreign affairs will now be briefly reviewed.

Each main issue or group of issues will be discussed chronologically to give the reader a sense of what has actually been happening in international shipping politics since World War II, even though the dominant mode of analysis in this study is not historical. A second purpose of this section is to show where the political implications, previously discussed at a theoretical level, actually have consequences in real-life politics.

The discussion proceeds under the headings of "contaminated issues" and "pure issues." The former covers issues which carry over from non-shipping arenas of politics and affect shipping simply because it is a vital link between nations. The latter are issues peculiar to shipping as such.[5]

Contaminated Issues

These simply reflect the broader flow of world events. Wars, crises, and tensions always show up in special ways in the world of shipping. Blockades and embargoes are favorite instruments in isolating a target country and cutting it off from supplies.[6] They are methods typically used in situations of war or serious crisis. According to present data, the following conflict situations had, *inter alia*, the effects on shipping indicated in each case:

Nationalist uprising in Indonesia, 1946	Dutch blockade of Indonesia.
Berlin Blockade 1948	Numerous incidents of ship seizures, shellings, charges of interference and harassment of ships, etc., between the US and the USSR.
Palestine War 1948-49	Arab countries' blockade of Israel.
Chinese Civil War 1946-49	Nationalist blockade of mainland China (1949-50); communist counter-blockade (1950-60).

Korean War 1950-53	The US tightens up control over foreign ships in US waters; institutes embargo against China as well as other communist countries; gets involved in dispute with UK and others as to the problem of "non-belligerent" shipping in the area.
Algerian War	French blockade of Algeria, 1956-61.
Cuban missile crisis, 1962-	US embargo, blockade, and blacklist.
Vietnam War 1965-68	US proposal for a blockade, US bombing of North Vietnamese harbors; US blacklist of non-belligerent shipping on North Vietnam.
India-Pakistan War 1965	Pakistan seeks to blockade Indian ports.
Rhodesia's unilateral declaration of independence, 1965-	Blockade and embargo of Rhodesia.
Biafra War 1967-68	Nigeria declares area closed to foreign shipping.
Arab-Israeli Six-Day War 1967	Closing of Suez Canal; issue of free passage in Straits of Tiran.

Similarly, relationships marked by tensions and "cold war" rather than full-blown crisis or war create more unexplained little incidents; more charges and accusations of espionage, harassment etc.; more blacklisting and similar long-range conflict activities—with correspondingly less of the open conflict found, for example, in a blockade.

Some examples of tension relationships which have had clear effects on shipping:

1. USA-USSR   1946-1968[7]
2. Indonesia-Netherlands   1946-1963
3. China-Taiwan   1949-1968
4. Arab-Israeli standoff   1957-1967
5. USA-Cuba   1960-1968
6. China-USSR   1966-1968
7. China vs. other states during cultural revolution.

All of these issues have their main cause *outside* the field of shipping. For this reason they will not be the center of attention here.

Considerably more important are those issues that arise from problems inherent in shipping as such. Above, I have attempted to show where international shipping activities may have political implications. Here, international shipping problems in the 1946-68 period will be taken up for brief consideration before a more thoroughgoing analysis in the subsequent chapters. Our question at this point is: In what areas have there been most conflict, most disagreement, or simply: most activity?

Pure Issues

Two complexes of interrelated problems have been continuously present and important ever since 1946: the problems of flag discrimination, and the problems of liner conferences and freight rates.

A central item in the large number of flag discrimination disputes is the United States cargo preference legislation and its opposition in (mainly) Western European shipowner and transport administration circles. In principle, the cargoes covered are only the government-financed portion of American trade. In practice, however, it has proven very difficult to draw a clear line separating government-financed cargoes from other cargoes, especially since such complicating factors as government-subsidized products and government-guaranteed loans in various forms have already been taken into account in the administration of the rules, thus widening the original concept and making it less precise.[8] Reserving a 50 percent share of such cargoes for US-flag ships has been the general guideline.

As mentioned, it is mainly West European governments and shipowners, lately joined by Japan, who feel their interests threatened by this policy and who have consequently been most active in opposing it. Every year in the 23-year period covered by this study the US cargo preference dispute has been actively present—the most stable item of conflict in the entire data collection.

Another problem-area related to flag discrimination is the maze of specific disputes connected with Latin American countries, particularly Brazil, Argentina, and Chile. Typical of the Latin American problem is a certain discontinuity which is not found in the US case: whereas US policy has been fairly stable and consistent, the former countries' policies have usually been made by decrees, instituted and repealed in rapid and confusing succession. Not infrequently, pressures from abroad have succeeded in the repeal of a specific decree that is subsequently merely replaced with a slightly revised version. The Latin American countries have also used a greater variety of instruments, such as foreign exchange manipulations, export-import licenses, port dues, etc., in a discriminatory fashion—i.e., lower charges for national-flag ships or for cargoes shipped in such vessels.[9]

The foreign opposition here—as in the US case—has consisted mainly of West European governments. In the first years after World War II, Argentina seems to have been the focus of conflict, but she was joined in the 1950s by Brazil and Chile and, to a lesser extent, by Ecuador, Venezuela, and Uruguay.

In the 1960s, the patterns of interaction between Latin America and Western Europe over these problems have undergone a basic shift. Previously, the typical pattern was that of a Western European "bloc"[10] confronting each single Latin American country in particular cases. Recently, however, economic cooperation has increased among the Latin American nations, which now give preference to regional flags over others. A regional conference discussing these matters was held in 1963, and two years later the interested countries concluded an agreement establishing general principles for the common policy to be pursued among LAFTA countries.[11] Meanwhile, Brazil has been increasingly active in the UNCTAD Committee on Shipping to achieve international recognition of preferential treatment as a legitimate instrument of policy.

In other parts of the world, flag discrimination is less common. African countries seem generally to have refrained from such policies. Among Middle Eastern and Asian countries, however, the bilateral cargo-sharing clause in trade agreements has been fairly widely used, and a regional cargo reservation arrangement is found also among the East European countries.

Predictably, the size of a country's fleet seems to be an important determinant of discriminatory policies: below a certain minimum size there is no point in discriminating as there is no one to reap the benefits. Similarly, there may be an upper limit—though the US fleet indicates it is more vague—above which more may be gained by engaging in open competition with foreign operators. Thus, African fleets are generally too small to derive any real benefits from discrimination, while several Asian and Arab fleets and most of the Latin American fleets are in the middle-sized category where advantages may be greater.

On the other hand, most West European fleets are large and efficient enough to be able to gain more from competition than from discrimination—indeed, some of them are entirely dependent on maintaining a competitive edge over others, as they carry most of their cargoes between foreign countries. Hence the stable pattern of opposition between West European countries on the one hand and all discriminating countries on the other.

So much for the problem of flag discrimination. The interesting thing, however, is that the same general rift is found in liner conference problems, with the important difference being that the US is here aligned more clearly with the countries of the third world. This constellation was not found in the earlier postwar years, but has, rather, developed gradually.

Initially, the West European governments were not so involved in liner conference problems. Interaction—and conflict—in the late 1940s and the 1950s centered on relations between the United States and the liner conferences, and between countries poorly represented in the liner conferences and the conferences themselves.

The United States approached the problems from a legalistic angle: the conferences must be made to conform to US legislation pertaining to trusts and cartels in general, and to liner conferences in particular. Each conference was reviewed as a separate case, often upon complaints from nonconference US liner operations such as Isbrandtsen Lines. Thus, until the late 1950s there was no general confrontation between the US government and the liner conferences, but rather a fragmented series of cases where the government usually came out on top.

The same pattern seemed to apply to relations between a number of developing countries and the conferences, though the questions at stake tended to be somewhat different: freight rate increases and access to membership for nonconference, national-flag lines seem to have dominated. As in other areas, the Latin American countries were active here as well, though both African and Asian countries were represented in the interaction. The general pattern, however, seems to have been the same as was found in the United States case: isolated disputes pop up and die down, and new disputes arise at irregular intervals.

The great shift in these patterns that brought the West European countries into the center of events, and that suddenly seems to have made the liner conferences *the* issue (rather than merely the source of many separate, little problems), occurred around 1960 as far as the US is concerned, and some five years later in the case of the developing countries.

In the US, the Supreme Court decision in the *Isbrandtsen Case*,[12] and the Congressional investigations triggered[13] by it, led to a thorough reorganization of the shipping-supervisory organs of the US government and a harder line in the government's supervision of the conferences.[14] The question that first brought the West Europeans into the picture was the American demand that the conferences hand over important internal documents whenever requested to do so. A number of West European governments, led by the United Kingdom, protested vigorously and even ordered the lines under their jurisdiction specifically *not* to comply with the American demand.[15] This dispute remained unresolved by the end of the period under study.

A second broad line of attack was drawn up in 1963, when US Senator Paul H. Douglas, as chairman of the Joint Economic Committee, uncovered evidence "that rates on many steel products were higher outbound than inbound,"[16] raising American suspicions that a number of their exports ended up in an unfavorable competitive position abroad due to the structure of conference freight rates. The subsequent investigations and the 1965 decision by the Federal Maritime Commission were again opposed by the conferences, backed as before by key West European governments.[17]

At about the same time (1966), the UNCTAD Committee on Shipping decided to sponsor a more general study of the level and structure of freight rates in shipping, with particular emphasis on the position of the developing countries.[18] Of necessity, this meant another incursion into liner conference territory, and again the harder-line West European governments (the UK and the

Scandinavian countries in particular) lined up with the conferences in opposition to a united front of developing countries. The study nevertheless went ahead. The issue will continue to be treated by the committee because of the interest of developing countries in undertaking similar studies in the years ahead. The general question of demands for documentation from the conferences has also entered the Committee's discussions[19] and further widened the rift.

These are, then, the two main continuous and important problems in international shipping since the war: flag discrimination and liner conferences. In this connection, mention might be made of one rather isolated issue that nevertheless has bearing on both problems: the non-ratification campaign against the IMCO Charter, spearheaded by the Scandinavian countries in the years 1954-58. The objectionable clause in this Charter was, from the Scandinavian point of view, article 1 (c), which specifies "matters concerning unfair restrictive practices by shipping concerns" as part of the organization's field of interest.[20] In the Scandinavian view, IMCO should not be concerned with "political" matters, but restrict itself to technical aspects of shipping. Norway, Sweden, Denmarks, and Finland for several years sought to round up support for their view, but with only limited success. Eventually the Charter was ratified by enough states to go into effect in 1958, and so the Scandinavians gave up their resistance "from the outside" and also ratified it—but with important reservations. Thus, Norway's reservation threatened withdrawal if IMCO were to venture beyond clearly technical matters.[21] This "resistance from within" may have proven more effective: to date, IMCO has not attempted to deal with any of the more politically tinged problems of shipping, and so article 1 (c) has thus far been a dead letter.

Still, the issues of shipping are far from exhausted. Among the more publicized problems remaining are, for instance, the controversies over the flags of convenience. Beginning shortly after the Second World War, the dispute at first centered on working conditions aboard convenience-flag ships. The United Kingdom, among others, claimed the right to inspect such vessels when in British ports. The UK was supported by the labor movement and the ILO, and strenuously opposed by Honduras and Panama. During the 1950s, the dispute between the ILO and the flags of convenience continued, with the flag-of-convenience countries apparently taking steps to improve working conditions on their ships. As a result, the labor issue seems gradually to have died down, and the interest shifted to the competitive advantages enjoyed by shipowners under these flags. Two important international meetings brought this question to a head: the first was the international conference on the Law of the Sea in Geneva in 1958, at which the demand for a "genuine link" between a ship and its state of registry was formulated; the second was the opening session of the IMCO Assembly in 1959, at which members of the IMCO Council were to be elected. According to the IMCO Charter, the countries with the largest of the world's merchant fleets would automatically become Council members, and both Liberia and Panama now claimed such status, supported by the United States. Needless to say, the opposition from the traditional maritime countries was unyielding. The dispute was finally submitted to the International Court of Justice which ruled, one year later, in favor of the flags of convenience. As a matter of fact, the decision seems to have effectively defused the issue, and no interaction of importance in this area has appeared since 1961.

None of the "pure issues" discussed so far have had any impact beyond the area of shipping itself. One group of problems, however, shows clearly the weakness of such a distinction between pure and contaminated issues, namely the questions relating to free passage in international waterways. The complexity of the free passage problem derives from its obvious links both with shipping as such and with military-strategic considerations.

Three geographical bottlenecks have commanded most of the attention in this area since 1946: the Suez Canal, the Panama Canal, and the Straits of Tiran between the Red Sea and the Gulf of Aqaba. The Suez Canal became increasingly a politically tender spot in Anglo-Egyptian relations in the early 1950s when British troops were stationed in a zone along the Canal after King Farouk's ouster in 1952. Shooting incidents and harsh exchanges between political leaders in the two countries were daily occurrences. Only a few months after British troops were finally withdrawn in May 1956, President Nasser effected his nationalization of the Suez Canal, which resulted in the Anglo-French-Israeli attacks of October 31 and November 1. In subsequent years, after the reopening of the canal, the issue of free passage in general gradually crystallized into the issue of free passsage "for all except Israel and Israeli-bound (or -originating) cargoes." This Egyptian formulation of the problem made it vital to more countries than just Israel and Egypt and contributed to prolonging the dispute well into the 1960s.

The question of free passage in the Straits of Tiran has cropped up whenever the Suez issue has been at its hottest, meaning early 1957 and May-June 1967. On the first of these occasions, it was Saudi Arabia that raised the issue by encouraging Jordan and Egypt to join it in declaring both the Straits and the Gulf of Aqaba to be their territorial waters. At this time Israel was, at least initially, the main party claiming the right of free passage. The stationing of UN troops at Sharm-el-Sheikh resolved the problem for the next decade.

In 1967, on the other hand, the Straits of Tiran rather than the canal was initially disputed, and this time it was the UAR which took the initiative to close the Straits after the UN troops were pulled out. Israel was on this occasion strongly backed by the United States. After the Six-Day War in June the issue again subsided when Israel gained control over the shore batteries at Sharm-el-Sheikh.

The Panama Canal has not been as spectactular a scene of events as Suez, but there has been a continuously active dispute between Panama—which wants national control for economic and national prestige reasons—and the United States, which still defines the canal as vital to its national security. Actual violence has taken place only once in January 1964, but the issue has been politically alive ever since 1954 in the postwar period. Interaction is mostly marked by alternating cycles of *distance* (exchanges of diplomatic notes, and of hostile references to the other side), and *proximity* (sporadic direct talks or negotiations officially designed to give Panama a more equitable status in the relationship). An acceptable solution has still to be found.

This completes the discussion of the more prominent problems of shipping, which have turned out to be difficult to solve even in the long run. They are likely to continue to be important political problems of shipping because they are so closely connected with key structural aspects of international maritime trade.

Briefer mention will be made of some issues that have proven soluble in the short run, as each case has arisen. Some of these are linked to international credit arrangements or leasing arrangements; a rather curious case in this category was the attempt by the US government in 1950 to repossess ships bought but not paid for by nationals of Taiwan. The United States traced the whereabouts of each vessel, then proceeded to persuade the authorities in each of the countries where the ships were located at the time to impound them and turn them over to the US. In most cases, cooperation was refused.

Another case which went on for quite some time was the attempt by the US to make the Soviet Union return ships made available under the World War II lend-lease arrangements. Endless negotiations from the end of the war until 1954, with a brief revival in 1961, had no practical results, and the ships remained Russian.

Other typical one-shot affairs are disputes over shipwrecks and collisions. Diplomatic activity can reach amazing levels in such cases as, for instance, that of the Swedish freighter *Naboland*, which was involved in a collision in the Sea of Marmara, and whose captain spent three years in a Turkish prison.

Maritime affairs are also marked by a considerable number of international conferences—some of them rather general in scope, such as the conferences on the Law of the Sea in 1948 and 1958; others more specifically defined, such as the 1947 conference on tonnage measurement, the Scandinavian conference in 1952 on the welfare of crews, the conferences in 1953 and 1954 on oil pollution, the 1956 conference on weather services in the North Atlantic (emphasis on iceberg control), and numerous conferences in the 1960s on the oil pollution problem.

The above historical outline may serve as a backdrop for an analysis of the frequency of conflict in shipping, with the problem viewed initially from a systemic perspective.

Notes

1. For further details on this part of the research, see Appendix A.
2. For exact wording of question, see Appendix B.

3. For a methodological reservation, see Appendix A, pp. 177-179.

4. Along the argument that "if it hurts them and helps undermine their predominance, it will ultimately benefit us."

5. The sources are, if not otherwise indicated, the two newspapers used for the interaction analysis: the NEW YORK TIMES, and the NORGES HANDELS OG SJØFARTSTIDENDE.

6. The term "blockade" is here used in a loose, non-legal sense, referring to attempts to sever all maritime connections with a certain country, or even what one claims to be part of one's own country, (e.g., China-Taiwan, France-Algeria, Nigeria-Biafra).

7. The period covered by this study does not extend beyond 1968.

8. Samuel A. Lawrence, op. cit., p. 167 and ff.

9. One good summary is found in J.R. Patton and F.T. Schornhorst, "Cargo Preference and Flag Discrimination in International Shipping—Actions and Reactions," GEORGE WASHINGTON LAW REVIEW, December 1965.

10. Actually, the association among West European governments was more like an *ad hoc* movement: whenever one or a few of these countries felt the situation was unbearable, the other governments were consulted and their support in a common representation was requested. (Information supplied by a representative of an intergovernmental organization with interests in shipping.)

11. See also Patton and Schornhorst, op. cit., on this point.

12. FEDERAL MARITIME BOARD V. ISBRANDTSEN; see Lawrence, op. cit., p. 199; Frihagen, op. cit. pp. 255-56 and ff.

13. Lawrence, op. cit., p. 199.

14. Frihagen, op. cit., pp. 303-04.

15. Especially ibid., pp. 210-11 and 311-19.

16. Lawrence, op. cit., p. 260 (note).

17. Ibid., p. 121 and 236 (note).

18. See FREIGHT MARKETS AND THE LEVEL AND STRUCTURE OF FREIGHT RATES. REPORT BY THE UNCTAD SECRETARIAT (op. cit.).

19. See, for example, the summary record of the third session in April, 1969.

20. Frihagen, op. cit., p. 183.

21. Ibid., pp. 184-85.

5

The Interaction System of International Shipping Affairs

In this chapter, the overall traits of interaction and the specific trends of conflict in international shipping will be analyzed at the level of the international shipping system.[1]

An introductory section will present gross trends in the interaction data to describe the basic characteristics of the system. The test of the main hypothesis will then become the central theme of the chapter. After the selection of an indicator for the distribution of shipping values, the amount of skew and its duration will first be tested against the frequency of conflict. Additional independent variables will subsequently be introduced, one by one, under the heading of *sub-system penetration*.[2] Finally, the main findings of the chapter will be presented in a summary.

Description of General Interaction Characteristics

What is the overall interaction picture for the 23-years period under study? (See Table 5-1.)

Table 5-1
Interaction in International Shipping 1946 through 1968, by Action Type[a]

	Number of Acts		Percent	
Conflict actions	538		6.7	
Verbal conflict/offensive	1579		19.7	
Verbal conflict/defensive	953		11.9	
All conflict		3070		38.2
Participation[b]	2687		33.4	
Active cooperation	2278		28.4	
All non-conflict		4965		61.8
Total	8035	8035	101.1	100.0

[a]Sources for interaction data, throughout, are the NEW YORK TIMES INDEX, January 1, 1946–December 31, 1968; and NORGES HANDELS OG SJØFARTSTIDENDE, same period. The method of data collection is explained in Appendix A.

[b]Consists of "consultation/negotiation," "comments on situation," and "policy statements."

Clearly, the issue-area of shipping is not, on the whole, dominated by conflict. Only 38 percent of all interaction is of the conflict type. Yet a comparison with Charles McClelland's data from the World Event-Interaction Survey (covering international politics in general) for the year 1966 yields some interesting further clues. (Table 5-2.)

McClelland's categories are only slightly different from mine—his two "verbal participation" and "participatory actions" were combined by me in Table 5-1 as "participation."

It should be noted that McClelland does not make any assessment of how "typical" the year 1966 may be as compared to other years and how this could affect the validity of his findings. One important qualification regarding the 1966 WEIS data, which probably enhances comparability in this case, is pointed out: the data do not include "the specific military events and acts of the Vietnam war . . ."[3]

Table 5-2

Interaction in International Shipping 1946 through 1968, and Separately for 1966; and Interaction in Overall International Politics in 1966, by Action Type[a] (Percent)

	International Shipping Interaction 1946-1968		International Shipping Interaction 1966		International Politics (Generally) Interaction 1966	
Conflict actions	6.7		8.0		7.5	
Verbal conflict/ offensive	19.7		20.2		16.4	
Verbal conflict/ defensive	11.9		14.2		7.7	
All conflict		38.2		42.4		31.6
Verbal participation/ Participatory actions	33.4		33.5		17.4 18.0	
Verbal cooperation	22.9		22.2		24.2	
Active cooperation	5.4		1.9		8.8	
Total	100.0		100.0		100.0	
N	8035		212		5550	

[a]Source: For shipping data as in Table 5-1; other data from Charles McClelland and Gary Hoggard, "Conflict Patterns in the Interactions Among Nations," in Rosenau II, op. cit., p. 716.

On the whole, variations in the three data sections in Table 5-2 within categories are small enough to allow a general characterization of *basic similarity*. The differences, however, are considerably more interesting. First, and most important, shipping issues appear to generate more conflict than international politics generally. The difference is sharpest when comparing the two data sets from the same year, although the overall frequency of conflict in shipping in the entire 1946-68 period is also substantially higher than the frequency of conflict in international politics for 1966. Indeed, the difference between shipping conflict and general international conflict for 1966 is statistically significant at the .01 level.[4] Thus, although shipping is not dominated by conflict, *such behavior appears to occur more frequently in shipping matters than in international politics in general.*

If an explanation may be suggested, the most plausible one seems to be that international shipping is not a field where governments are continuously engaged in interaction, but rather one in which interaction tends to take place only when disputes and acute problems come up. Very little energy and resources are, in other words, devoted to anticipating problems, simply because the problems involved do not appear to be really important to most governments. Furthermore, shipping problems often spur interaction between countries geographically distant from each other and therefore not accustomed to interacting in other political contexts. In short, interaction generally takes place only when specific problems or disputes occur, and then often involves parties not used to dealing with each other—both of which may be conducive to a greater frequency of conflict. With these overall characteristics in mind, attention should now be directed to the central hypothesis of this study and to a more detailed analysis of the frequency of conflict.

The Hypothesis

If a skewed distribution of values persists or is reinforced over time, then the frequency of conflict in the respective interaction system will increase.

As mentioned earlier, the interaction system of shipping is here viewed formally as a subsystem of the overall international political system. Still, the terms "system" and "systemic" will be used in the following in reference to the *international system of shipping.* When reference is to other systems, this will be explicitly stated.

Systemic conflict is here defined as the number of conflict actions in the system in a given (5-year or 1-year) period, in percent of the total number of actions. The term *conflict actions* covers Charles McClelland's three main categories: "verbal conflict defensive," (protests, rejections, denials, etc.), "verbal conflict offensive," (charges, criticisms, threats, etc.), and "physical conflict," (mobilization, seizure of property, shelling, battle engagements, etc.).

The main hypothesis allows for two interpretations. The first of these may be described as *broad*: it assumes that decision-makers do not respond directly and spontaneously to any change—large or small—in the value distribution, but that longer-term trends in the latter will gradually be perceived as a change in the decision-maker's operative environment. Hence, this version would state that when inequality has been either increasing or decreasing over a period of years, specific conflict will begin to pick up the same trend (increase or decrease) and accelerate for a shorter period, then taper off. A change of long-term trends in inequality will be followed by a delayed change of trends in conflict—rapid at first, then tapering off.

The other interpretation assumes that decision-makers respond directly to any year-to-year change in the value-distribution with a proportionate and corresponding change in conflict activity, although delays in perception may result in a time-lag. This is a narrower version of the main hypothesis.

The two interpretations require different procedures for hypothesis testing. The narrow version will be tested by regression analysis, whereas for the broad version we shall have to rely simply on the visual inspection of graphs. To guard against undue arbitrariness the 21-year period will be divided into as few "trend periods" as possible, preferably only one or two.

First, however, an indicator must be found for the distribution of values in shipping.

The Distribution of Values in Shipping

Since the values accruing to a country from shipping activities are many and varied, there are actually many distributions of values in shipping. What is wanted here, however, is one measure to cover as many of these values as possible.

Basically, the values accruing from shipping activities may be described as follows:

1. The *transport function* of ships; i.e., the benefit of having goods transported between two points at the right time and price.
2. The *freight earnings of ships.*
3. The *national registry* of the ships themselves.

Several more values derive from these:

a) The earnings of *land-based facilities* for ships, such as ports, shipyards, canals, bunker and supply facilities.
b) The implications and impact of freight earnings and earnings of land-based facilities on *the national economy*, especially on balances of payments.
c) The military *defense advantages* of a national-flag merchant fleet.
d) The *national prestige* presumably deriving from a national-flag merchant fleet.

To take in as many of these values as possible in one measure, I have chosen to use the *distribution of world shipping tonnage.*

As may be seen from the list above, most of the values accruing from shipping are closely related to the national registry of ships. This measure, furthermore, is simple to use and fairly accurately measured by Lloyds of London.

It should be noted, however, that most of the values labeled *earnings of land-based facilities* are independent of the size of the national flag merchant fleet. On the other hand, they may be less significant politically because they are less susceptible to change—few countries, for instance, can have international canals of any importance; and the earnings of ports such as Singapore, Rotterdam, or Antwerp are largely determined by geographical location and the patterns and habits of international trade. Ships, on the other hand, are concrete, highly visible and very moveable objects, and their international distribution may also for this reason affect international behavior in matters concerning shipping.

Measuring the Distribution of Values in Shipping

Measuring the degree of conformity of a given distribution to some kind of ideal or equal distribution can be done in many ways.[5] The particular measure chosen here is *Gini's coefficient of inequality* (the Gini index), which is based on a Lorenz curve diagram showing the share of a given value enjoyed by a given percentage of the population. The ideal distribution is assumed to be one where 1 percent of the population has a 1 percent share of the value, 10 percent of the population has a 10 percent value share, and so on.

The problem in this case, however, is to define the "population." Should it be countries, and show the share of the world merchant fleet owned by increasing percentages of the total number of countries? Such a definition of "population" would not yield an adequate measure of inequality by our criteria. Obviously, the ideal distribution is not one where all countries regardless of size, population, trade, etc., are counted as equal percentage units. Before the Lorenz curve and the Gini index can be used to measure the distribution of shipping tonnage, it is therefore necessary to find a way of weighting each country in a way that reflects, somehow, its size and maritime importance.

A solution to this problem is offered in the size (in weight) of a country's seaborne trade. Expressed as the *average annual volume of goods loaded and unloaded* in a given country, weighting with this figure ensures that each country is now counted for the percentage of world seaborne trade it represents. The "population," in other words, is really the total trade carried by ships in a given year, and the ideal distribution of values is one where 1 percent of the world's merchant fleet is available to carry 1 percent of the world's seaborne trade. Obviously, because national jurisdictions restrict the movement of tonnage registry, this ideal is impossible to attain exactly, but it may be sufficiently closely approximated to make it useful for the purposes of this study.

It should be clear that in reality, even if 1 percent of the world's shipping tonnage is registered in a country accounting for 1 percent of world seaborne trade, these nationally registered ships can (apart from the inefficiency which would obviously result) in practice hardly manage to obtain exclusive carriage of national trade.

The present method of measuring inequality is a somewhat crude attempt to draw a picture (one of many possible ones) of reality to which governments might conceivably respond with external action—to the extent that thinking in distributive terms takes place at all.

Figure 5-1 shows the trend of the Gini index of world tonnage distribution. First of all, the distribution of values for the whole 21-year period must be characterized as distinctively lopsided. Two main trends can be distinguished: a period of decreasing inequality which subsequently becomes temporarily stabilized (1947-1956), and a period of increasing inequality (1956-1966). Anticipating the test of the broad interpretation, we shall reject the main hypothesis if the overall trend of the first period is one of increasing conflict and if the overall trend of the second is one of decreasing conflict.

Systemic Conflict

Table 5-3 shows the main patterns of conflict and non-conflict over time, divided into five sub-periods.

Two relevant observations may be made from this table. First, it appears that the total volume of interaction has been increasing from 1946 at least until the middle 1960s—as an issue-area, shipping is evidently becoming a field of increasing intergovernmental activity. The yearly average of interaction volume clearly reflects this, if we disregard the period 1955-59 for the moment as a special case.

Secondly, the period 1955-59 shows the tremendous impact of the Suez crisis on the volume of interaction. Almost half of the total interaction volume in the 23-year period occurred during these five years—and most of that again in 1956! At first, this may appear strange. Although the Suez Canal was clearly the main stake in the conflict, one does not usually think of the 1956 crisis as a matter of shipping. It is easy to forget, however, that the events around November 1 of that year were only a dramatic climax to a longer period of intense interaction that spanned several months.

The November war may have been a complex mixture of issues, but its prelude, a process which started with Nasser's nationalization of the Canal in late July, was predominantly a matter of shipping, though with strategic overtones: should Britain and France, with their strong interest in shipping, let Nasser take over the Suez Canal Company and with it control of the canal?

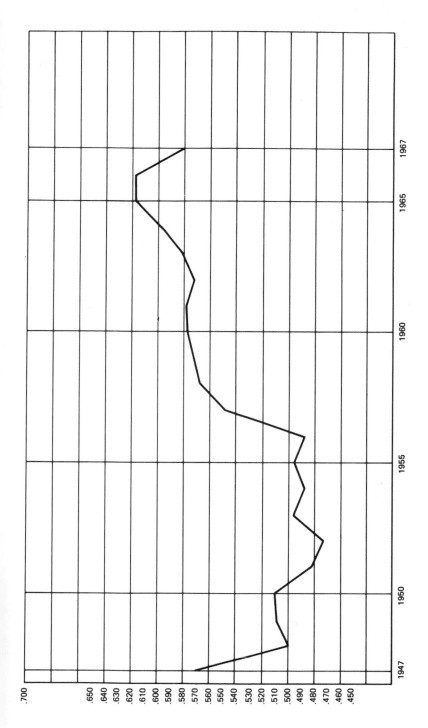

Figure 5-1. Gini Index of the Distribution of Shipping Tonnage (g.r.t.) Among the States of The World, 1947-1967.

Table 5-3
Main Action Types Over Time[a]

	1946-49	1950-54	1955-59	1960-64	1965-68	Total
Conflict actions	207	607	1296	540	420	3070
Non-conflict actions	512	500	2673	770	510	4965
Total	719	1107	3969	1310	930	8035
Total actions, yearly average	179.7	220.4	793.8	262.0	232.5	349.3

[a]Source: As in Table 5-1.

Actually, it would be practically impossible to disentangle the commercial and strategic aspects of the situation. What seems to be clear, however, is that both Britain and France *made* it an issue of shipping by seeking to round up support for their views first and foremost from the leading maritime countries— and the interaction during these first months revolved mainly around the various schemes for cooperative international control of the Canal and the creation of the Suez Canal Users' Association. The Association was obviously designed to attract the support of leading shipping nations, which it did, though they had their reservations.[6]

What is important here, however, is that the bulk of the interaction coded for this issue in 1956 occurred between July 27 and October 31. As for the remainder of the crisis, extreme care was taken to code only items that had direct effects on shipping. Thus, all possible precautions have been taken to isolate the shipping-related aspects from the other issues of the crisis. Still, the fact that the interaction volume was so great in the 1955-59 period represents a characteristic of the data deserving special attention in the analysis. Wherever possible, therefore, the Suez Crisis and the 1955-59 period will be given separate treatment from the remainder of the data, without forgetting the natural place of this crisis in any study of shipping conflict.

The actual measure of systemic conflict, operationalized as the percentage of conflict actions in the total volume of interaction for each period is shown in Table 5-4.

Testing the Main Hypothesis

The trend of the Gini index of the distribution of values in shipping demanded, as will be recalled, that systemic conflict should decrease in the 1947-56 period and increase in the 1956-66 period. Figure 5-2 shows the actual frequency of conflict for each year along with the Gini index.

At first glance the picture seems ambiguous, both because of the steep initial

Table 5-4
Main Action Types Over Time, in Percent[a]

	1946-49	1950-54	1955-59	1960-64	1965-68	Total 1946-68
Conflict	28.8	54.8	32.7	41.2	45.2	38.2
Non-conflict	71.2	45.2	67.3	58.8	54.8	61.8
Total	100.0	100.0	100.0	100.0	100.0	100.0
N	719	1107	3969	1310	930	8035

[a]Source: As in Table 5-1.

increase in conflict and because of the fluctuations of the trend after 1956. In both trend periods, however, the pattern of conflict is quite close to the requirements of the hypothesis. After the dramatic peak in 1950 the trend is reversed to a seven-year steady decline of conflict. The second period shows an uneven yet clear overall increase. The fact that the effects lag in both cases is essential to this interpretation.

Time-series regression analysis will be employed to test the narrower interpretation. The possibility that the value distribution could have a delayed effect on conflict will be taken into account by testing various lags in the Gini index. It may be recalled that the question involved in this test is whether there is a direct correlation between year-to-year variations in the Gini index and the corresponding variations in the frequency of conflict.

The test gives a negative correlation for the unlagged relationship, $r = -.452$ ($N = 21$, $F = 4.89$),[7] in marked contrast to our hypothesis. When the Gini index is lagged by one, two and three years the correlation coefficient remains negative but approaches zero.

Further complications arise at this point. One of the assumptions of regression analysis is that the "error terms" (the part of the variation in the dependent variable which cannot be accounted for by the least-squares solution) are serially independent. In time series this assumption may not hold, a problem usually referred to as *autocorrelation*.[8] The value of a given variable in a given year may be dependent on the value for the previous year. Autocorrelation has the effect of inflating the correlation coefficient.

Durbin and Watson[9] have developed a test for autocorrelation which will be employed here. In addition to the Durbin-Watson statistic, a correction factor[10] will be used in order to eliminate the autocorrelation whenever found.

The Durbin-Watson statistic for the regression of tonnage distribution on conflict was 1.09, indicating that positive autocorrelation was indeed involved. When the variables were transformed by means of the correction factor, the autocorrelation was removed ($d = 1.80$, $N = 20$), but the relationship was no longer significant at the required level ($r = -.357$, $N = 20$, $F = 2.63$).

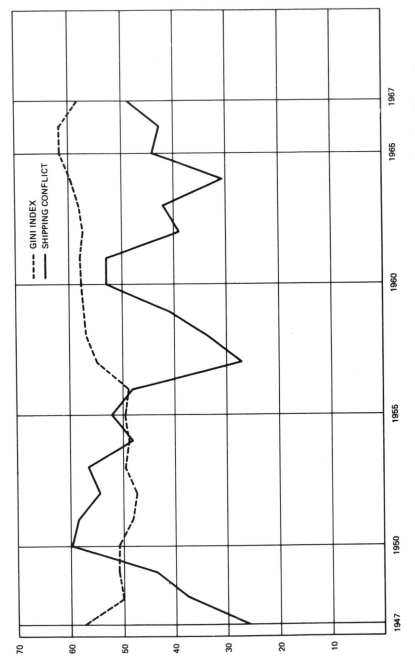

Figure 5-2. Gini Index of the Distribution of Shipping Tonnage, and Systemic Shipping Conflict (Percent), 1947-1967.

In other words, there is no support for the narrower interpretation of the main hypothesis. The broader version, however, will be retained. From a theoretical point of view this may even be considered fortunate: the broader version of the hypothesis is more satisfying theoretically in that it makes more realistic assumptions about the behavior of decision-makers. First of all, decision-makers can hardly be assumed to be continuously attentive to changes in the value distribution. Distributive aspects are only part of their entire operative environment. It also seems unrealistic to assume that decision-makers are as likely to respond to smaller variations as to larger ones. Finally, one may question the assumption that the amount of behavioral response will always be proportionate to the amount of change in the value distribution. The broad interpretation of the main hypothesis is an attempt to avoid these problems, a task admittedly achieved only at the cost of a rather crude hypothesis test.

Penetration by the International Political System

A crucial question regarding the increasing frequency of conflict in shipping must still be answered: to what extent is this increase a function of influences from the international political system? To the extent that such influences are active ingredients in shipping interaction, even the broader interpretation of the main hypothesis will be weakened.

The term "penetration" will be used to signify such influences. Specifically, *the degree of penetration of a sub-system by the international political system* is defined as the extent to which processes of interaction in the subsystem reflect basic characteristics of structure and interaction in the international political system.

Structural characteristics of the international political system will be operationalized in terms of persistent international conflict dimensions (rifts). These are not the only important structural characteristics of the overall system, but they are sufficiently important in themselves to be used as indicators of the degree of penetration.

A measure of violent international conflict will be employed to describe the characteristics of interaction in the international political system. Since this measure only takes in a kind of behavior that is distinctly marginal even in international politics, a control will be introduced in the shipping interaction data to separate issues that are typical appendices of wars and acute international crises from issues that are more typical of commercial international shipping. This is intended to compensate for the fact that the violent conflict measure does not cover nonviolent crises such as the Cuba missile crisis in 1962.

Penetration may be deemed to exist in the system of shipping to the extent that variations in the frequency of conflict are attributable to the effects of main international rifts; or to the extent that variations in conflict can be traced to the issues that are most closely related to conflict in the international political system; or to the extent that shipping conflict is correlated with violent international conflict.

Violent Conflict in the System as an Indicator of Penetration

In this section, the possibility that variations in the frequency of shipping conflict are related to variations in violent international conflict will be examined. The following hypothesis is offered:

If the frequency of conflict in the international system increases, then the frequency of systemic shipping conflict will increase.

Few measures of violent international conflict in the post-World War II period are available. Among those that do exist, there are considerable differences as to sources of data and definition of conflict. The set of data chosen here has been collected by J. David Singer and Melvin Small as part of their major study of the international system since 1815. Based on a comparatively stringent set of criteria,[11] the Singer-Small data may be summed up in a list of twelve interstate conflicts between 1945 and 1965.[12] Three versions of this measure have been computed by Professor Maurice A. East of the University of Denver,[13] based on, respectively, monthly, quarterly, and yearly frequency counts.

To extend the measure up to 1968, I have added two conflicts that satisfy the Singer-Small criteria: the Vietnam war from February 1965 through 1968, and the Arab-Israeli war in June 1967. The monthly version of East's frequency count, extended to 1968, is shown in Figure 5-3. It indicates a trend of gradually decreasing international conflict over the years.

Figure 5-3 also shows the frequency of conflict in shipping, and the Gini index. Here, the overall trend of shipping conflict is different from the overall trend of international violent conflict: the former increases gradually over the years, while the latter decreases. On this evidence, the hypothesis seems not to be supported.

A time-series regression of world conflict on shipping conflict yields a similar result. If world conflict is lagged by three years, the correlation with shipping conflict turns out to be .534 (product-moment correlation). When corrected for autocorrelation, the relationship is no longer significant and the hypothesis is therefore rejected.

Issue Type as an Indicator of Penetration

As was mentioned earlier, the data on shipping conflict are to some extent "contaminated" by extraneous events, in the sense that wars, international

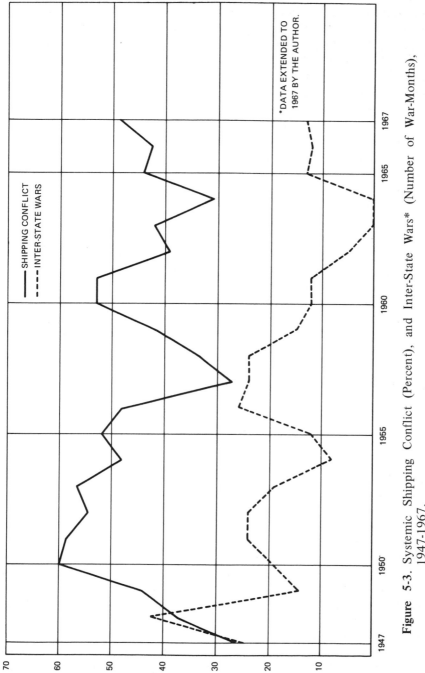

Figure 5-3. Systemic Shipping Conflict (Percent), and Inter-State Wars* (Number of War-Months), 1947-1967.

*DATA EXTENDED TO 1967 BY THE AUTHOR.

SHIPPING CONFLICT
INTER-STATE WARS

crises, and tensions between states tend to have side effects on shipping in the form of blockades, blacklisting of ships serving "unfriendly" countries, embargoes, etc. Since each action included in the data set has been coded separately, it has also been possible to give each a code for the context (or issue) in which it occurred. This means that actions attributable to wars, crises, and international tensions may in large part be separated from actions related to shipping questions as such. As in Chapter 4, the former type of shipping issues will be referred to as "contaminated" issues,[14] to indicate their closeness to world politics, while the latter will be called "pure" shipping issues,[15] in reference to their more technical nature. The central question at this point is to what extent the variation in the frequency of shipping conflict is really only due to variation in conflict on contaminated issues, which are typical conflict issues anyway.

All the data on shipping interaction have now been divided into two subsamples, one consisting of interaction on contaminated issues, the other consisting of interaction on pure issues. For each year in the period studied, the percentage of conflict actions (out of the total number of actions in the subsample) has been computed; e.g., in 1947 there was 15.1 percent conflict on pure issues and 45.1 percent conflict on contaminated issues. (Figure 5-4.)

There is a marked difference between the contaminated shipping issues and the pure shipping issues in all years, with conflict consistently higher (except for 1946) on the contaminated issue type, as one might have expected. In one case, 1946, the pure issues have a higher proportion of conflict, but even that figure is the lowest for all years. At only one point do the conflict proportions for the two issue types approach each other in size. As expected, shipping issues that by their nature are closely related to international conflict have a far higher conflict rate than pure shipping issues. The t-statistic for the difference of means in the two subsamples is 7.016, which is clearly significant at the .05 level.[16] Thus, the initial assumption that contaminated issues would differ significantly from pure issues in conflict terms is strongly corroborated by the data.

This raises a number of additional questions, however. First, one may ask whether the Singer-Small measure of violent conflict and the present measure of contaminated shipping conflict are actually reflections of the same general phenomenon. Here, the question can only be answered in part by looking at variations in both measures over time, to see whether and to what extent the measure of contaminated shipping conflict reflects wars as such, and to what extent it reflects other types of conflict as well. If contaminated shipping conflict is largely a side effect of wars, then one would expect a high correlation with the Singer-Small measure. If international *crises* and *tensions* dominate in contaminated conflict, one would expect a low correlation, since the Singer-Small measure only covers wars.

The data indicate that wars do not have a dominant effect on contaminated shipping conflict. With world conflict lagged from 0 to 4 years, none of the

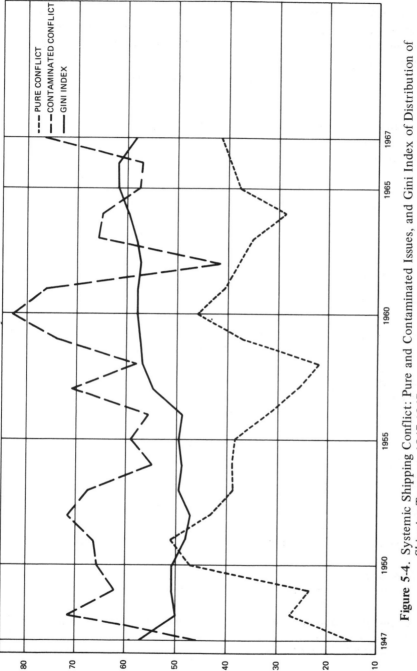

Figure 5-4. Systemic Shipping Conflict: Pure and Contaminated Issues, and Gini Index of Distribution of Shipping Tonnage, 1947-1967.

correlation coefficients turned out to be significantly non-zero by the F-test. We may therefore conclude that contaminated shipping conflict reflects a broad variety of international conflict types, most of which are nonviolent.

A second question arising from the difference between pure and contaminated shipping conflict pertains to the central hypothesis. What is the nature of the relationship between *pure* shipping on the one hand, and the distribution of shipping values on the other? Does the removal of contaminated conflict improve the fit between shipping conflict and value distribution?

Figure 5-4 indicates that the relationship between value distribution and pure shipping conflict remains essentially unchanged by this operation. In the 1947-56 period we would expect a change to decreasing conflict; it occurs in 1951. In the 1956-66 period a new increase would be expected, and this takes place from 1958 on. In the first period the change in conflict lags by four years, in the second by two.[17] In other words, the relationship between shipping conflict and value distribution is not substantially affected when contaminated shipping conflict is kept out of the test.

*Main International Rifts as an
Indicator of Penetration*

The question to be posed here is this: to what extent is the frequency of conflict in shipping affected by main rifts in international politics?

The relationship between rifts (cleavages) and conflict has been expressed in hypotheses of varying formulations.[18] Originally applied to the study of individuals in politics, its basic idea states that conflicting loyalties will serve to moderate political behavior, while reinforced loyalties have no such restraining effects.

Extended to a social system, the proposition becomes that the existence of partially overlapping group memberships and loyalties will reduce the amount of conflict in the system, while coinciding group loyalties will reinforce conflict. If, for example, all lower-class people in a society are Catholics while all middle- and upper-class people are Protestants, conflict between socioeconomic groups is amplified by conflict between religious groups and vice versa. The greater the number of group loyalties that coincide in this fashion, in other words, the deeper the cleavage between clustering group loyalties, and the greater the amount of conflict.

The particular formulation of the rift hypothesis to be used here is as follows:

When the actor state and the target state belong to different main groups of states, the act performed by the actor state is more likely to be a conflict act than if they both belong to the same group.[19]

In the international system, many such clusters of group loyalties have been identified, often by quite sophisticated methods such as factor analysis.[20] Here, only the two most important international rifts will be selected, their actual existence being assumed to be a matter beyond controversy. There is first the persistent conflict dimension between the industrialized West European, North American, and Oceanic states on the one hand, and the socialist states mainly of Eastern Europe on the other, here designated "the East-West rift." Secondly, there is the rift between the more developed states of the world and the less developed states, "the North-South rift."

Assignment of a given state to a given group is performed in the simplest possible way. The group definitions are taken from the UN General Assembly resolution creating UNCTAD, in which a system of group consultations is established.[21] States are explicitly assigned to one of four groups, labeled A, B, C, and D.[22] Group A covers the Latin-American states; group B covers the West European, North American, and Oceanic states; group C spans the African and Asian states (excepting the USSR); and Group D covers the socialist states of Eastern Europe. For our purposes, groups A and C are combined into one group labelled "South," while Group B is called "West" and group D "East."

It is assumed that the two rifts have been sufficiently persistent in the post-1945 period to permit extension of the group classification back to 1946 and up to 1968, allowing, of course, for the varying dates of independence of the new nations. There have been a few changes in group association on the part of some states, however. Because of the large volume of the interaction data, states had to be assigned to only one group for the entire period, and borderline cases have been weighed carefully regarding the possible consequence to the analysis of assignment to one group rather than another.[23]

Now that the group of states have been identified, the rift hypothesis can be summed up in the expectation that conflict will be more frequent in inter-group interaction than in intra-group interaction. Table 5-5 may give a first indication of the extent to which the expectation holds up.

Table 5-5
Conflict Actions in Shipping, by Group Affiliation of Actor State and Target State, All Issues, 1946-1968 (Percent)[a][b]

	Target State's Group:	
Actor State's Group	Same as Actor's Group	Other than Actor's Group
South	24 (N = 330)	62 (N = 1585)
West	35 (N = 1597)	56 (N = 1249)
East	0 (N = 14)	62 (N = 482)

[a]Each percentage represents the number of conflict actions out of the N for that percentage.
[b]Source: As in Table 5-1.

A clear relationship appears: throughout, the frequency of conflict interaction is higher between groups than within groups. At this stage, then, the hypothesis on the effects of international rifts on interaction seems to receive unqualified support. If we break down interaction by main issue types, however, the picture becomes somewhat different. Deviation from the expected pattern appears first of all in the case of contaminated issues. (Table 5-6.)

Table 5-6

Conflict Actions in Shipping, by Group Affiliation of Actor State and Target State, Contaminated Issues, 1946-1968 (Percent)[a]

	Target State's Group:	
Actor State's Group	Same as Actor's Group	Other than Actor's Group
South	83 (N = 66)	71 (N = 384)
West	46 (N = 385)	72 (N = 367)
East	— (N = 0)	82 (N = 178)

[a]Source as in Table 5-1.

Here, interaction within the Southern group clearly falls outside the general pattern discovered in the previous table. Rather than being lower than the conflict level between South and other groups, the intra-group percentage is significantly higher.[24] Although it is difficult to explain why this figure is so high, some light may be thrown on this problem by a comparison with the figures for the two other groups.

The Western states seem to be considerably more prone to conflict in their interaction with out-group nations than with in-group nations. This signifies exactly what the terms "in-group" and "out-group" imply: Western nations have a degree of solidarity with each other on issues of blockades, embargoes, etc., that is not present among the less developed countries on these issues. First of all, most of these countries are either members of NATO or otherwise allied with the United States, a fact which would have special relevance for the contaminated issues. Secondly, the West European countries share a common political culture and form a kind of political community that limits the amount of overt conflict even on more salient issues. They are also traditional maritime countries that have a stake in not hurting each other's shipping business, so that strong policy instruments like blockades are usually rejected by them as a matter of principle.

The striking absence of any actions within the group of East European states on these issues is evidence of an even higher degree of solidarity. Not a single act of in-group conflict was recorded for the socialist states in the entire 23-year period—regardless of issue! In contrast, the Southern nations, by the present definition a group embracing three continents, may be too diverse in makeup to allow solidarity to prevail on contaminated shipping issues. If they represent a community of economic interest on the basis of their poverty, it does not extend to the point where they are willing to restrain the use of negative economic sanctions among themselves.

The rift hypothesis emerges a bit weakened from this part of the test. To get the complete picture, however, both the pure issues and the special case of the Suez affair should be taken into account. (Tables 5-7 and 5-8.)

In both cases, the rift hypothesis has unqualified support. Even the smallest of the differences, that for West in Table 5-7, is significant at the .01 level.[25]

Table 5-7
Conflict Actions in Shipping, by Group Affiliation of Actor State and Target State, Pure Issues,[a] 1946-1968 (Percent)[b]

	Target State's Group:	
Actor State's Group	Same as Actor's Group	Other than Actor's Group
South	11 (N = 106)	57 (N = 389)
West	41 (N = 750)	48 (N = 495)
East	0 (N = 14)	36 (N = 135)

[a]Excluding interaction on Suez issue 1956-1959.
[b]Source: As in Table 5-1.

Table 5-8
Conflict Actions in Shipping, by Group Affiliation of Actor State and Target State, Suez Issue, 1956-1959 (Percent)[a]

	Target State's Group:	
Actor State's Group	Same as Actor's Group	Other than Actor's Group
South	7 (N = 158)	58 (N = 482)
West	14 (N = 462)	52 (N = 387)
East	— (N = 0	63 (N = 169)

[a]Source: As in Table 5-1.

Without exception, then, the frequency of conflict is significantly higher *between* groups than *within* groups.

Still, it can hardly be denied that the difference between intra-Western conflict on the one hand and conflict between West and other groups on the other hand is considerably smaller on pure issues than on contaminated issues. Western states discriminate much more clearly between in-group and out-group on contaminated issues than on pure issues. Why this difference?

The most obvious explanation is that the difference of issues causes the difference in conflict behavior. Contaminated issues usually imply a threat to the entire business of ocean transport, raising the specter of international conflicts and wars disrupting regular shipping activities. In such cases it is natural for the main shipowning countries to stick together. Pure issues, on the other hand, are not tinged with such associations: most of them are interwoven with everyday shipping activities in any case, such as freight rate matters, treatment of ships in port and questions of navigation. Here, each maritime country looks out for itself and pursues policies maximizing short-term national shipping interests. Consequently, intra-group conflict is more frequent among maritime states on these issues.

In sum, it can now be concluded that the rift hypothesis is confirmed by the present data. Shipping interaction, which does cross the main rifts in the international system generally, has a higher conflict frequency than shipping interaction, which does not—with one exception, namely, the Southern group on *contaminated* issues. Clearly, the international political rifts thoroughly penetrate the international system of shipping, with important effects on the essential nature of shipping politics.

But the context of shipping politics also gives an interesting twist to the significance of international rifts: the East-West cleavage is not of major importance in shipping interaction. This interpretation is based, not on the level of conflict between groups, but on the volume of interaction. (Table 5-9.) The East-West rift may be important in the sense that whenever interaction occurs it has a high conflict content. But since East-West interaction occurs considerably

Table 5-9
Volume of Interaction, by Direction, 1946-1968[a]

Issues	Intra-South	Intra-West	Intra-East	South/West West/South	South/East East/South	East/West West/East	Total
Pure	106	750	14	768	56	195	1889
Con-tam.	66	385	0	603	45	281	1380
Suez	158	462	0	797	69	172	1658
All	330	1597	14	2168	170	648	4927

[a]Source: As in Table 5-1.

less frequently than both South-West interaction and intra-West interaction, the conflict dimension between East and West is simply not "activated" that often. The same observation applies to the East-South dimension. Thus, judging both by frequency of conflict and frequency of interaction, there are only two cases in which both tend to be high, namely interaction between South and West, and intra-West interaction.

Overall Assessment: Relative Impact of the Main Independent Variables

Since it has been established beyond doubt that international rifts affect the frequency of conflict in shipping, it is necessary to assess the relative influence of this variable compared to the effects of the variables previously considered.

A new time series variable was therefore constructed, measuring—for each year—the amount of interaction flowing *between* the three groups (East, West, and South) in percent of the total volume of interaction for that year. Note that conflict actions are not reflected in the measure, which only takes in the *volume* of interaction.

In view of the findings so far, the hypothesis on the effect of this new variable must be that the higher the percentage of between-group interaction in a given year, the higher the frequency of conflict in the international system of shipping. This hypothesis is clearly supported in the data. Pearson's r for the relationship between shipping conflict on all issues and volume of cross-rift interaction is .619, significant by a wide margin at the .05 level.[26]

The analysis is now locked in a situation of stalemate. Both the main hypothesis in its broad interpretation and an alternative hypothesis have been confirmed by the data. Since the former hypothesis does not lend itself readily to a regression, we are prevented from carrying the analysis further.

It is worth noting, however, that the two hypotheses are not contradictory—if one is true the other is not necessarily false. Consequently, there is no reason to make a choice in favor of one or the other.[27] We prefer instead to opt for the coexistence of theories in recognition of the probability that both contain an element of "truth."

This concludes our analysis at the systemic level. In view of the hazards of making inferences from a higher to a lower level of analysis, it remains to be seen (in the following chapter) what the present findings mean at the actor level.

Notes

1. See Chapter 2 for details of the approach used in this study. The author is indebted to Jörg W. Bronebakk and Fredrik Björkan for research assistance, to

Eyolf Steen-Olsen for programming assistance, and to Andrew Cowart for ideas and comments in regard to the analysis presented in this chapter.

2. The concept is defined below.

3. Ibid., p. 713.

4. Difference-of-proportions test: $z = 3.125$, one-tailed test.

5. See, for example, H.R. Alker, MATHEMATICS AND POLITICS, (New York: Macmillan, 1965), Chapter 3.

6. See: Terence Robertson, CRISIS: THE INSIDE STORY OF THE SUEZ CONSPIRACY (New York: Atheneum, 1965).

7. Significant at the .05 level.

8. J. Johnston, ECONOMETRIC METHODS (New York: McGraw-Hill, 1963), Chapter 7.

9. J. Durbin and G.S. Watson, "Testing for Serial Correlation in Least-squares Regression," BIOMETRIKA, 1950 (part I) and 1951 (part II).

10. See K.W. Smillie, AN INTRODUCTION TO REGRESSION AND COR-RELATION (New York: Academic Press, 1966), pp. 96-97.

11. J. David Singer and Melvin Small, "Alliance Aggregation and the Onset of War, 1815-1945," in Singer, ed., op. cit., pp. 258 ff. The main criteria are: (1) the best estimate of total battle-connected deaths must be 1,000 or more; (2) at least one participant on at least one side of the conflict must be "an independent and sovereign member of the international system" (p. 258). The Singer-Small category of *civil war* is thus excluded here.

12. See Appendix F.

13. Maurice A. East, "Stratification and International Politics: An Empirical Study Employing the International Systems Approach." Unpublished Ph.D. dissertation, Princeton University, 1969, pp. 104-107.

14. Covers: blockades; embargoes; blacklisting of ships; incidents of searching, seizing, or shelling of ships; refusal to grant access to ports; actual or alleged espionage by ships; incidents of harassment of ships by military aircraft or naval vessels; wartime restrictions on shipping; and disposal of merchant fleets of defeated World War II powers.

15. Covers the following groups of issues: flag discrimination; liner conferences and freight rates; flags of convenience; shipbuilding and financial matters (e.g., insurance credits, chartering, pooling); international law and organizations as such; development aid in shipping; uses of ports; safety and navigation; and labor questions.

16. One-tailed test, 38 degrees of freedom.

17. Tests of the narrower interpretation by regression analysis yielded no statistically significant results for pure shipping conflict.

18. See, for example, Karl W. Deutsch and J. David Singer, "Multipolar Power Systems and International Stability," in Rosenau II, op. cit., p. 317; Russett, TRENDS IN WORLD POLITICS (New York: Macmillan, 1965), pp. 87 ff.

19. "Actor state": the state which performs the item of action. "Target state": the state toward which the action is directed.

20. For an excellent example of this, see Alker and Russett, op. cit.

21. General Assembly Resolution no. 1995-XIX, December 30, 1964.

22. A list of the states within each group is included in Appendix G.

23. Special cases are indicated in the list included in Appendix G.

24. Significant at the .05 level, two-tailed difference-of-proportions test, $z = 2.04$.

25. One-tailed difference-of-proportions test, $z = 2.44$.

26. $F = 11.789$, $N = 21$, 1 and 19 degrees of freedom. Durbin-Watson test: $d = 1.58$, no autocorrelation.

27. Galtung, op. cit., pp. 456-458. I am indebted to Mr. Morten Egeberg for this point.

Analysis of Behavior at the Actor Level

In this chapter, the characteristic traits of the participants' behavior will be examined from several perspectives, but the primary focus will be on their propensity to conflict. Basically, efforts will be made to search out possible links between the behavior of states and their distinctive features with regard to shipping activities.

It should be noted that the expression "behavior of states" in the following refers to the behavior of officials acting in behalf of the state.[1] As pointed out in Chapter 2, it is assumed that this behavior is rational in the sense of seeking to maintain or improve the position of the country in the international distribution of shipping values. This is a somewhat narrow interpretation of rationality; but for reasons given above, problems of rationality and irrationality are assumed not to have any serious impact on decision-making in shipping affairs.

The participants are the immediate sources of actions studied. This is why it is important to take a closer look at them here: whereas Chapter 5 examined gross, systemic behavior patterns in terms of global explanatory factors, this chapter will focus on the behavior patterns of states and relate them to pertinent characteristics of states.[2]

The main questions arising at this level of analysis are as follows:

1. Who are the participants in each of the five periods selected (1946-49, 1950-54, 1955-59, 1960-64, 1965-68)? Which of the participants are stable over time? Who are the "activists," the participants with the highest frequency of participation? Are these stable over time? Is there, in other words, a nucleus or smaller central system of interaction that is more stable than the peripheral parts of the system? If there is, how large is the nucleus compared to the total system?

2. What are the factors most closely associated with conflict behavior on the part of participants? Specifically, what role does the *shipping situation* of a state play as a possible determinant of its behavior?[3] What is the importance of liner conference issues and each country's relationship with the liner conferences in this connection? A crucial question is, of course, whether certain corollaries of the central hypothesis regarding the international distribution of values hold up at this level of analysis.

Participation in the System

Participatory aspects of behavior will first be inspected in terms of frequency. Four types of participants are covered in this study:

1. *Nation-states*, for the whole period or from date of independence.
2. *"Quasi-states"*: certain units that have not been formally independent throughout the 1946-68 period have been included as participants, for reasons given below.[4]
3. *Intergovernmental organizations*, from the starting date of effective operation.
4. *Liner conferences* have been included as participants whenever they have acted as such through their secretariats.[5] Individual member companies have not been regarded as participants at any time.

The 1946-1949 Period

Table 6-1 shows the frequency of participation in the 1946-49 period. Concentrating for the moment on the columns labeled "all issues," what appears first of all is the rather wide difference between median (6.2) and mean (13.0), showing that there are only a few really high participants and very many low ones. Secondly, although the above-mean participants are typically western industrialized states, they are not exclusively so: e.g., China and Egypt, and to some extent also Argentina. And if all above the median are considered, this tendency is even more pronounced: the group of participants added here is mostly neither western nor industrialized. Especially notable is the activity of India, independent for less than two years in this period. If participation is related, among other things, to a sense of competence, a confidence in one's ability to have an impact on international political processes (as Almond and Verba suggest in a different context),[6] then Indian decision-makers must have acquired such subjective competence at a very early date. This may also apply to the case of Egypt, but it should be remembered that Egypt was at this time involved in an intense conflict with Israel, which may also have affected the frequency of its participation in this period.[7]

Two "informal" participants are listed whose involvement may seem surprising: West Germany and Japan. Although neither state was formally independent at this time, they did have administrators for transportation matters appointed by the occupation powers, and since these administrators were able to present public demands regarding their country's shipping activities to the occupation powers, they have been included here as participants. Two other nonindependent participants are included from 1946 on for somewhat similar reasons: Hong Kong and Singapore. Neither has been an independent state for most of

Table 6-1

Frequency of Participation by 54 Participants 1946-1949 (Rank Order by Number of Actions)[a]

Rank All Issues	Country	Number of Actions All Issues	Rank Pure Issues
1	USA	134	1
2	UK	81	2
3	Republic of China	54	16
4	Norway	52	3.5
5	USSR	38	3.5
6.5	Netherlands	31	6.5
6.5	UAR	31	41.5
8	France	27	5
9	Sweden	24	6.5
10	Denmark	20	9
11	Belgium	16	10
12	Argentina	15	8
13.5	India[b]	12	13.5
13.5	Poland	12	31.5
15.5	Greece	10	16
15.5	Yugoslavia	10	24.5
17.5	Japan	8	13.5
17.5	Spain	8	20
19.5	Canada	7	31.5
19.5	Colombia	7	11.5
22	Inter-Allied Rep. Agency	7	–
22	Panama	7	11.5
22	South Africa	7	24.5
26	Australia	6	31.5
26	Brazil	6	41.5
26	Chile	6	31.5
26	Finland	6	20
26	Western World War II Allies	6	16
31	Ecuador	4	20
31	Italy	4	24.5
31	New Zealand	4	–
31	Venezuela	4	20
31	West Germany	4	20
35	Iceland	3	24.5
35	North Korea	3	–
35	United Nations	3	31.5
39	Czechoslovakia	2	31.5

Table 6-1 (cont.)

Rank All Issues	Country	Number of Actions All Issues	Rank Pure Issues
39	Ireland	2	31.5
39	The Liner Conferences	2	31.5
39	OEEC	2	31.5
39	Switzerland	2	31.5
48	Ceylon	1	–
48	Cuba	1	41.5
48	Honduras	1	41.5
48	ILO	1	41.5
48	Jordan	1	–
48	Lebanon	1	–
48	Luxembourg	1	41.5
48	NATO	1	–
48	Peru	1	41.5
48	Portugal	1	41.5
48	Singapore	1	41.5
48	Thailand	1	–
48	Uruguay	1	41.5

Mean, all issues	13.0	Median, all issues	6.2	
	Range, pure issues	1-86		
Mean, pure issues	7.9	Median, pure issues	4.7	

[a]Source: As in Table 5-1.
[b]Where several participants have the same frequency, they are listed alphabetically.

the 1946-68 period, yet both are in rather special positions with regard to shipping. They are both crucial ports in the shipping of the Far East, they have traditionally—though not formally—had a relatively autonomous status with regard to their internal affairs and with regard to such "non-political" external affairs as trade and shipping. The registration of ships, for instance, is undertaken locally, and at least in the case of Hong Kong has been subjected to regulations quite different from those obtaining in the United Kingdom.[8]

Hence, for the entire period under study, there are five participants of a "quasi-state" type: Japan (1946-52 only), West Germany (1946-51 only),[9] Hong Kong (1946-68), Singapore (1946-65 only), and Malta (1955-64 only). Malta is included by virtue of the fact that it began acting independently of, and in opposition to, the United Kingdom in matters of shipping in 1956. The quasi-states that have since become independent are included as nation-state participants as of their date of independence.

One of the intergovernmental participants figuring fairly prominently in the

1946-49 period is the Inter-Allied Reparations Agency. This organization actually had a rather brief spurt of involvement in shipping matters right after the war, when it presided over the division of former enemy merchant fleets among the allies and then faded out of the picture soon thereafter.

Another relic of the Second World War is found in the participant labeled Western World War II Allies, which is the western portion of the Allied Control Council. The interaction involving West Germany in its period as "quasi-state" was mostly undertaken *vis-à-vis* this participant, and *vice versa*.

On the whole, intergovernmental organizations are not totally inactive in this period, despite the absence of any formal organization to deal with maritime transport questions. Both the UN,[10] the OEEC, NATO, and the ILO have engaged in shipping interaction in this period. While the UN has been participating mainly in reactive patterns (i.e., without taking initiatives) during most of the 23-year period, the OEEC in this early postwar span gives indication of a lasting interest in shipping which leads it, in 1954, to the establishment of a Maritime Transport Committee—the first permanent and formal intergovernmental organization set up in shipping affairs to take effect after World War II.

NATO's involvement, on the other hand, concerned the status of NATO merchant fleets in time of war. The single action coded here was NATO's announcement of its plans in the fall of 1949. Diplomatic negotiations took place in late 1949 and early 1950, but from March 1950 the discussions continued at a lower level in NATO's *Planning Board for Ocean Shipping* (PBOS), which has been a forum for regular discussions on this topic ever since.[11] Interestingly, Høegh argues that without this agreement on the common uses of NATO fleets in wartime, the United States would have had a powerful argument for expanding its merchant fleet to cover purely military contingencies.[12] One might therefore venture the guess that the West European strategy in these discussions has been to keep on reassuring the US of West European loyalty to the initial agreement, just as it has been in the interest of Liberia and Panama to let their American shipowners pledge the availability of their ships to the US Government in wartime.[13]

ILO's interest in shipping is, not surprisingly, mainly restricted to the working conditions on board ships. This is, however, not quite the cut-and-dried issue it might seem. The ILO was for years involved in a dispute with flag-of-convenience countries—described in a previous chapter—concerning the welfare and wages of sailors employed on convenience-flag ships.[14]

Finally, this temporary focus on uncommon participants in international shipping brings attention to the three landlocked states taking part in interaction in the 1946-49 period: Czechoslovakia, Switzerland, and Luxembourg. The old joke about the "Swiss merchant marine" is not a joke at all: both Czechoslovakia and Switzerland have respectable oceangoing merchant fleets and therefore have an obvious interest in maritime matters. Luxembourg, on the other hand, is primarily interested in a frictionless movement of goods through the closest possible ports, and in the most unrestrained movement of goods possible between ports. It was on the latter type of question—flag discrimination—that Luxembourg took action in 1949.

On the whole, however, the typical participants seem to be the larger shipowning nations, the larger trading nations, coastal states with important ports, and island states.

Turning to the right hand column of Table 6-1, showing ranks on pure issues only, a few drastic differences appear. Nationalist China, in the final spasm of civil war, instituted a vigorous blockade against communist-controlled areas of the mainland on June 20, 1949. As will be seen below,[15] this blockade kept the nationalists among the highest-frequency participants in the issue-area of shipping for several years. At this point, during six months in 1949, China scores a total of 49 actions on the blockade issue alone. At the same time, China was impressively unconcerned with matters more pertinent to shipping as such.

For Egypt, a strikingly similar pattern is shown in the drop from a rank of 6 on all issues to the lowest rank on pure issues. Like China, Egypt was involved in a blockade or, actually, in a combination of blockade and embargo against Israel. If this specific issue is disregarded, Egypt appears to take practically no interest in maritime questions at this time.

In essence, the rank order on the pure issues is intended to isolate participants with a *broad scope* of interest in shipping. Obviously, neither the Republic of China nor Egypt qualify for this distinction in the 1946-49 period. No other participants give evidence of an equally narrow scope of interests, although several states drop considerably in rank—such as Yugoslavia, Poland, and Canada. Predictably, the Inter-Allied Reparations Agency disappears altogether.

It may be appropriate to comment a bit further on what is meant by a broad scope of interests. As explained above, the totality of specific issues in shipping is considered in two main classes—contaminated issues and pure issues.[16] The contaminated issues were so called because they are related in one way or another to the threat or use of interstate violence or—in other words—to war and international crises that commonly involve non-shipping issues. The specific issues may bear reviewing:

1. blockades and quasi-blockades.
2. embargoes.
3. blacklisting of ships; refusing entry to ports.
4. searching, seizing, or shelling of ships.
5. demanding special wartime documentation for ships, (navicerts, etc.).
6. espionage of and by ships, harassment of ships by navies or air forces.

Naturally any country whose shipping or trade is directly affected by such events, or which is undertaking policies or actions intended to bring about such effects on foreign trade and shipping, will be highly active in the contaminated issues.

But a country having interests in shipping or seaborne trade that go *beyond* the immediate concerns of such situations must be expected to be active also in the pure issues. It must not be presumed to act only when prodded—in a stimulus-response fashion.

The test of narrowness of interest scope is therefore: does the state participate in the issue-area of shipping only when its normal maritime transactions are violently disrupted, or when the danger of violent disruption is perceived? If so, it will be deemed to have a narrow scope of interests in shipping.

The 1950-1954 Period

Table 6-2 shows the rank of participants by frequency for the 1950-54 period. The group at the top is still there, but with Egypt heading the list this time; Taiwan following not far behind. Two active new participants are worth noticing: Israel and China. Israel could have been expected to be active as early as the first period, when Egypt's blockading efforts were started. Why this did not happen, or at least why it is not reflected in the data, is not immediately apparent. It may be that the Egyptian blockade initially affected the main maritime nations more than it affected the Israeli merchant fleet, which was of a size hardly worth mentioning in the first years. In the second period, however, the Israeli response is up to par. Here, Israel follows the nationalist Chinese pattern described above with an almost exclusive concentration of interest on the blockade issue.

Egypt, on the other hand, now also discovered the potentialities of the Suez Canal. Moreover, Egypt changed its attitude towards the presence of British troops when the old regime was deposed in 1952. Because of the introduction of the Canal issue in this period, Egyptian shipping interests could be said to have broadened in scope since the previous period. Still, non-shipping issues were clearly mixed in through the presence of British troops in the Suez Canal zone at this time. The Canal issue, at any rate, is where Egypt's non-blockade activities are massively concentrated in the second period.

Another newcomer in the blockade business at this time is mainland China. Mao Tse-Tung's government imposed a kind of "counter-blockade" against western shipping that brought the traditional maritime nations literally under double fire. The communists were less persistent blockaders than the nationalists, however, and these efforts—which were closely related to the Korean War—died down fairly quickly after the war was ended. Nevertheless, both Chinas are about equally one-sided in their shipping pursuits—both drop to the lowest or near-lowest ranks when contaminated issues are disregarded.

Greece is another narrow-scope participant in the second period. The reason for Greece's relatively high involvement in contaminated issues may be a tendency on the part of some Greek trampship owners to take cargoes to and

Table 6-2
Frequency of Participation by 69 Participants 1950-1954 (Rank Order by Number of Actions)[a]

Rank All Issues	Country	Number of Actions All Issues	Rank Pure Issues
1	UAR	175	2
2	USA	174	1
3	UK	135	3
4	Taiwan	99	25
5	USSR	60	4
6	Israel	54	49.5
7	Norway	40	6
8	Sweden	31	5
9	Denmark	29	7
10.5	France	24	13
10.5	Poland	24	9
12	China	23	49.5
13	United Nations	20	19
14	Netherlands	17	10
15	Japan	12	8
16	Greece	10	49.5
17.5	Brazil	8	11
17.5	Turkey	8	13
19	West Germany	7	19
23.5	Arab League	6	25
23.5	Australia	6	25
23.5	Chile	6	15.5
23.5	India	6	25
23.5	Italy	6	34.5
23.5	The Liner Conferences	6	13
23.5	Panama	6	34.5
23.5	Saudi Arabia	6	15.5
28.5	Canada	5	34.5
28.5	Iran	5	25
33.5	Bolivia	4	19
33.5	Finland	4	49.5
33.5	NATO	4	—
33.5	New Zealand	4	—
33.5	OEEC	4	19
33.5	Singapore	4	49.5
33.5	South Korea	4	49.5

Table 6-2 (cont.)

Rank All Issues	Country	Number of Actions All Issues	Rank Pure Issues
33.5	Venezuela	4	19
43	Argentina	3	34.5
43	Belgium	3	34.5
43	Colombia	3	25
43	Czechoslovakia	3	49.5
43	Ecuador	3	25
43	Hong Kong	3	–
43	ILO	3	34.5
43	South Africa	3	34.5
43	South Vietnam	3	34.5
43	Spain	3	34.5
43	Yugoslavia	3	49.5
51.5	Cambodia	2	34.5
51.5	Honduras	2	–
51.5	Indonesia	2	–
51.5	Laos	2	34.5
51.5	Pakistan	2	49.5
51.5	Western World War II Allies	2	34.5
62	Albania	1	49.5
62	Burma	1	49.5
62	Ceylon	1	49.5
62	Dominican Republic	1	49.5
62	Iraq	1	–
62	Ireland	1	49.5
62	Jordan	1	–
62	Lebanon	1	–
62	Luxembourg	1	–
62	North Korea	1	49.5
62	Paraguay	1	49.5
62	Peru	1	49.5
62	Portugal	1	–
62	Romania	1	49.5
62	Syria	1	–

Mean, all issues	15.7	Median, all issues	4.25	
	Range, pure issues	1-90		
Mean, pure issues	8.6	Median, pure issues	2.5	

aSource: As in Table 5-1.

from high-risk tension areas, such as the Far East at this time. Blockade- and embargo-running brought other governments into trouble as well, during the Korean War and the US embargo of Red China undertaken at the same time. Thus, both Panamanian and Norwegian ships were seized temporarily by the United States on several occasions on charges of violating the embargo. Panama, in addition to Greece, was particularly exposed to this problem, as is seen in its drop in rank on the pure issues.

Poland, on the other hand, shows a more stable interest in shipping in the 1950-54 period. In the two-and-a-half decades since World War II, Poland has gradually acquired a special position as the leading East European nation in maritime affairs. Professor Arnljot Strømme Svendsen pointed out the openness of Poland to less doctrinaire ways of thinking about ocean transport as early as 1962.[17]

A more curious participant in the second period is Saudi Arabia. This country's distinguishing marks from a shipping point of view are its huge oil exports and its control of the Straits of Tiran—the latter normally shared with Egypt. In 1954, however, Saudi Arabia became a pioneer in the field of cargo reservation for petroleum. The story of this initiative, which involved the Greek shipowner Aristotle Onassis, was related in Chapter 4. Saudi Arabia's rank in the 1950-54 period is largely a product of this episode.

Among the non-state participants, the OEEC, ILO, the UN, and the Liner Conferences remain moderately active. The Liner Conferences are typical reactive participants, mostly responding to US attempts to regulate their activities. They are not really participants here by way of choice; they are rather prodded into action by the policies and actions of the nation-state participants.

The major participants in the second period, as in the first, are a characteristic mix of great powers and leading maritime nations. Their stability on a broader scope of issues also leads to the conclusion that it is their great interest in shipping and seaborne trade—not the great-power status of several of them—which makes them the active participants they are.

Still, it is surprising to see Japan ranking so high just a few years after the end of US occupation, and ahead of a country like the Netherlands. If this activity is compared with Japan's general stature in world politics at the time—which was not impressive—the postwar Japanese image as economic giant and political dwarf seems to fit very well.

Finally, in the 1950-54 participation picture, one should note the position of Bolivia. This landlocked state was at the time involved in a dispute with Chile concerning the development of northern Chilean ports to facilitate the movement of Bolivian foreign trade—the perennial problem of landlocked states. This particular dispute also had roots in an old territorial quarrel. The interaction in the 1950-54 period involved the United States as well, acting as a peripheral participant trying to mediate.

The 1955-1959 period

Turning now to Table 6-3, which gives participation frequency for the 1955-59 period, the reader will observe that issues are here considered in three degrees of inclusiveness: all issues, pure issues, and pure issues excluding the issue group "international law and organization." The latter conceals the specific sub-issue "free passage in international straits and canals," which is the classification of the 1956 Suez nationalization dispute in the present data collection. As noted in the previous chapter, the volume of interaction on this particular question was so great that the possible need for special treatment of the issue was foreseen. Here that need has obviously arisen. Even the leading participant after both the contaminated issues and the Suez issues have been cut away, (USA) is reduced to 1/10 of its total activity in the process. Significantly, also, the total number of participants is practically halved by this manipulation (from 93 to 48).

On all issues considered jointly, the major contenders in the Suez affair predictably top the list, headed by the UAR. It should be noted that in the shipping aspects of the 1956 Suez crisis, Israel was *not* an important participant. The shipping problem which consumed much more of Israel's attention and energy was the dispute with Saudi Arabia and Jordan regarding their closure of the Straits of Tiran, beginning around New Year 1957. Later, however, and particularly in 1959, Nasser's policy of keeping the canal closed to Israeli ships and trade, yet open to all other nations, did become a bothersome Israeli headache. As one might expect, the UAR and Israel drop way down on the list if these issues are excluded, and Saudi Arabia, among others, disappear altogether.

Several other participants appear to have a very special interest in the Suez issue. Jordan, Iraq, and Syria clearly fall within this narrow-interest group, as do Australia and Canada—the latter two possibly more unexpectedly. One should not forget, however, that both of these leading Commonwealth countries played special roles during the Suez crises. Australia did so because Prime Minister Menzies headed the mission which sought a compromise solution with Nasser, and because of the special importance of the canal to Australian external trade. Canada's participation may be traced to the behind-the-scenes work of Lester Pearson, who was especially active in the United Nations setting.[18] Even Panama was exceptionally aroused by the canal commotion, probably hoping that a possible internationalization of the Suez Canal could set a powerful example for the United States to follow.

When the two versions of the pure issues are compared, it is interesting to note how France's rank declines relative to a country like Norway in the absence of the Suez issue. Here the broad scope of the shipping interests of Norway stand out strongly, and the indication is obviously that although France has important interests in both shipping and trade, these are mellowed by other foreign policy concerns common to great powers. Norway, on the other hand,

Table 6-3

Frequency of Participation by 93 Participants 1955-1959 (Rank Order by Number of Actions)[a]

Rank All Issues	Country	Number of Actions All Issues	Rank Pure Issues	Rank Pure Issues Excl. Suez
1	UAR	649	1	18.5
2	USA	528	2	1
3	UK	446	3	3
4	France	288	4	11.5
5	USSR	239	6	4
6	United Nations	238	5	23.5
7	Israel	209	7	34.5
8	India	142	8	15
9	Norway	104	9	2
10	Saudi Arabia	57	10	–
11	Denmark	56	11	5.5
12	Australia	54	12	–
13	Sweden	52	13	5.5
14	Indonesia	46	22.5	23.5
15	Yugoslavia	43	15.5	43
16	Iraq	40	20	–
17.5	Italy	36	17.5	15
17.5	Netherlands	36	19	8
19	Panama	35	14	23.5
20.5	Canada	33	15.5	29.5
20.5	Jordan	33	17.5	–
22	Lebanon	31	22.5	–
23	Syria	29	21	–
24	Taiwan	26	53.5	23.5
25	West Germany	25	26	11.5
26.5	Iran	24	24	–
26.5	Pakistan	24	26	–
28	IBRD	23	26	23.5
29	Ceylon	22	28	–
30	Japan	20	29	8
31	Poland	19	30	15
32.5	China	17	36.5	43
32.5	Spain	17	31	29.5
34	Belgium	16	32	15
35.5	Greece	15	36.5	23.5
35.5	Liberia	15	33	10
37.5	Tunisia	14	36.5	–

Table 6-3 (cont.)

Rank All Issues	Country	Number of Actions All Issues	Rank Pure Issues	Rank Pure Issues Excl. Suez
37.5	Turkey	14	34	34.5
39.5	New Zealand	13	36.5	–
39.5	Philippines	13	59.5	–
41	OEEC	11	39	8
42	Suez Canal Users' Association	10	40	–
43	Libya	9	41	–
44.5	Brazil	8	42	15
44.5	Czechoslovakia	8	53.5	43
47	Ethiopia	7	44	–
47	IMCO	7	44	18.5
47	Sudan	7	44	–
51	Colombia	6	46.5	29.5
51	Hungary	6	49	–
51	Morocco	6	53.5	–
51	Peru	6	46.5	–
51	South Africa	6	49	–
54.5	Argentina	5	49	23.5
54.5	Switzerland	5	59.5	–
58	Chile	4	53.5	23.5
58	Finland	4	53.5	43
58	Iceland	4	53.5	–
58	Ireland	4	53.5	–
60.5	Guatemala	3	59.5	29.5
60.5	Portugal	3	59.5	–
69	Afghanistan	2	66.5	–
69	Austria	2	78.5	43
69	Bolivia	2	–	–
69	Burma	2	66.5	–
69	East Germany	2	66.5	34.5
69	Ecuador	2	66.5	34.5
69	Ghana	2	66.5	34.5
69	Honduras	2	66.5	43
69	The Liner Conferences	2	66.5	34.5
69	Malta	2	66.5	–
69	NATO	2	66.5	–
69	Nepal	2	–	–

Table 6-3 (cont.)

Rank All Issues	Country	Number of Actions All Issues	Rank Pure Issues	Rank Pure Issues Excl. Suez
69	South Korea	2	78.5	43
69	Thailand	2	66.5	–
69	Venezuela	2	–	–
85	Albania	1	–	–
85	Costa Rica	1	78.5	43
85	Council of Europe	1	78.5	–
85	Cuba	1	78.5	–
85	Dominican Republic	1	78.5	43
85	ILO	1	78.5	43
85	Luxembourg	1	–	–
85	Malaya	1	78.5	–
85	Mexico	1	78.5	–
85	Monaco	1	–	–
85	Nicaragua	1	78.5	–
85	Paraguay	1	78.5	43
85	Romania	1	78.5	–
85	San Marino	1	–	–
85	Uruguay	1	78.5	–
85	Vatican	1	–	–
85	Yemen	1	78.5	–

Mean, all issues	41.2	Median, all issues	7.5	
	Range, pure issues	1-632		
Mean, pure issues	42.1	Median, pure issues	7.33	
	Range, pure issues (excl. Suez)	1-60		
Mean, pure issues (excl. Suez)	7.2	Median, pure issues (excl. Suez)	4.5	

aSource: As in Table 5-1.

probably has fewer conflicting goals and engagements to hamper the pursuit of its "freedom of the seas" policy, and the result is a broad scope of participation in shipping questions.

In the most "purified" version of the ranking list, then, the top states are the typical maritime participants. Note the prominent ranking of the Soviet Union, however. There is no evidence that the Soviet government treats shipping merely as a means to an end—which would otherwise be a fitting judgment on many states involved only in contaminated issues.

The 1955-59 period is also the one in which Liberia appears for the first time as an active participant, reflecting the Liberian challenge to Panama's tonnage leadership among flags of convenience. Yet the two dominant countries in this special group are not typical high participants, but rather tend to fall in the moderately-active class. One suspects that they resemble the liner conferences to some degree in that they are *reactive* participants—their ships ply all over the world, yet it is only when a ship or a company is in trouble that the government reacts, or acts. Shipping apparently is to them more a matter of revenue than a matter of serious national interest. Problems of convenience flags also marked the debut of the new Intergovernmental Maritime Consultative Organization (IMCO) in 1959. Panama and Liberia played leading roles in the dispute which centered on the acceptance of flag-of-convenience countries as genuine maritime nations.[19]

The 1960-1964 Period

Turning to the subsequent time period (Table 6-4), a new variation in the previously established group of leading participants appears: Panama approaches the top. The issue that brought Panama so suddenly near the top on the pure issues was not related to flags of convenience but to trouble over the Canal Zone, most of it in January 1964. This issue also carried the OAS into the activist group, way ahead of any other international organization.

Two other specific shipping issues are related to the fairly frequent participation of the liner conferences and the IBRD in this period.

The liner conferences became involved in a new phase of their cat-and-mouse game with the US government when the latter started demanding confidential information from the conferences regarding their internal arrangements and operations.[20] At the same time, the previous dispute regarding freight rates blossomed forth again—and both of these sub-issues involved the major West European maritime states to a considerable degree.

The IBRD, on the other hand, was engaged in less controversial activities. With the granting of independence to a large number of new states in the 1960-64 period, the IBRD became more heavily engaged in problems of economic development. In the area of shipping, the IBRD devoted particular attention to port development projects in the new states.

Although the same group of high participants is found here as earlier, the Soviet Union now appears to be more heavily involved in contaminated issues than previously, which brings it to a lower rank, relatively speaking, on the pure issues. The Cuba crisis and blockade in 1962 is obviously behind this. But there is also another and probably less known sequence of events involved: throughout the 1960s, the Soviet government complained and protested again and again to the United States that Soviet merchant vessels were being harassed by US military aircraft and naval vessels. The allegations may well have been true, at least if US reactions are adequately reported in the data, since the US government responded only infrequently and weakly to the Soviet charges.

Table 6-4
Frequency of Participation by 85 Participants 1960-1964 (Rank Order by Number of Actions)[a]

Rank All Issues	Country	Number of Actions All Issues	Rank Pure Issues
1	USA	353	1
2	UK	90	3
3	Panama	86	2
4	USSR	85	10.5
5	Norway	84	4
6	Netherlands	35	5
7	Denmark	34	6
8.5	Sweden	33	8
8.5	UAR	33	7
10	France	30	13.5
11	West Germany	29	12
12.5	Italy	27	10.5
12.5	Japan	27	9
14	OAS	22	13.5
15	Cuba	21	30
16	Greece	19	15
17	Belgium	14	16
19	The Liner Conferences	13	17.5
19	Poland	13	22
19	United Nations	13	17.5
21	IMCO	11	19
22	IBRD	10	20
24	Brazil	9	22
24	Canada	9	35.5
24	Indonesia	9	35.5
27.5	China	8	26
27.5	Israel	8	22
27.5	Liberia	8	24
27.5	Yugoslavia	8	42.5
32	Arab League	6	26
32	Chile	6	26
32	India	6	35.5
32	Peru	6	30
32	Spain	6	30
36.5	Bulgaria	5	42.5
36.5	Finland	5	30
36.5	Mexico	5	35.5

Table 6-4 (cont.)

Rank All Issues	Country	Number of Actions All Issues	Rank Pure Issues
36.5	Switzerland	5	30
41.5	Albania	4	51.5
41.5	Argentina	4	51.5
41.5	Costa Rica	4	42.5
41.5	Czechoslovakia	4	35.5
41.5	Morocco	4	42.5
41.5	Uruguay	4	35.5
48	Bolivia	3	42.5
48	Cambodia	3	42.5
48	Ecuador	3	51.5
48	Iceland	3	42.5
48	Lebanon	3	51.5
48	Malaysia	3	51.5
48	Romania	3	42.5
59	Australia	2	51.5
59	Ceylon	2	51.5
59	Dominican Republic	2	67
59	East Germany	2	67
59	Ghana	2	51.5
59	Guatemala	2	–
59	Iran	2	51.5
59	Iraq	2	51.5
59	Ivory Coast	2	51.5
59	Jordan	2	67
59	Paraguay	2	51.5
59	Portugal	2	–
59	Syria	2	67
59	Turkey	2	–
59	Venezuela	2	67
76	Burma	1	67
76	Colombia	1	67
76	Congo (Kinshasa)	1	–
76	Haiti	1	67
76	Honduras	1	–
76	Hungary	1	67
76	International Court of Justice	1	67
76	Ireland	1	67
76	Malagasy Republic	1	67
76	NATO	1	–

Table 6-4 (cont.)

Rank All Issues	Country	Number of Actions All Issues	Rank Pure Issues
76	New Zealand	1	67
76	Nicaragua	1	67
76	OECD	1	67
76	Saudi Arabia	1	67
76	Senegal	1	67
76	Somalia	1	67
76	South Korea	1	67
76	South Vietnam	1	67
76	Tunisia	1	67
	Mean, all issues	15.1	Median, all issues	4.33
		Range, pure issues	1-249
	Mean, pure issues	12.0	Median pure issues	3.8

aSource: As in Table 5-1.

Thus, the whole affair had the public appearance of a one-way flow of Soviet actions.

The low participants in this period—as indeed in all previous periods—are typically non-Western states, with the weakest regional representation in Africa. There is no repetition of the Indian example from the 1946-49 period by the states which have now gained independence. But neither is there any new state at this time (1960-64) which can be said to rival India in maritime importance, with the possible exception of Nigeria.

The 1965-1968 Period

Finally, participation in the interaction system of shipping in the 1965-68 period should be taken into account.

Again, a single sequence of events predominates: the closing of the Straits of Tiran and later of the Suez Canal itself, in connection with the 1967 Arab-Israeli war. This time, however, (as opposed to the 1956 Suez crisis), the shipping aspect is highly secondary in what happens. The closing of the canal was a direct

Table 6-5

Frequency of Participation by 80 Participants 1965-1968 (Rank Order by Number of Actions)[a]

Rank All Issues	Country	Number of Actions All Issues	Rank Pure Issues
1	USA	174	1
2	UK	75	4.5
3	USSR	64	6
4	UAR	56	2
5	Israel	53	4.5
6	Norway	51	3
7	China	29	26
8	Brazil	26	7
9	France	22	8
10	Sweden	17	9
11	United Nations	16	16
12	Japan	15	11.5
14	The Liner Conferences	14	11.5
14	West Germany	14	10
14	Zambia	14	39
16	Greece	13	26
18	Italy	12	22.5
18	Netherlands	12	13.5
18	Portugal	12	—
20.5	Denmark	11	16
20.5	IMCO	11	13.5
22	Nordic Council	10	16
23	India	9	18
25	Chile	8	20
25	Panama	8	20
25	UNCTAD	8	20
29.5	Argentina	7	22.5
29.5	Belgium	7	26
29.5	Finland	7	29.5
29.5	Nigeria	7	51
29.5	Pakistan	7	39
29.5	FNL (Vietnam)	7	—
34.5	Canada	6	26
34.5	Indonesia	6	—
34.5	Iraq	6	26
34.5	Rhodesia	6	—
38.5	Kuwait	5	29.5

Table 6-5 (cont.)

Rank All Issues	Country	Number of Actions All Issues	Rank Pure Issues
38.5	Poland	5	39
38.5	Spain	5	32.5
38.5	Uruguay	5	32.5
43	Bulgaria	4	39
43	IBRD	4	32.5
43	Mexico	4	39
43	South Africa	4	51
43	Tanzania	4	32.5
49.5	Ceylon	3	39
49.5	Czechoslovakia	3	39
49.5	East Germany	3	51
49.5	Jordan	3	39
49.5	Kenya	3	51
49.5	Mali	3	66.5
49.5	North Vietnam	3	—
49.5	OECD	3	39
62	Bolivia	2	66.5
62	Colombia	2	51
62	Cuba	2	66.5
62	Ecuador	2	51
62	EEC	2	51
62	Hungary	2	51
62	Lebanon	2	66.5
62	Liberia	2	66.5
62	Malaysia	2	66.5
62	New Zealand	2	66.5
62	OAS	2	51
62	Paraguay	2	51
62	Peru	2	51
62	Singapore	2	51
62	Somalia	2	51
62	Turkey	2	51
62	Venezuela	2	51
75.5	Algeria	1	66.5
75.5	Australia	1	66.5
75.5	Ghana	1	66.5
75.5	Ivory Coast	1	66.5

Table 6-5 (cont.)

Rank All Issues	Country	Number of Actions All Issues	Rank Pure Issues
75.5	Libya	1	66.5
75.5	Romania	1	66.5
75.5	Saudi Arabia	1	66.5
75.5	Senegal	1	66.5
75.5	Uganda	1	–
75.5	Yugoslavia	1	66.5
	Mean, all issues 11.6	Median, all issues 4.5	
	Range, pure issues	1-115	
	Mean, pure issues 8.8	Median, pure issues 3.67	

aSource: As in Table 5-1.

product of the war and cannot be regarded as a shipping-political move. This is reflected in the volume of interaction, which is by no means abnormally high. The way the events in the Middle East in 1967 show their presence is through the identity of the high participants, with both the UAR and Israel near the top.

There is also another nontraditional high participant present, namely Brazil. During the 1960s Brazil has been increasingly active in matters of shipping, and seems to be challenging the role of India as a leading spokesman for the developing countries. Brazil's main strength (or weakness) in this apparent endeavor is a markedly less conciliatory attitude towards Western shipping than India's. As a result, India has been pushed towards a mediating position, away from its role as spokesman for the less developed countries.

In this last period there is also an addition to the group of international organizations active in shipping, as UNCTAD created a Committee on Shipping which held its first session in 1965. The UNCTAD Committee on Shipping quickly turned out to be a forum for political confrontation, thereby assuming a function which previous IGOs in the field had strenuously sought to avoid. IMCO, after the initial dispute about flags of convenience, soon settled down to a happy existence amidst thoroughly de-politicized issues. The OEEC's Maritime Transport Committee was, during the first seven years of its existence, a homogeneous group of like-minded Western European maritime states, all equally strong in their support of the OEEC liberalization code for international trade and shipping. The OEEC ran into some problems, however, when it was reorganized and became the OECD in 1961 and suddenly included USA and Japan as potential members of the Maritime Transport Committee. Neither country had a convincing record of practicing liberalization, but Japan showed its willingness to reform by revising some discriminatory legislation upon becoming an OECD member. The United States retained its less cooperative attitude, and has been steadfastly out of line with the rest of the organization on the issues pertaining to liberalization.

Still, no other international organization has rivalled UNCTAD when it comes to political confrontation, which only reflects a general characteristic of the organization.

The Nordic Council is another new name among IGOs in shipping in this period, but its involvement is not tied with a stable concern for shipping problems. The issue that brought the Nordic Council to life in shipping was the matter of oil pollution of the oceans, in which it launched a proposal for expanded international control. The Nordic Council otherwise stays clear of most shipping issues.

Events in Africa in later years have affected shipping on several points. The closing of the Suez Canal has already been referred to, but in addition both Rhodesia's "unilateral declaration of independence" and the Biafra tragedy brought new participants into the system.

The Rhodesian case concerned the petroleum embargo applied by the UN and sought enforced by the Wilson government. Rhodesia itself naturally had a special interest in this matter, but Zambia's activity is possibly more noteworthy. It appears that Zambia used every opportunity it had in the United Nations to criticize UN members for not supporting the embargo—even long after the rest of the world had accepted the effort as a failure.

The case of Biafra, on the other hand, received little widespread attention in its shipping aspects. It was simply a logical consequence of the civil war that shipping had to be suspended or redirected from the area. Nigeria's activity was restricted correspondingly to periodic warnings and decrees covering the movement of foreign shipping in the area.

Stable Participants 1946-1968

Attention should now be directed to Table 6-6 which shows the states that have participated on a continuous basis in shipping interaction in the entire 1946-68 period, or from their respective dates of independence (excluding states independent in 1960 or later).

Confining the ranking list in this way to stable participants yields a remarkable consistency across the sub-issues. Clearly, being active on pure issues is positively related to being active on all issues. Or, to put it differently, a state is not very likely to be active on contaminated issues only, once it has been established as an active participant on other issues.

Still, there are eight participants which qualify as stable on all issues and which do not so qualify on the pure issues.[21] Of these only Jordan could possibly be expected to have rather narrow interests in shipping. All the others are island states or coastal states with important ports and could have been

Table 6-6

Frequency of Participation by 40 Stable Participants 1946-1968 (Rank Order by Number of Actions)[a]

Rank All Issues	Country	Number of Actions All Issues	Rank Pure Issues
1	USA	1362	1
2	UAR	940	2
3	UK	826	3
4	USSR	486	4
5	France	390	5
6	Norway	331	6
7	Taiwan	179	35
8	India	175	7
9	Sweden	157	9
10	Denmark	150	10
11	Panama	142	8
12	Netherlands	131	11
13	Italy	85	13.5
14	Japan	82	12
15	West Germany	78	13.5
16	China	77	28
17	Poland	73	20
18	Australia	69	15
19	Greece	67	27
20	Yugoslavia	65	19
21	Indonesia	63	22.5
22	Canada	60	18
23	Brazil	57	17
24	Belgium	56	16
25	Jordan	40	21
26	Spain	39	22.5
27	Lebanon	38	24
28	Argentina	34	25
29	Chile	30	29
30	Ceylon	29	26
31	Finland	26	30.5
32	New Zealand	24	32
33	Czechoslovakia	20	33
34.5	Colombia	19	30.5
34.5	Portugal	19	39
36.5	Ecuador	14	34
36.5	Venezuela	14	36

Table 6-6 (cont.)

Rank All Issues	Country	Number of Actions All Issues	Rank Pure Issues
38	East Germany	7	37.5
39	Malaysia	6	40
40	Ghana	5	37.5

[a]Source: As in Table 5-1.

expected to be consistently active in the issue-area of shipping. The reason they are not will be given closer examination later in this chapter.

Among the upper one-fourth of the stable participants on pure issues (10 states), seven are Western industrialized states, one is a "canal state" (UAR), while the last two—India and the Soviet Union—do not fall into such a ready pattern. The predominance of the Western states, observed earlier for specific periods, is a characteristic feature of the interaction system.

Table 6-6 also suggests another possible relationship—one between stability of participation on the one hand, and scope of interests on the other. There seems to be a distinct tendency for stable participation and a broad scope of interests to go together.

On this point, however, some caution would be appropriate. The table does not tell us anything about the scope of interests of non-stable participants. If these are included, the actual situation becomes as shown in Table 6-7. There is no relationship between stability of participation and scope of interests; the Chi square of 0.0019 is not significant at the .05 level.[22]

Table 6-7
Stability of Participation and Scope of Interests, 1946-1968 (Number of States)

		Scope of Interests		
		Broad	Narrow	Total
Stability of participation over time on all issues	Stable	33	7	40
	Not stable	46	11	57
Total		79	18	97

(Q = +.06, chi square = 0.0019)

Broad scope: State participated on pure issues in all time periods in which it participated.

Narrow scope: State did not participate on pure issues in at least one of the time periods in which it participated.

Sources: For both variables, as in Table 5-1.

**Hypotheses Pertaining to Frequency
of Participation**

Consider the following two hypotheses:

If a government has formulated a general national policy on shipping questions as part of its overall foreign policy, then it will be more likely to participate in interaction over shipping questions.

If a country's fleet is engaged in considerable third-flag carriage, then that government is more likely to take part in interaction over shipping questions.

The idea behind the first hypothesis is simply that a government more active in participation will be more likely to have formulated certain general principles regarding its conduct with shipping. Stated differently: to what extent are participants in the issue-area haphazardly, or passively, involved? Active, deliberate involvement would seem to require an explicitly formulated policy. The question is related to the distinction made somewhat loosely above between participants which are only reactively involved and those which are "activists." The former were held to be participants mainly because they were affected by actions to which it would be very difficult not to respond.

The variable "formulation of a general national policy on shipping questions" will be operationalized by examining the various statements made by governments in meetings of the UNCTAD Committee on Shipping 1965-69. The criterion is whether or not the government in question actually stated its views on some aspect of international shipping during a session of the committee. Although less than 50 states are formal members of the committee, any UNCTAD member may take part in the debates simply by requesting the committee's permission. Furthermore, a considerable number of countries regularly attend the committee's sessions as observers. In the 1969 session of the Committee on Shipping, 27 states participated as observers.[23]

The variable "frequency of participation" is broken down to the categories "high"/"medium"/"low" to get three groups of states of roughly the same size. (Table 6-8.)

Clearly, the two variables are associated. The gamma of .63 indicates a moderately positive relationship. The formulation of general policy tends to go along with a high frequency of participation.

But the hypothesis must not be viewed in explanatory terms. Participation and policy formulation are two faces of the same coin, and neither should be considered a causal variable in relation to the other. In causal terms the two variables should probably rather be seen as complementary dependent variables, both affected by the same set of independent variables. (Whether this in fact is true is, of course, an empirical question.)

Therefore, the correlation found to exist between participation and policy

Table 6-8

Frequency of Participation by Governments (1960-68), by Frequency of Policy Statements (1965-69)[ab]

| | | \multicolumn{5}{c}{Number of Sessions of the Committee on Shipping at which Policy Was Stated} | |
		4	3	2	1	0	Total
Frequency	High	13	5	1	0	4	23
of parti-	Medium	4	6	2	7	16	35
cipation	Low	2	1	1	3	17	24
Total		19	12	4	10	37	82

[a]Sources: For interaction data, as in Table 5-1; for policy statements: UNCTAD, Trade and Development Board, Committee on Shipping, SUMMARY RECORDS (TD/B/C.4/SR.1 through TD/B/C.4/SR.55).
[b]Participation on pure shipping issues only.

formulation is taken to mean that the more active participants are not haphazardly or reactively involved in shipping interaction, but are consciously engaged in pursuit of explicit policies. Conversely, the low-frequency participants do show signs of being reactively or incidentally involved in the system.

While the first hypothesis concerned a relationship of correlation, the second hypothesis brings in a possible explanatory variable, extent of third-flag carriage. The rationale behind the second hypothesis is as follows: When a country is involved in considerable third-flag carriage, this means that a substantial portion of its merchant fleet is engaged in carriage between other countries, rather than between the home country and other countries. In July 1970, for example, 92 percent of the Norwegian oceangoing fleet was engaged in cross-trade carriage.[24]

The expectation is, then, that a country whose fleet sails predominantly in a third-flag pattern will seek to promote unrestricted shipping transactions above all. Any restriction which reduces the freedom of that country's ships to pick up cargo at any given port and carry it to any other port would be harmful to the country's shipping interests. Such a country is therefore assumed to follow all developments in international shipping quite closely and attentively.

Secondly, this kind of country will, through its shipping, get in regular contact with a much larger number of foreign countries than one whose fleet is engaged primarily in trades on the home country. This means that the likelihood of becoming involved in interaction is probably higher for the former than the latter type of country.

The main problem here is how to measure extent of third-flag carriage, given that the kind of figures quoted for Norway is not available for other countries. The solution employed here is to compare a country's percentage share of world shipping tonnage with its share of world seaborne trade, measured in volume terms. This resembles the procedure behind the Gini index.[25] Rather than go on to compute an index for the world as a whole, however, the index required here should be calculated separately for each country.

Using the two measures of tonnage and volume of seaborne trade means that *carrying capacity* is compared to *demand for carrying capacity*. It is true that no country carries all its seaborne trade in national-flag ships even when it has the theoretical capability to do so. Yet, it is held here that the comparison of carrying capacity with size of seaborne trade will give an approximate indication of the extent of a country's dependence on foreign shipping. It is not claimed, in other words, that the carrying capacity which exists is actually used to carry the nation's foreign seaborne trade. The claim is, rather, that the intended comparison will show which countries are more, or less, dependent on foreign shipping than others, and—conversely—which countries are more (or less) dependent on securing foreign employment for their ships than others.

The actual third-flag index is derived by standardizing the percentage difference between ships and trade so that the highest excess of ships over trade in a given year is set to +1.00, and the highest excess of trade over ships is set to −1.00. Approximately equal shares of ships and seaborne trade will give a country a third-flag index close to .00. The index will therefore yield .00 both for a country with equally *large* shares of ships and trade, and for a country with equally *small* shares of ships and trade. It is the countries with discrepant shares which deviate from a .00 score.[26]

The index has been computed for five selected years: 1947, 1952, 1957, 1962, and 1967. Tables 6-9 and 6-10 show the frequency of participation of states with positive, balanced, and negative scores on the third-flag index in 1962 and 1967, respectively.

Both chi square figures are significant at the .05 level, which means that the

Table 6-9
Frequency of Participation by Governments (1960-1968), by Score on Third-Flag Index 1962[ab]

| | | Score on Third-Flag Index | | | |
		Positive	Balanced (Zero or Near Zero)	Negative	Total
Frequency	High	9	8	5	22
of parti-	Medium	1	20	7	28
cipation	Low	0	13	9	22
Total		10	41	21	72[c]
Gamma = .48	Chi square = 15.94, df = 4				

[a]Sources: For frequency of participation, as in Table 5-1. For third-flag index, UN STATISTICAL YEARBOOKS.
[b]Participation on pure shipping issues only.
[c]Excluding countries with missing data.

Table 6-10
Frequency of Participation by Governments (1960-1968), by Score on Third-Flag Index 1967[a]

| | | | Score on Third-Flag Index | | |
		Positive	Balanced (Zero or Near Zero)	Negative	Total
Frequency	High	9	6	7	22
of parti-	Medium	1	19	5	25
cipation	Low	0	9	7	16
Total		10	34	19	63
Gamma = .39		Chi square = 15.70, df = 4			

[a]See notes to Table 6-9.

null hypothesis of no relationship between the variables can be rejected. But the gamma coefficients are so low that the relationship must be deemed a rather weak one. Extent of third-flag carriage is therefore not irrelevant to the attempt to account for frequency of participation—it is only insufficient in itself.

The three categories of scores on the third-flag index suggest an alternative interpretation of the index. So far, the negative category has been treated as something conducive to a low frequency of participation. But the positive and negative categories actually share an important common characteristic: both indicate a discrepancy between ships and trade, although in opposite directions. Thus, an alternative formulation of the second hypothesis would state that it is the discrepancy between ships and trade, rather than merely an excess of ships, that makes a state more disposed to participate in shipping interaction. Dependency on foreign tonnage would then be considered a motivating factor for participation, equally as strong as dependency on cross-trade cargoes. To test this hypothesis, the positive and negative categories from Tables 6-9 and 6-10 will be combined into one category labelled "discrepancy," as distinguished from the category "balance." The expectation is now that "discrepancy" will be associated with a high frequency and "balance" with a low frequency of participation. (Tables 6-11 and 6-12.)

Only one of the two chi square figures is significant at the .05 level, namely that for Table 6-12. The outcome is somewhat ambiguous, but must be interpreted in the direction of support for the hypothesis, since one of the gamma coefficients is quite high and the other is not distinctly low. The present interpretation of the third-flag index is evidently better suited to explain the frequency of participation than was the original interpretation.

Could another hypothesis produce a similar result? There are two competing hypotheses that ought to be considered. One states that the frequency of participation increases as size of fleet increases. The other states that the frequency of participation increases as size of seaborne trade increases.[27] (Tables 6-13, 6-14, 6-15 and 6-16.)

Table 6-11

Frequency of Participation by Governments (1960-1968), by Score on Third-Flag Index 1962[a]

| | | Score on Third-Flag Index | | |
		Discrepancy	Balanced (Zero or Near Zero)	Total
Frequency of participation	High	14	8	22
	Medium	8	20	28
	Low	9	13	22
Total		31	41	72

Gamma = .54   Chi square = 4.81, df = 2

[a]See notes to Table 6-9.

Table 6-12

Frequency of Participation by Governments (1960-1968), by Score on Third-Flag Index 1967[a]

| | | Score on Third-Flag Index | | |
		Discrepancy	Balanced (Zero or Near Zero)	Total
Frequency of participation	High	16	6	22
	Medium	6	19	25
	Low	7	9	16
Total		29	34	63

Gamma = .70   Chi square = 9.21, df = 2

[a]See notes to Table 6-9.

Table 6-13

Frequency of Participation by Governments (1960-1968), by Size of Fleet 1962[a]

| | | Size of Fleet | | | |
		Large	Medium	Small	Total
Frequency of participation	High	18	5	0	23
	Medium	4	10	14	28
	Low	0	5	18	23
Total		22	20	32	74

Gamma = .87   Chi square = 39.86, df = 4

[a]See notes to Table 6-9.

Table 6-14
Frequency of Participation by Governments (1960-1968), by Size of Seaborne Trade 1962[a]

		Size of Seaborne Trade			
		Large	Medium	Small	Total
Frequency	High	16	5	1	22
of parti-	Medium	4	10	14	28
cipation	Low	4	8	10	22
Total		24	23	25	72
Gamma = .56	Chi square = 19.82, df = 4				

[a]See notes to Table 6-9.

Table 6-15
Frequency of Participation by Governments (1960-1968), by Size of Fleet 1967[a]

		Size of Fleet			
		Large	Medium	Small	Total
Frequency	High	18	5	0	23
of parti-	Medium	4	16	9	29
cipation	Low	0	6	12	18
Total		22	27	21	70
Gamma = .88	Chi square = 37.11, df = 4				

[a]See notes to Table 6-9.

Table 6-16
Frequency of Participation by Governments (1960-1968), by Size of Seaborne Trade 1967[a]

		Size of Seaborne Trade			
		Large	Medium	Small	Total
Frequency	High	18	3	1	22
of parti-	Medium	4	5	17	26
cipation	Low	4	4	9	17
Total		26	12	27	65
Gamma = .61	Chi square = 22.50, df = 4				

[a]See notes to Table 6-9.

All relationships tested in these tables are significant at the .05 level. The differences between them appear in the gamma coefficients. Both seaborne trade and fleet are positively related to participation in 1962 as well as in 1967. Moreover, although not shown here, seaborne trade and fleet are positively related to each other in both years. Size of fleet, however, is definitely more strongly related to participation than is size of seaborne trade.

Two questions arise at this point. First, do the present findings contradict the relationship found above between participation and a discrepancy between ships and trade? Second, how can these relationships be understood in causal terms?

As to the first question, the relationships between discrepancy and participation may be partly spurious. In this connection it is important to note that a number of states (13 in 1967) are classified as having a discrepancy between ships and trade (Tables 6-11 and 6-12), yet are also classified as having both a large fleet and a large seaborne trade (Tables 6-13 through 6-16).[28] Furthermore, in the case of 1967, all of these thirteen countries are also high-frequency participants. Hence it is impossible to tell from Table 6-12 alone whether the high level of participation is associated with discrepancy or simply with sheer size. The succeeding tables (i.e., 6-13 through 6-16) amply illustrate this point.

To compare the relative impact of discrepancy and size, the third-flag index (discrepancy/balance) may be used as a control variable. (Table 6-17, 6-18, 6-19, and 6-20.)

If discrepancy were the most important variable, one would expect to find only a weak relationship in the two tables (6-20 and 6-22) where discrepancy is "removed." This is not the case. Both the tables give evidence of strong relationships (gamma coefficients of .77 and .94, respectively).

On the other hand, if discrepancy were of little or no importance one would expect the gamma coefficients to be very nearly the same when comparing Table 6-19 with Table 6-20, and Table 6-21 with Table 6-22. In fact, however, the relationship becomes considerably weaker in the first case (size of fleet), and

Table 6-17

States with Discrepancy: Frequency of Participation 1960-1968, by Size of Fleet 1967[a]

| | | Size of Fleet | | | |
		Large	Medium	Small	Total
Frequency	High	14	2	0	16
of parti-	Medium	1	4	2	7
cipation	Low	0	2	6	8
Total		15	8	8	31
		Gamma = .95			

[a]See notes to Table 6-9.

Table 6-18

States with Balance: Frequency of Participation 1960-1968, by Size of Fleet 1967[a]

		Size of Fleet			
		Large	Medium	Small	Total
Frequency	High	4	2	0	6
of parti-	Medium	3	9	7	19
cipation	Low	0	3	6	9
Total		7	14	13	34
		Gamma = .77			

[a]See notes to Table 6-9.

Table 6-19

States with Discrepancy: Frequency of Participation 1960-68, by Size of Seaborne Trade 1967[a]

		Size of Seaborne Trade			
		Large	Medium	Small	Total
Frequency	High	14	2	0	16
of parti-	Medium	2	4	1	7
cipation	Low	4	4	0	8
Total		20	10	1	31
		Gamma = .83			

[a]See notes to Table 6-9.

Table 6-20

States with Balance: Frequency of Participation 1960-68, by Size of Seaborne Trade 1967[a]

		Size of Seaborne Trade			
		Large	Medium	Small	Total
Frequency	High	4	1	1	6
of parti-	Medium	2	1	16	19
cipation	Low	0	0	9	9
Total		6	2	26	34
		Gamma = .94			

[a]See notes to Table 6-9.

considerably stronger in the second case (size of seaborne trade) when discrepancy is removed.

In short, discrepancy appears to have a limited impact on frequency of participation, compared to the effects of both fleet and seaborne trade. The presence of a discrepancy seems to reinforce the effect of size of fleet, and to reduce the effect of size of seaborne trade. Thus, the main correlates of a state's propensity to participate in shipping interaction are size of fleet and size of seaborne trade—not the hypothesized excess of ships over trade.

This may seem trivial. Its importance lies first in the way it de-emphasizes excess of ships over trade in particular, and discrepancy between ships and trade in general, as factors motivating for participation. Furthermore, it indicates that a number of states with small fleets and a small seaborne trade remain quite passive in maritime affairs, when in fact shipping—at least as seen by an outside observer—may be rather crucial to their national economies and foreign economic relations. To paraphrase a statement made in a different context, one is left with the impression that "the best shipping policy of a small state is to have no policy at all."[29] There seems to be a capability threshold, in other words, below which the political (and other) costs of pursuing an active shipping policy become (subjectively) greater than the costs of acquiescing in the policies and practices of foreign shipping interests. This is not to deny that such acquiescence may be economically advantageous to the small state, or to certain consumer and business elites within it—assuming that foreign shipping is the cheapest available transport alternative. On the other hand, one should also keep in mind that the "activist" posture of many developing countries in shipping may reflect the pressures of local shipowners as much as—or even more than—a government's concern for the nation's economic interests. This pertains in particular to some Latin American countries.

The central point, however, is this: Whether the low-frequency participant states (and the non-participants) are satisfied or dissatisfied with their shipping situation, the thought of allocating scarce resources to the pursuit of an active shipping policy, combined with the possibility of adding an extra conflict dimension to their relations with the developed world may simply seem too costly to a great number of less-developed countries. Hence, their behavior in shipping becomes largely a matter of apathy or a mere reaction to intermittent external stimuli.

The correlation between a high frequency of participation and a large fleet and seaborne trade may be less interesting than some more specific aspects of high-participant behavior. In the following section, thirty-six high-frequency participants will be singled out for closer study. The focus moves back to conflict; specifically, to the participant's propensity to engage in conflict behavior.

State Behavior: Shipping Background
and Propensity to Conflict

The value allocation hypothesis has so far been tested only at the systemic level. The main task of this section is to test some derivatives of this hypothesis at the actor level. Briefly stated, the value allocation hypothesis suggested that as the distribution of values in the system becomes more skewed, the frequency of conflict in the system will increase.[30] At the actor level the question then becomes: What is the relationship between a given state's share of the distribution of values and its propensity to engage in conflict behavior?

In examining possible derivatives the terminology will, for the sake of convenience, be simplified. Thus, participants with large value shares will be referred to as "rich" in the following formulations, while those with small value shares will be referred to as "poor."

It should be stressed that the hypotheses to be considered are not derivatives of the systemic hypothesis in the strict sense. That is, they do not follow with logical necessity from the systemic hypothesis, but are rather ideas about behavior at the actor level which may be evoked by the systemic hypothesis. As will be seen, they are also cast in synchronic terms while the "mother hypothesis" is diachronically formulated.[31]

The systemic hypothesis—"the more inequality, the more conflict"—says nothing about who participates in this conflict, so that all of the following interpretations appear equally possible:

1. the rich have a greater propensity to engage in conflict than the poor.
2. the poor have a greater propensity to engage in conflict than the rich.
3. the rich and the poor have about the same propensity to engage in conflict.

In a situation of considerable inequality, hypothesis number one could be said to correspond to the notions of "domination" and/or "squabbling over the spoils," while number two could be characterized as "revolution" and/or "the struggle for survival," depending on who are the targets of conflict. Number three may represent a mixture of the other two, or it may mean that the value distribution is irrelevant to behavior at the actor level. Notice that the third hypothesis is also the null hypothesis in relation to both of the others.

The systemic behavior pattern must not be assumed to be a simple sum or product of actor behaviors. As the three hypotheses above show, a rejection of the first two of them implies support for the third, but the latter is also compatible with the systemic hypothesis. No matter which one is confirmed, the outcome has no necessary bearing on the systemic hypothesis itself.

The purpose of the following test is therefore to see whether the ideas evoked by the systemic hypothesis and expressed in hypotheses one and two could be supported by the data. Such a test, however, requires more precise phrasing. The number one hypothesis may be restated thusly:

States with large shares of the international distribution of shipping values will tend to have a higher propensity to conflict than states with small shares of values.

Similarly, the number two hypothesis may be restated as follows:

States with small shares of the international distribution of shipping values will tend to have a higher propensity to conflict than states with larger shares of values.

A state's share of the value distribution will be measured by the size of its merchant fleet in percent of total world tonnage. Propensity to conflict is operationally defined as the percentage of conflict acts in a state's total behavior output[32] in the years 1960-1968, inclusive. Thus we eliminate the possibility that the measure reflects frequency of participation rather than propensity to conflict, since high-frequency participants may be expected to engage in all kinds of behavior—including conflict—more frequently than lower-frequency participants. Stated differently, this is a measure of degree of aggressiveness in the sense of a preference for using conflict acts rather than other types of action to deal with other states.

A word on the sample: As mentioned earlier, this section concentrates on the study of a smaller sample of states than previously. In the terminology of the previous section, the present sample embraces the category "high-frequency participants" plus about half of the category "medium-frequency participants," in all thirty-six states. An important consideration behind this reduction of the sample was the desire to concentrate on states that are more actively and consciously engaged in shipping politics, in view of the finding above that lower-frequency participants tend to participate in a random and unreflected manner. Inclusion of the latter type of states would therefore have meant the inclusion of important sources of error. But practical considerations also played a role: Each state's behavior output had to be of a certain minimum size to make it possible to speak meaningfully of its propensity to conflict. Thus, *five acts in relation to pure shipping issues* is the lower limit for the inclusion of a case in the present sample. Below is a list, by main group,[33] of the thirty-six states included:

East	Bulgaria	Poland
	Czechoslovakia	USSR
South	Argentina	Kuwait
	Brazil	Liberia
	Ceylon	Mexico
	Chile	Panama
	China	Peru
	Cuba	UAR

South	India	Uruguay
(cont.)	Iraq	
West	Belgium	Netherlands
	Canada	Norway
	Denmark	Spain
	Finland	Sweden
	France	Switzerland
	Greece	United Kingdom
	Israel	USA
	Italy	West Germany
	Japan	

A first series of simple tests, using only dichotomized variables, lent some support to the hypothesis that a large fleet is correlated with a high propensity to conflict. Although the trend was not very strong, it remained stable over several alternative tests.

Keeping these test results in mind as a first indication, we shall now subject the relationship to a more demanding test at the interval level of measurement, introducing at the same time two sets of additional shipping variables. One set of variables pertains specifically to liner shipping, while the other covers maritime relations in general.

The liner variables include the number of liner conferences serving a country (inbound and outbound), the percentage of these conferences employing some kind of tying arrangement (e.g., dual rate, deferred rebate, contract), the percentage of the conferences which maintain a closed membership policy, and the number of foreign liner operators serving the country. Finally, there is a variable that to some extent belongs in both groups: the number of calls (as defined in Chapter 3) made abroad by a country's national-flag liner fleet.

The variables relating to liner shipping were chosen in view of the controversial nature of liner issues,[34] the idea being that states in close contact with conferences would be likely to engage more frequently in conflict—whether to attack or defend the conference system. Data on the liner conferences have—with one exception—been collected from *Croner's World Directory of Freight Conferences.*[35]

But this source gives no information on membership policies, nor does such information seem to be available elsewhere. Furthermore, the distinction between open and closed membership policy is not altogether clear. In fact, this is not so much a matter of either closed (i.e., fixed) or open membership as a matter of degree: even if a conference does not declare its membership to be fixed, it is often very difficult for a non-conference operator to become a conference member unless he offers real competition as an outsider. Also, some countries (such as the United States) require by law that membership be open, at least in principle, to any applicant. The question is complex, since there are numerous subtle ways of shutting out an unwanted applicant, in spite of a declared "open-door" policy. Therefore, the emphasis in operationalizing this variable is on the results of conference recruitment practices: *if a conference serving a given country does not have any members from that country, and provided the country does have a merchant fleet, that conference is considered closed for the purposes of this study.*

The additional variables pertaining to maritime relations in general are as follows: The size of a country's seaborne trade (average of imports and exports, in percent of world total in volume terms); score on third-flag index where -1 is the low point of the scale; and score on third-flag index where zero is the low point of the scale. These variables were included because they may contribute to a more complete, general picture of each country's shipping situation, and therefore also to a better understanding of the relationship between share of values and conflict. The modifier "general" is meant to suggest that the variables in this set are probably not linked to any single, specific shipping issue, but to all of them.

Since the variables are all at the interval level, Pearson's r will be employed. Note that the liner variables are all measured in 1968, while the others are measured both in 1962 and 1967. Table 6-21 shows the correlation matrix for all the variables now introduced.[36]

To concentrate first on the hypotheses being tested, Table 6-21 clearly supports only the null hypothesis, since neither of the correlations between size of fleet and conflict is even near being significant at the required level. The difference between this and the previous tests is somewhat puzzling, but at least the two tests agree on one point: the hypothesis associating a small value share with a high propensity to conflict should be rejected.

To account for the different test results one may point to the evident weakness of the relationship in the first test, and also to its relative crudeness compared to the more stringent requirements set by the product-moment correlation, especially regarding the shape of a relationship. For instance, a curvilinear relationship might be missed by the correlation coefficient, but be picked up by the dichotomization. The scattergram (see Figure 6-1) could be interpreted in this direction: Small-fleet states tend to cluster in the lower range of propensity to conflict, states with medium-size fleets have a fairly high propensity to conflict, while states with very large fleets again show a somewhat lower propensity to conflict. From this viewpoint, the correlation coefficient could be said to be "too low," because it "ignores" curvilinearity.

On the other hand, even the curvilinear tendency is quite weak, a fact that detracts from its usefulness in this connection. "No relationship" is still a plausible alternative interpretation, especially since none of the other hypotheses receive strong support in the data. This is after all the paramount criterion for a test of hypotheses, and the conclusion must therefore be to retain the null hypothesis and reject the two others.

Table 6-21

Matrix of Product-Moment Correlation Coefficients for Fourteen Variables Relating to Shipping Background and Propensity to Conflict, 1960-1968[a][b]

	2.	3.	4.	5.	6.	7.	8.	9.	10.	11.	12.	13.	14.
1. Prop. to confl. pure issues	.127	.169	.270	.293	-.031	-.075	.223	.362	.159	.404	-.139	.094	.205
2. Size of fleet 1962		.928	.681	.650	.766	.528	.708	.456	.614	.094	-.429	.842	.227
3. Size of fleet 1967			.516	.541	.814	.695	.745	.620	.461	.147	-.342	.702	.155
4. Size seaborne trade 1962				.970	.149	-.107	.278	.052	.681	-.008	-.330	.631	.345
5. Size seaborne trade 1967					.131	-.104	.214	.047	.641	.000	-.368	.593	.324
6. Third-flag index 1962 (-1 = low)						.915	.714	.539	.212	.101	-.244	.568	.048
7. Third flag index 1967 (-1 = low)							.613	.537	-.013	.109	-.057	.281	-.038
8. Third-flag index 1962 (0 = low)								.872	.178	.164	-.043	.555	-.029
9. Third-flag index 1967 (0 = low)									.003	.259	.075	.302	-.057
10. No. of liner conferences										.326	-.567	.741	.791
11. Pct. conferences using tying arr.											-.089	.159	.553
12. Pct. closed conferences												-.627	-.273
13. Calls abroad by own liner fleet													.350
14. No. of foreign liner operators													

[a]Underlined coefficients are significant at the .05 level or higher by the F-test, 1 and 30 degrees of freedom, N = 32.

[b]Bulgaria, China, Cuba, and Uruguay are excluded due to missing data.

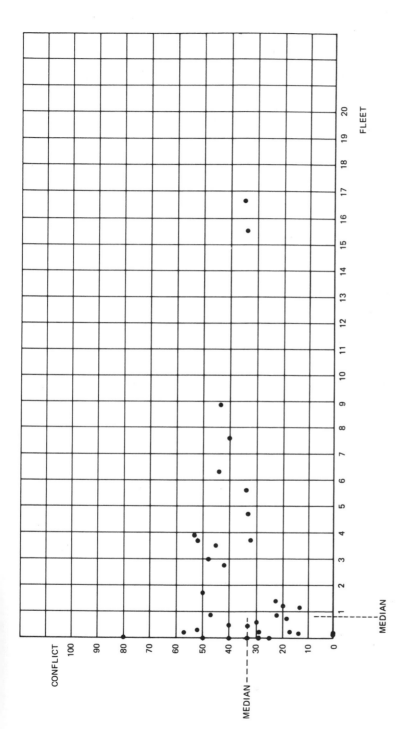

Figure 6-1. Scattergram of Relationship Between Size of Merchant Fleet (Percent of World Total) and Propensity to Conflict (Percent) for 36 States, 1962.

Although size of value share is not related to propensity to conflict, Table 6-21 indicates that other variables are. Both discrepancy between fleet and trade (third-flag index score different from zero) and percent of conferences using tying arrangements are significantly correlated with conflict. Note the characteristic overall pattern in the matrix, however: only two variables are significantly correlated with conflict, but a great number of independent variables are closely interrelated in a rather dense kind of pattern. Indeed, size of fleet is highly correlated with ten of the twelve other independent variables. If we consider the two main groups of independent variables, moreover, the general background variables (numbers 2 through 9) are more highly correlated among themselves than are the liner variables (numbers 10 through 14). The choice of the label "general background variables" seems quite appropriate. Among the liner variables, tying arrangements is unique since it is related only to one other independent variable. This is all the more interesting as tying arrangements has the stronger of the two correlations with conflict.

Since the second of the two correlations involves discrepancy between fleet and trade (1967), propensity to conflict may be said to be associated on the one hand with a general aspect of a country's shipping situation, and on the other with a very particular aspect of the liner business. This combination of the general and the particular is important. Although single-factor explanations are neither sought nor expected here, it would not have been unreasonable to expect shipping variables to coalesce around a single shipping dimension that would then be only one determinant among a number of other, non-shipping determinants. But Table 6-21 shows the contours of at least a two-dimensional relationship within the class of shipping variables. This may be seen in the lack of a significant correlation between tying arrangements and the discrepancy variable, and in the very low correlations between tying arrangements and most other independent variables.

The question which must first be clarified, however, is what the correlations mean. Discrepancy between fleet and trade is of course conceptually tied both to size of fleet and size of trade, yet the table shows that it is considerably closer linked to fleet than to trade: its correlations with trade are practically zero. This is also reflected in the rather high correlations (.714 and .613) with the third-flag index expressed as a scale from -1 to $+1$. But neither fleet nor the third-flag index in this latter form are correlated with conflict! Hence, the discrepancy measure must capture something which is lost in both of the other measures, and this something must be found in the difference between the two versions of the third-flag index.

The difference, of course, is that the discrepancy version rests on the expectation that excess of trade over ships will have the same effect on conflict as excess of ships over trade, while the other version expects them to have opposite effects on conflict. The correlation coefficients indicate that the former interpretation is the more appropriate one.

Moreover, the correlation between the two versions is simply a reflection of the fact that the sample contains more cases with excess of ships over trade than with excess of trade over ships. The latter cases, nevertheless, proved indispensable to the analysis.

The discrepancy version of the third-flag index is an indicator of a situation of need—there is either a need for foreign ships to carry the national seaborne trade, or a need for foreign cargoes to keep national-flag vessels employed. Both kinds of situation make international shipping questions important to a country—correcting or balancing a state of need becomes a matter of national interest, and the policies and actions of other states in shipping acquire a significance they would not otherwise have. Thus, discrepancy between fleet and trade can be an important motivation to engage in conflict with other states, as it appears to be here.[37]

Yet, tying arrangements has the higher correlation with the dependent variable. A straightforward interpretation—saying that propensity to conflict on pure issues must therefore in large part be the same as propensity to conflict concerning tying arrangements—does not make much sense. Only 27 percent of the actions committed by states on pure issues in this period can be attributed directly to liner conference issues, and the tying-arrangement question is only one of these.

An attractive alternative is to say that the percentage of conferences using tying arrangements reflects other, underlying phenomena that are not directly measured and that it is these phenomena which are associated with propensity to conflict. The clue to the broader meaning of the tying-arrangement variable may thus be its correlation with number of foreign (liner) shipowners. The foreign-shipowner variable brings in the phenomena of resentment and frictions between national and foreign shipping interests (covering both shipowners and shippers). There are interests which are directly opposed, there is competition, there is governmental involvement, there are numerous occasions for petty disputes—and beneath it all there is probably more than a little xenophobia.

But number of foreign shipowners is not in itself related to propensity to conflict. Its importance lies in what it tells us about the tying-arrangement variable. The foreign shipowner variable is highly correlated only with tying arrangements and with number of conferences, though it has a weak correlation also with calls abroad. This is crucial to the understanding of the larger pattern of interrelationships. The number of foreign liner operators is a variable which links the "xenophobia dimension" with the tangle of controversial liner conference issues.

This can also be seen if we look again at tying arrangements. Why is this variable correlated with conflict when closed membership is not? Because closed membership is an issue only between national and foreign shipowners, while tying arrangements is an issue pitting shippers against foreign shipowners, shippers against local shipowners, local shipowners against foreign shipowners.

Very centrally involved is also the question of conference service versus nonconference service. The use of tying arrangements is the conference's means of securing a stable flow of cargoes, its means of fighting non-conference competition, and—at least indirectly—its means of fighting competition from other conferences. Thus, the tying arrangements variable embraces a large spectrum of conflicts and issues concerning most governments engaged in international shipping politics, and herein lies the most likely explanation for its correlation with propensity to conflict.

A few other relationships in Table 6-21 are worthy of comment before the main findings of the chapter are summed up and synthesized. Observe how the closed-conference variable is related to the others: closed membership in liner conferences is found mainly in countries with small merchant fleets, little seaborne trade, and few other liner conferences. As a conference policy, in other words, it is effective only where the competition is insignificant—reflecting the monopolistic aspects of the conference system. The policy's effectiveness is emphasized since closed membership is not a policy reserved for application against less-developed countries. The fact that the correlation coefficients referred to are not exceptionally high underlines this point. Still, favorable conditions in less-developed countries may further encourage the practice of exclusive membership in these areas, unless steps are taken to prevent it.

One question remains for the discussion in this section to be complete: to draw a map of the more plausible causal connections between the main variables. Figure 6.2 gives an indication of how these connections may be represented by using causal arrows. Each arrow represents, with one exception,[38] a significant correlation coefficient. They are all positive correlations. Double-headed arrows may be read either as a two-way effect or an a correlation which is difficult to interpret in causal terms. The open-ended arrows are meant as a reminder of the existence of numerous factors which cannot be examined here.

It should be remembered that the discrepancy variable is by definition a function of both seaborne trade and merchant fleet, hence the double-headed arrow between discrepancy and ships. The arrow between fleet and trade is double-headed to indicate a two-way effect, since seaborne trade may both be a stimulant to, and be stimulated by, the existence of a national-flag merchant fleet. A third double-headed arrow (between tying arrangements and number of conferences) points to an interpretation problem. Although the existence of conferences is a logical precondition for the use of tying arrangements, this in itself is no compelling reason to consider the former to be a cause of the latter. A more reasonable line of thought seems to be to consider both as effects of a common cause (or complex of causal factors). One of these might be the number of foreign liner operators, as shown in the chart. The last double-headed arrow probably represents a partly spurious relationship with trade as the common factor in the background. But conferences are not formed only among foreign shipowners. Often, local owners may be even more active in this regard than foreign owners.

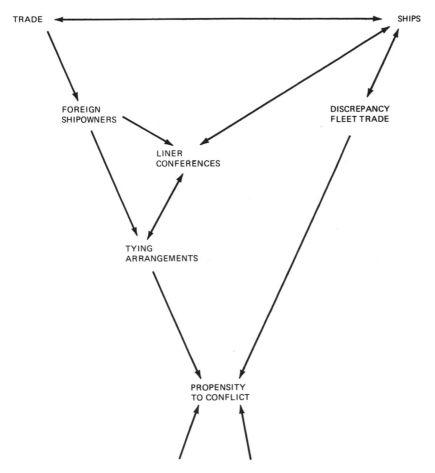

Figure 6-2. A Suggestive Map of Causal Relationships.

The single-headed arrows ought to be relatively noncontroversial. The figure depicts two main causal chains which are linked at the top by the relationship between ships and trade. The pattern in the left half of the figure (trade—foreign owners—conferences—tying arrangements—conflict) could be called an "external" causal complex because it emphasizes relationships with other countries and direct contact with the extra-national environment. Seaborne trade attracts foreign (but also national) liner operators that organize themselves in liner conferences—at or beyond the political and juridical control limits of the host country—using various means like tying arrangements to buttress their position. The combination of the foreign element and the multiple controversial issues surrounding the conference system serves both to provoke a state into offensive conflict and to involve it in conflict launched by others.

The pattern on the right-hand side could be referred to as an "internal" factor, since the dynamic element here seems to be the perception, by decision-makers, of a state of imbalance between available national ships and available national cargoes. The need to correct, to compensate for, or to adjust to such a situation is a motivating factor for engaging in conflict. Compared to the other pattern, this appears to be the more fundamental one, in that it conditions government and elites to thinking of shipping as a problem deserving constant attention. The external causal complex may then be seen both as conflict-inducing in itself and as a set of stimuli triggering the more basic motivation inherent in the enduring state of imbalance between ships and trade.[39]

The open-ended arrows in the figure may help to place the relationships analyzed into a broader perspective. The multiple correlation coefficient for propensity to conflict, discrepancy between ships and trade (1967) and tying arrangements is .484,[40] which is quite a bit higher than either of the bivariate relationships. Still, it is able to predict only about 23 percent of the variation in propensity to conflict. Many additional factors that cannot be accounted for here must therefore be imagined as part of the totality of causal factors behind a state's propensity to conflict in shipping.

This is as far as the analysis of the available data can take us within the limits of the present project. The final chapter will therefore aim to compare the findings of this and previous chapters at a more theoretical level, and to suggest which questions remain for further exploration.

Notes

1. See Snyder, Bruck, and Sapin, "Foreign Policy Decision-Making," in Snyder et al., eds., FOREIGN POLICY DECISION-MAKING (New York: Free Press, 1962), p. 65.

2. Behavior patterns of intergovernmental organizations and of liner conferences cannot be covered by more than a rather superficial examination, since most of the characteristics measured for states do not apply to the former participants (e.g., shipping situations).

3. The *shipping situation* of a state will be examined in terms of factors such as: size of fleet relative to size of seaborne trade; size of fleet considered separately; size of seaborne trade considered separately; several factors connected with liner conference activities.

4. See pp. 110-112.

5. Owing to the problem of squeezing several hundred liner conferences into a 3-digit code covering *all* participants, and to inconsistent naming of conferences by the newspapers, it has not been possible to consider the behavior of each conference separately. In the following they will therefore be treated collectively under the label "The Liner Conferences."

6. Almond and Verba, THE CIVIC CULTURE; POLITICAL ATTITUDES

AND DEMOCRACY IN FIVE NATIONS (Boston: Little, Brown and Co., 1963), p. 188.

7. See p. 115 for a further discussion of this.

8. Singer and Small regard Singapore as a "member of the interstate system" on its own from 1945. See J. David Singer and Melvin Small, "Formal Alliances, 1816-1965: An Extension of the Basic Data," JOURNAL OF PEACE RESEARCH, no. 3, 1969, p. 261.

9. West Germany's freedom to engage in international shipping was fully reestablished in 1951.

10. I.e., Secretariat or Secretary-General; or Security Council, General Assembly, Trusteeship Council, or Economic and Social Council acting through a collective decision.

11. Høegh, op. cit., pp. 66-67.

12. Ibid.

13. Boleslaw A. Boczek, op. cit., p. 200.

14. See Chapter 4.

15. See also Chapter 4.

16. See Chapter 5.

17. Arnljot Strømme Svendsen, "Shipping in the Countries of the Eastern Block," NORWEGIAN SHIPPING NEWS, no. 2, 1962.

18. See Robertson, op. cit., for a full account, especially of the Canadian role.

19. This issue was discussed a bit more extensively in Chapter 4.

20. See Chapters 3 and 4.

21. Ceylon, Indonesia, Jordan, Lebanon, New Zealand, Portugal, Taiwan, Venezuela.

22. Benson recommends the use of Yate's correction for the chi square when working with small expected frequencies, and in general when 2 X 2 tables are involved. Chi square computations in this chapter involve Yate's correction wherever appropriate. See Oliver Benson, POLITICAL SCIENCE LABORATORY (Columbus, Ohio: Charles E. Merrill Publishing Co., 1969), p. 158. See also Blalock, SOCIAL STATISTICS, pp. 220-221.

23. See UNCTAD, Trade and Development Board, Committee on Shipping, Third Session, PROVISIONAL LIST OF PARTICIPANTS (TD/B/C.4(III)/Misc. 1/Rev. 1), April 14, 1969, pp. 19 ff.

24. Information supplied by the Norwegian Shipowner's Association, Statistical Office.

25. See Chapter 5.

26. The third-flag index for all countries is shown in Appendix D.

27. Due to the canal traffic, Egypt and Panama are treated as special cases in seaborne trade. See Appendix A, p. 185.

28. The reason for this is mainly that the difference in size between the largest case and the smallest case within the categories "large trade" and "large

fleet" is considerable, leaving room for rather great discrepancies between ships and trade.

29. A slogan in the Norwegian foreign policy debate at the time of independence from Sweden in 1905: "The best foreign policy for a small state is no foreign policy at all."

30. See Chapters 2 and 5.

31. The main reason for this is that a number of variables to be used below are not available over time.

32. I.e., the total number of acts committed by a state.

33. See Chapter 5 regarding the criteria for assignment to main group.

34. See Chapters 3 and 4.

35. CRONER'S, op. cit.

36. For convenience, only one version of the dependent variable will be used in the following. The correlation (r) between conflict on all issues and conflict on pure issues is .872, and conflict on all issues is related to all independent variables in the same direction as conflict on pure issues.

37. The idea that a state of imbalance or disequilibrium may be an impetus towards action is a recurring theme in the theoretical contributions of Karl Deutsch. See, for instance, "Communication Models and Decision Systems" in James C. Charlesworth, ed., CONTEMPORARY POLITICAL ANALYSIS (New York: Free Press, 1967). A different, though not necessarily contrary, argument is advanced by Dean Pruitt who suggests that an actor will tend to refrain from conflict behavior the more dependent he feels himself to be on another actor's good will. (Dean G. Pruitt, "Stability and Sudden Change in Interpersonal and International Affairs," reprinted in Rosenau II, op. cit.) The finding above seems to contradict Pruitt's hypothesis.

38. The link Trade-Foreign Shipowners falls slightly short of our required level of significance.

39. Because both size of fleet and size of seaborne trade change rather slowly——i.e., only over several years—any state of imbalance is likely to be "enduring." This is not meant to imply permanence.

40. R = .484 is significant at the .05 level by the F-test, with 2 and 29 degrees of freedom (N = 32).

7

Summary and Conclusions

A Review of Questions and Findings

The central analytical questions of this endeavor concerned the determinants of the frequency of conflict in shipping interaction, in particular the relationship between distribution of values and frequency of conflict. The analysis began by regarding the problem from a systemic perspective, so that the initial main hypothesis was formulated in terms of "systemic conflict" and "distribution of values in the system." An inverse relationship was hypothesized between degree of equality in the distribution of values and frequency of systemic conflict. In its broadest interpretation this hypothesis received considerable support in the data.

Several competing hypotheses were also tested, all based on the argument that systemic shipping conflict may be a function of international politics in general rather than of specifically maritime factors. Most important among these hypotheses were (a) the suggestion that shipping conflict is a result of violent international conflict, and (b) the rift hypothesis stating that conflict is more frequent in "out-group" than "in-group" relations. Only the latter hypothesis was confirmed by the data.

These findings suggest that systemic shipping conflict may be explained in either of two ways: (1) as a function of cross-rift interaction, or (2) as a function of value distribution. Since these are non-contradictory theories, we have chosen not to reject either.

Actually, when we break down the variable *volume of cross-rift interaction* into its components we find that by far the largest component is the interaction between West and South (see Table 5-11)—which is also where distributive issues are most pronounced (e.g., colonialism, aid and development, increasing gap between rich and poor). Although the analysis has not ruled out the possibility of spuriousness, we prefer the interpretation that several causal factors are at work at the same time.

Shifting the analysis to the actor level, factors motivating a state to participate in interaction were initially examined. It was found that the larger a country's merchant fleet and (or) seaborne trade, the more likely its government will be to participate in shipping interaction; and also that the higher the frequency of participation, the more likely that a general shipping policy is formulated. The importance of these findings, it was suggested, lies especially in the fact that a number of countries of little *international* maritime significance, but to whom shipping may still be exceedingly important, are unlikely either to

155

participate in interaction or to formulate and pursue a general policy on shipping.

In Chapter 2, one of the theoretical assumptions regarding state behavior was that decision-makers will act in shipping matters with a view to maintaining or increasing their country's share of the international distribution of shipping values. The present finding does not quite agree with this assumption. It points to at least one intervening variable: governmental capabilities and resources in general. Many of the internationally unimportant maritime states are also among the poor countries of the world—countries with limited administrative and material resources. A certain minimum level of capabilities seems to be required before a state will allocate scarce resources to the task of policy-making in such a specialized area as shipping. In this sense it may be said that these states do not act in their own "objective" interests, as determined by an observer.

In connection with the second main question at the actor level—the factors determining propensity to conflict—two hypotheses were tested, both inspired by the original value-distribution hypothesis. One suggested that a large share of the value distribution would be associated with a high propensity to conflict; the other hypothesized that a small share of the value distribution would be associated with a high propensity to conflict.

The tests initially indicated some support for the former proposition (large value share, high propensity to conflict), but the support eroded when a more rigorous test was employed, and it was concluded that there is no relationship between share of the distribution of values and propensity to conflict. Significant correlations with conflict were found, however, both for discrepancy between size of fleet and size of trade, and for exposure to liner conferences employing tying arrangements. These variables were only weakly correlated with each other. The fact that tying arrangements was (excepting propensity to conflict) significantly correlated only with number of foreign liner shipowners was taken to indicate that more than conference practices alone were involved.

Thus, it was argued at the actor level that the two correlations with propensity to conflict represent different, but complementary, conflict dimensions—one with intranational reference (discrepancy fleet/trade), the other with extra-national reference (tying arrangements, contact with foreign shipowners). It was also argued that the discrepancy variable probably involves a more basic motivation than the other variable, since it gives a concentrated expression of the entire maritime transport situation of a country.

Some Further Questions

The theoretical framework adopted demands that certain crucial questions be answered by the study:

1. Does shipping interaction tend to follow the patterns of shipping trans-actions?
2. What are the implications of the confirmation or rejection of the value distribution hypothesis at one level of analysis for the confirmation or rejection of corollary or related hypotheses at the other level of analysis?

The answer to the first question is affirmative beyond doubt. A common trait of all shipping transactions is that they concentrate in two main patterns: carriage between the developing countries and the Western, developed world; and carriage between the Western countries themselves.[1] In Chapter 5, it was shown that by far the greatest volume of intergovernmental interaction takes place between the main groups South and West, and within the Western group. The frequency of conflict follows a similar pattern. Thus, the highest frequency of intra-group conflict was found in the Western group.

The answer to the second question involves the findings of Chapters 5 and 6. Specifically, the problem is the following: The central hypothesis has been confirmed for the systemic level, while two corollaries have been rejected at the nation-state level. J. David Singer has addressed himself directly to this problem in the well-known level-of-analysis article:

To illustrate . . . , one could, at the systemic level, postulate that when the distribution of power in the international system is highly diffused, it is more stable than when the discernible clustering of well-defined coalitions occurs. And at the sub-systemic or national level, the same empirical phenomena would produce this sort of proposition: when a nation's decision-makers find it difficult to categorize other nations readily as friend or foe, they tend to behave toward all in a more uniform and moderate fashion. Now, taking these two sets of propositions, how much cumulative usefulness would arise from attempting to merge and codify the systemic proposition from the first illustration with the sub-systemic proposition from the second, or vice versa? *Representing different levels of analysis and couched in different frames of reference, they would defy theoretical integration; one may well be a corollary of the other, but they are not immediately combinable. A prior translation from one level to another must take place.*[2] [Emphasis mine.]

Singer's view, in short, is quite pessimistic on this point. Still, in the theoretical foundations of this study I have attempted to build in what Singer calls a "prior translation" between the two levels of analysis. The key here is the assumption that *governments will act to maintain or increase their share of the international distribution of values in shipping.* This assumption has already had to be qualified on an important point: a considerable number of countries do not even participate in shipping interaction although they have every reason to do so.

The assumption might therefore be restated as follows: Governments tend to ignore international shipping matters (a) if they have limited administrative and material resources, and (b) if shipping is not crucially important to the country. Otherwise, governments will act to maintain or increase their country's share of the international distribution of shipping values.

This restatement accommodates the finding on participation. It also provides a theoretical basis for the finding that states with a large discrepancy between size of fleet and size of trade have a higher propensity to conflict than other states. The size of discrepancy, as was pointed out earlier, may give a good indication of the importance of shipping to the country.

In acting to maintain or increase their share of the value distribution, governments may be expected to become involved in conflict with each other, regardless of the size of their value share. As was emphasized in Chapter 6, there is no necessary reason to expect states with small value shares, or states with large value shares, to have a higher propensity to conflict than others. This can be expected only when rich (or poor) governments engage in conflict mainly with other rich (or poor) governments, or when conflict actions of the rich (poor) are directed at the poor (rich) *but without being reciprocated*. (See Table 7-1.)

All categories, whether appearing alone or in combination, are consonant with the systemic value-distribution hypothesis. The data indicate no difference in propensity to conflict between states with large value-shares and states with small value-shares. If only one pattern is involved (a most unlikely situation), only the "revolution" pattern can produce this result. If some combination of patterns is involved, however, a large number of them could produce the outcome of "no difference," (e.g., 1 and 5; 1 and 6; 1 and 7; 2 and 6; 4, 1, 2, 3, 5, 6, and 7; etc.)

There is evidence, however, that the combination of patterns in this particular case includes number 4 ("revolution") plus one or more of patterns 1, 2, and 3. The evidence consists of the finding that there is a slight tendency for states with large value shares to have a higher propensity to conflict,[3] added to the fact that

Table 7-1
A Tentative Classification of Conflict Patterns

Actor	Target	Reciprocal (Target also actor)	Pattern
1. Rich	Rich	Yes	"Squabbling over the spoils"
2. Rich	Rich	No	?
3. Rich	Poor	No	"Domination"
4. Poor	Rich	Yes	"Revolution"
5. Poor	Rich	No	"Impotent protest"
6. Poor	Poor	Yes	"Struggle for survival"
7. Poor	Poor	No	?

the West-South rift is the predominant one in international shipping politics.[4] To round out the picture, the high frequency of intra-group conflict among the Western states fits in rather nicely in support of the higher propensity to conflict of rich states.[5] Thus, the overall conflict pattern in shipping may be said to have a strong element of "revolution" and a weaker element of "squabbling over the spoils."

In this way we can meaningfully link the findings at two levels of analysis. Clearly, the assumption that governments act to increase or maintain their share of values was an insufficient, if not irrelevant, aid in this task. The assumption, moreover, is just as unable to help explain actor behavior as is the systemic value-distribution hypothesis. The attempt to explain why some states have a higher propensity to conflict in shipping than others must rely on other variables. We have seen that whether rich or poor, a state is likely to have a high propensity to conflict only when there is a sizable discrepancy between the size of its fleet and the size of its seaborne trade, and when it has a high degree of exposure to liner conferences using tying arrangements. Thus, while the implications of the systemic hypothesis at the actor level are not meaningless, they are useless as predictors of propensity to conflict.

In sum, the answer to the central question of this study is that the international distribution of values is an important—though not the only—determinant of conflict in shipping. The effects of the value-distribution variable cannot, however, be properly discerned if the analysis is confined to the level of the actors.

Some Further Implications of the Study

There are four points which will be emphasized here: the problem of levels of analysis, the phenomenon of nonviolent international conflict, the issue-area perspective, and the findings on "non-participants."

The problem of levels of analysis, and in particular the question of links between levels, have been an ever-present irritant and stimulant throughout this study. What seems clear, at least, is that the recommendations to use shift-of-level techniques and "Chinese-box" approaches[6] may reflect an overly optimistic view both in regard to the complexity (simplicity) of the problem involved and in regard to the kind of work needed. It may even be that the specific theoretical topic involved here was especially amenable to a shift of levels, and that other questions may not be analyzed in this way at all.

The second point is to stress the importance of studies of non-violent international conflict. Two characteristics of such conflict are especially noteworthy: its pervasiveness, and the irrelevance of physical sanctions.

Since World War I governments have, for many reasons, become increasingly involved in a large number of apparently technical international relations—controlling narcotics traffic, standardizing units of measurement, regulating the movement of labor, attempting to control pollution, regulating civil aviation, removing tariffs, establishing international currency regulations, giving and receiving development aid. Such issues take up much time, make heavy demands on human and material resources, and—studies of functional integration notwith-standing—greatly increase the number of possible conflict points between nations. Because of their limited relevance to questions of national survival, they are normally dismissed as unimportant.[7]

The argument here is that such questions and the conflicts they generate are important, because they represent political processes that are different, in significant respects, from the more familiar processes of international politics.

Maybe the most crucial difference lies in the irrelevance of physical sanctions in these low-level international conflicts. A threat to use military sanctions to enforce one's views on international currency regulations is not very credible. This, indeed, involves a charge which could be leveled at much of even contemporary thinking on international politics: if the threat of physical force does not lurk somewhere in the background, the issue is considered to be "technical."

Another point that bears repeating is the usefulness of the issue-area perspective. This perspective was part of the present approach, and it has yielded considerable payoff. The key to the issue-area perspective is the assumption that political processes will vary with the nature of the subject matter involved.

It has been shown that conflict in the issue-area of shipping tends to occur significantly more often than in world politics generally. Furthermore, the analysis of rifts showed that the East-West rift is only of secondary importance in shipping politics—contrary to the general notion that this has been a main line of division in postwar international politics. In addition, the North Atlantic community is split by a set of the most enduring and apparently insoluble controversies in the entire field of shipping affairs. What matters, therefore, is not only who is involved in interaction and what political means they use, but also what the interaction is about.

This study has not considered some of the most intriguing questions of issue-areas more than in passing. How can issue-areas be classified for more systematic study? How can the differences between issue-areas most fruitfully be highlighted by a typology? How can the differences between issue-areas be explained? The latter question is not the least important.

Finally, any study of issue-areas must include general as well as issue-specific political variables in order to bring out both the aspect of penetration by the international political system and whatever is unique about the issue-area. The penetration aspect was not unimportant in the issue-area studied here. In particular, the comments above on rifts must not be allowed to cover up the clear trend of greater hostility in relations across all main rifts.

The fourth and last point to be stressed concerns the finding that low-capability actors tend to refrain from participating in interaction. The relevance of this phenomenon to questions of dominance and hegemony in international politics should be beyond doubt. It appears likely that this kind of "non-behavior" is not restricted to shipping politics alone, but is rather a general characteristic of the present-day world with its large number of low-capability states. A promising way of approaching this phenomenon would be to study the behavior of higher-capability states towards the non-participants, as well as structural aspects of such relationships, as possible determinants of the passiveness of non-participants.

Where a scientific study ends is mainly a matter of definition. It will hopefully lead to more research, at least on the part of the author and possibly by others as well. The present study is neither a complete analysis of postwar shipping politics nor a presentation of anything more than fragmentary conclusions. As a building block that could fit into a number of larger scientific structures, however, it should be regarded as complete.

Notes

1. See Chapter 3.
2. Singer, "The Level-of-Analysis Problem," in Knorr and Verba, eds., THE INTERNATIONAL SYSTEM, p. 91.
3. See Chapter 6.
4. See Chapter 5.
5. See Chapter 5.
6. See, for example, Charles McClelland, THEORY AND THE INTERNATIONAL SYSTEM, op. cit.
7. A notable exception is the volume edited by Keohane and Nye, TRANSNATIONAL RELATIONS AND WORLD POLITICS, op. cit.

Appendixes

Appendix A

Methodology

This chapter is intended to fill one specific purpose, namely to discuss methodological questions pertaining to the three sets of data in this dissertation that are original in compilation. These are the *interaction data*, the *liner conference data*, and the *interview-questionnaire data*.

The reader will notice that these do not comprise the totality of data employed in the present study. What is common to the data excluded from this chapter is that they were all used as found in available statistical sources, and only minor processing chores had to be done to prepare them for use here.[1]

The following discussion will cover both the actual procedures of compilation and processing and the methodological issues implicit in the choice of given types of data, types of sources, and types of compilation and processing procedures. Finally, there will be some comments on statistical tests and on technical aids in data processing.

Interaction Data

The interaction data have a crucial place in this study because they form the basis of the central dependent variable, the frequency of conflict in interaction.

The category system and coding rules of the World Event/Interaction Survey (WEIS) provided, with minor modifications, a ready-made program of work for the interaction analysis.[2]

The category system breaks down the flow of interaction between states into discrete types of actions.[3] Already, the first methodological issue arises: Is it possible and defensible, on conceptual as well as practical methodological grounds, to dissect the events taking place between states and put each resultant item into a neatly designed box for further treatment?

As indicated, the question has two main aspects, one relating to conceptual processes, the other to the practical task of discerning between items of action in the coding process. This latter aspect will be left aside for a moment, though there is a degree of overlap between the two.

The conceptual part of the question could be rephrased in the following way: Doesn't the adopted procedure "do violence to reality" by assuming that actions are discrete, by pulling them out of context, so to speak? It could well be argued that very few actions made by states are actually discrete, and that the type of action chosen by a state in a given situation is closely tied to the many unique or special characteristics of that situation.

Interaction always occurs in sequences of events which are closely interrelated and rather complex. The WEIS arrangement in itself does not take *sequences* of interaction (or series of interrelated actions) into account. Any user of the category system could, however, do so if he wanted to. There is nothing in the WEIS setup that precludes building interaction sequences into the analysis, provided one has a workable definition of sequences.[4] Indeed such a study of interaction sequences would take in certain variables that are otherwise lost, and that can be summed up in the propositions that the frequency and intensity of conflict in interaction is determined (a) by positive or negative feedback from the process itself, and (b) by the types of participants involved in interaction in a given situation.

One of these variables is lost in the present analysis, namely that of feedback of interaction upon itself. (The variable "types of participants" is covered in the section on rifts in Chapter 4.) It can hardly be denied that the omission of the feedback variable is actually a weakness. The possibility exists, in other words, that some of the relevant findings of this study can later be proven invalid because this variable is left out.

As was just mentioned, the WEIS system does not take all of these situational variables into account, and it must therefore make certain assumptions to compensate, as it were, for this weak area.

The assumptions are as follows. First, it is argued that, regardless of the situation, a state will always have a *finite* number of action types from which to choose. The actions themselves are almost always recognizable from situation to situation. It is not the action as such, but the circumstances in which it takes place that support the argument that an interstate act is unique and incomparable. However, it is argued here that these situational circumstances are summed up in the sequences of actions preceding the act in question. Thus, assuming further that norms governing inter-state behavior have not changed drastically during the period studied, the argument continues by stating that *within the category system*, similar actions or constellations of actions will tend to produce similar responses.

A second main assumption builds upon the first by saying that if each action type tends to occur typically only in certain interaction contexts (i.e., that actions of types X and Y are the most likely responses to action type Q), then all instances of each action type must be *comparable*, and can therefore be considered collectively and treated in quantitative terms.

The practical question of discerning between different items of action has more immediate impact on the study. The set of categories in the WEIS system is accompanied by coding rules and examples explaining the application of each category. In most cases the category system is easy to use, but certain problems kept reappearing and will be considered shortly.

First, however, a note on coding procedure will be in order. The general coding rules for WEIS are as follows,[5] subject to the proviso that all coded items must pertain to the subject matter of shipping as defined in Chapter 2 (my own comments to each coding rule are put in parentheses after each quote):

"1. An acceptable act must be discrete. The act must be in some manner part of a political event-interaction." (In practice, as long as the act was discrete and acceptable by the other coding rules, no judgment was passed on whether it was "part of a political event-interaction," a fuzzy notion by any standard.)

"2. Activities and statements by the chief of state, assistant chief of state, foreign minister, or an official government representative will be collected. The information collection will contain only official actions." (See also Rule 9, below.)

"3. Statements made by official governmental newspapers (e.g., Pravda) will be included as representing official policy." (In the present study only newspapers of communist countries have consistently been embraced by this rule. Other, more dubious cases, such as *Al Ahram* of the UAR included in the WEIS project are excluded here.)

"4. Diplomatic visits of designated parties (see point 2 above) will be included." (These are normally coded 030-CONSULT. In the later version of the category system, visits are given more specific codes than that employed here.)

"5. Interactions of the United Nations, as well as those of other major international organizations, will be treated in the same manner as one treats those of a national entity. Therefore, any act of these organizations will be considered internal and thus excluded, unless it is considered an organizational action directed into the international system." (The practice followed in this study has been somewhat different, owing to a proposed comparison of intra-organizational vs. extra-organizational interaction, which was later deleted from the design. Thus, interaction *between states* taking place within the organizational framework of an intergovernmental organization has been included to the extent it was reported in the newspaper. Another exception from WEIS rules on this point is that *liner conferences* have been included as actors in the interaction system on shipping, owing to their considerable political importance in shipping affairs in interaction with governments.)

"6. The actions of internationally recognized revolutionary elites (e.g., the Viet Cong and NLF, the PLF, etc.) will be treated in the same manner as one treats any national entity." (The National Liberation Front of Vietnam was the only such entity that actually took part in shipping interaction, according to the sources used here.)

"7. All military interactions among stages will be included if there is not a state of war (continuous engagements). If there is a state of war, as in Vietnam, military actions are not recorded. Record is kept of the first day the conflict became a continuous affair and the day such a situation ends. All nonmilitary actions are, however, recorded in the normal manner." (For a qualification, see my list of qualifications of the action categories, below p. 172.)

"8. Both direct statements made by decision-makers to governments and 'tour of the horizon' statements will be recorded . . . "

"9. Statements by minor or nonofficial persons will not be recorded unless they elicit a specific response from a foreign government." (Actions and statements by persons not acting in any official capacity—e.g., Bertrand Russell appealing to the Soviet government—are always excluded in this study.)

"10. Attacks on government consulates, embassies, and foreign installations will be recorded."

"11. Reports which contain material that diffuses over a time period of more than a few days (i.e., situational reports) will be excluded."

"12. No editorial or 'news analyses' (commentary) will be collected. The exclusion of news analyses reduces the likelihood of 'interpretative' and/or false information." (In addition, any item qualified by the word "reportedly" or a similar term is excluded from this study, unless the item is explicitly confirmed in a subsequent report.)

"13. Newspaper reports of speeches will be recorded in the language of the newspaper rather than by reference to the texts of speeches."

"14. Any act that is unacceptable according to these rules, but that elicits a specific acceptable response, will become eligible by virtue of having drawn an official response and will be included in the collection." (*This rule is rejected in the present study*, since it would bring in a host of domestic political acts in all countries, which the WEIS category system is by no means designed to handle.)

Items of action were coded *directly* from the source onto a coding sheet for punch cards. This eliminated an extremely time-consuming part of the WEIS procedure, which requires that each item be recorded first *verbatim* on an index card, then—as a secondary step—that the item be coded in the WEIS code for punching. This is a safety device that certainly enhances the reliability of the coding procedure by making it very easy to go back and check each item—provided, of course, that the verbatim recoding is correct. The main drawback of this method is that with a large number of items, it is simply not a one-man job. Consider the following example: A coded item from late June 1949 was based on a newspaper report to the effect (roughly) that "Chiang Kai-Shek's government today ordered a blockade of all communist-controlled ports in China." In the proper WEIS procedure the date, page, and column of the source[6] would be recorded on an index card, and the item would then be taken down word for word as found in the source. In the procedure employed in this study, the essential data such as date of source, date of occurrence, page and column numbers would be coded in the appropriate spaces on the coding sheet, but the act itself would simply be taken down in the following form: "CHT-150-NSC." ("150" is the code for "DEMAND; issue order or command, insist; demand compliance.")[7] This, of course, would also be the ultimate result of the WEIS coding procedure, when the information on the index cards was prepared for punching. In my procedure, however, the intermediate step would be eliminated and a huge amount of work saved. To compensate for the loss of reliability on this score (among other things), I used *two* primary sources for the interaction data rather than only the single source used for the WEIS project.[8] Thus, a combined coding and source-accuracy test was performed on all items mentioned in both sources. It should be noted that a considerable number of items were mentioned in only one of the two sources.[9] Hence, this reliability test was not complete; i.e., it did not cover all 8035 coded items. For the cases that were double-checked in this manner, it is noteworthy that only one single item was reported in a contradictory fashion in the two sources. (The item concerned was excluded from the data.) Where minor differences appeared, the most detailed of the two sources (the *Norges Handels og Sjøfartstidende*)[10] was allowed to overrule the other.

The practical task of coding was somewhat different for the two sources employed. Common to both, however, were the simple safeguards of reviewing the coding rules and the category set every day, and of recording in a note book all coding decisions that created particular problems, along with the serial number of the item coded.

The *New York Times Index* is arranged by subject matter and therefore rather easy to use. Cross references in the index complicated the picture somewhat, however. In general, coding started, for each annual volume, with the heading "Ships and Shipping." Immediately following this heading, the *Index* always had a list of cross-references. These were examined first, with each item being coded as I went along. Then followed the main heading itself—"Ships and Shipping." Coding was done on sheets printed for programming purposes by the University of Oslo. The sheets were unusual in that they allowed the coding of 23 complete punch cards on one sheet, rather than just one card, which is commonly found. This greatly facilitated the task of checking that no item was coded twice due to the cross reference system used by the *Index*.[11]

The coding was done chronologically by year for the *New York Times Index* (within each year, the *Index* naturally juggles all dates because of the subject matter divisions), starting with 1946. For the *Norges Handels og Sjøfartstidende* coding was done in complete chronological order, beginning with January 1, 1946, and going day by day until December 31, 1968.

The latter source was not indexed and had to be studied from page to page. Fortunately, its volume is at the most one-tenth that of an average *New York Times*. Coding on the *Norges Handels og Sjøfartstidende* was not started until the entire data collection from the *New York Times Index* was complete. The items coded up to that point were then chronologically arranged by year. For each item found eligible in the Norwegian source a check therefore had to be made to see whether it had already been coded from the *Index*. Normally, this was not as time-consuming as it may sound, owing to the practical format of the coding sheets and the limited number of actions coded for each year. It was only the 1956 Suez Crisis, with its enormous volume of interaction (see Chapter 5, above) that made this task more than commonly frustrating at times. In all, the coding of the interaction data, a total of 8035 items, took approximately nine months of sustained work.

In general, coding inter-state interaction on the basis of the WEIS category system was found to entail two general kinds of difficulties: (a) what can be called the "action-within-an-action" problem; and (b) inadequacies of the category system itself.

The first problem is not insoluble, but demands alertness on the part of the coder. It can best be illustrated by examples of some main varieties. First, a fictitious example of a variety mentioned in the coding instructions for the WEIS project: "The Italian Foreign Minister and the US Secretary of State had talks today on the subject of shipping. During the talks, Italy requested exemptions for her ships from US cargo preference legislation . . . " Clearly, two action categories in the WEIS system are involved: 030-CONSULT,[12] and 093-REQUEST (material assistance), but *the latter is subsumed by the former.* Here, the coding instructions are clear.[13] Category 030-CONSULT should only be used when the details of the talks are *not* known—i.e., if one or more verbal acts taking place during the talks are known, the code 030 is omitted, and only mutually exclusive items of action are coded.

Other cases—not mentioned in WEIS handbooks—can be a bit more tricky to handle. Consider the following (fictitious) example: "The Soviet Ambassador yesterday delivered a note of protest against alleged US harassment of Soviet merchant ships in international waters. The note charged that the incidents are deliberate provocations designed to . . . (etc.)." This kind of problem crops up quite frequently, and again is an example of an "action within an action." In this case, however, it is fairly clear that two discrete acts are involved (132-FORMAL PROTEST, and 121-ACCUSE; charge; blame) and that the latter is part of the former only in a narrow, technical sense. *Both* would be coded by the procedure adopted here.

The other kind of difficulty referred to above concerns inadequacies of the WEIS category system itself. In all fairness, the vast amount of work spent over many years by Professor McClelland and his associates at the University of Southern California in order to refine and improve the category system should be stressed again. For all its advantages, however, the category system is not perfect. Still, only one category turned out to be ambiguous on all occasions when it seemed to be applicable. This was category 150-DEMAND, which has not been revised in the final version of the WEIS category system.

Two different meanings of this category turn up on closer investigation. The first meaning of a "demand" in inter-state interaction involves a situation where the actor has no way of securing compliance with the demand, except through his influence over the target state or by committing forcible acts outside his own territory. Example: "United Kingdom insists Rhodesia government abandon unilateral declaration of independence."[14]

The second meaning of "demand" is found in situations where the actor can easily secure compliance, because the specific objects of the demand (often foreign officials, or other foreign nationals, including corporations and ships) are located within the actor's own territory. Example: "Turkey today demanded the withdrawal of certain US Peace Corps workers."[15]

The examples used to illustrate the two meanings of the demand-category were both borrowed from handbooks on the WEIS coding procedure, one dated January 1968, the other January 1969. In neither handbook, nor in McClelland's own "Comments on Meanings and Rationales in the WEIS Category Systems" (cited above) is there any acknowledgement of this ambiguity, and the irony of it is, of course, that of the two examples used each fits its own meaning of the term. In the present study, the code 150-DEMAND has been used for both meanings, but for future studies it is proposed here to use a new code (151) for *demands which are part of interstate influence attempts*, and another code (152) for demands that by their nature are easily enforceable by the actor state. It is true that judgment will always have to be exercised in the use of the WEIS category system; that there will, in other words, always be tricky items to code—but such cases are quite different from the two varieties of the demand-category just indicated, which should clearly be kept distinct. Doing so would also make the WEIS system better suited to studies of influence attempts.

One other distinction which is not altogether clear is that between 01-YIELD and 06-GRANT. Thus 013 is a code for "admitting wrongdoing, retracting statement," while 061 covers the "expression of regret, apologizing." Similarly, category 012 is described as "yield position, retreat, evacuate"—usually, but not always, applicable to physical locations[16]—while 064 is described as "grant privilege; diplomatic recognition; de facto relations, etc." Not seldom, these distinctions are difficult to make. The rule which is most helpful here is McClelland's statement that "the 06 categories are held together by the idea of some extension of courtesy, privilege, or gratification which the initiating government might readily withhold."[17] In comparison, 01-YIELD is characterized more by submission.[18] The distinction can at times become awfully subtle.

The following minor adjustments of coding practice, pertaining directly to the action categories, were also made:

1. The blacklisting of ships was coded *202-EXPEL* organization or group.
2. Blacklisting was coded *by country*—not by ship, so that the country of registry was in effect regarded as blacklisted from the date the first ship of

that registry was blacklisted until the last ship of that registry was removed from the list.

3. Double-coding: In action types 030-CONSULT, 081-AGREE, 082-AGREE and 223-MILITARY ENGAGEMENT, all states participating are (usually) at the same time both actor and target. In the WEIS procedure, the act is therefore coded twice for each pair of participants. Where many actors are involved, however, the number of items coded would be quite large, and WEIS rules therefore allow the use of the code "MLG" (multilateral group) as a generalized *target* code in such situations. Each state is then coded only once as interacting with MLG, and the number of items is thereby reduced.[19] As an additional guideline on when to double-code and when to use MLG, the author followed the rule that *double-coding is used* when *the number of participants in interaction is three or less*. For four or more participants, the MLG practice is followed.

4. Exceptions from double-coding not covered by point 3, above:
   a) Double-coding is not used when a country is conferring (030) with many or all member states or an intergovernmental organization of which it is not itself a member. The interaction must, of course, take place in connection with regular sessions of the organization.
   b) Double-coding is used, however, for interaction between a state and a high-level official representative of an intergovernmental organization, whether the state is a member or not.
   c) Ratifying or acceding to a multilateral agreement or convention already in existence is coded 081, without double-coding.

5. By the WEIS rules, the military engagements in an ongoing war are coded only for the first and last day of action. However, *all military acts between belligerents and third countries have been included in this study*.

6. Routine meetings of international organizations are not coded unless more specific reports of interaction appear. E.g.: "The UN General Assembly held its 1345th plenary meeting today in New York" is an item which would be excluded unless more interaction reports came forth.

The coding work was concluded by a process of reviewing the notes on dubious or problematic items and making final decisions as to which were to be retained and which to be deleted. The data collection was then ready for punching.

For most of the punching I was helped out by two assistants, one of them a full-time key punch operator. The punching task was completed over five weekend sessions. Punching reliability was checked in two ways. First, all the most important codes in the card layout were checked on a counter-sorter to make sure that no column included inadmissible punches. (The first digit of the action code, for instance, could only be a 0, a 1, or a 2.) Secondly, a random check of *all punches* on 10 percent of the cards (i.e., 804 cards) was performed.

The randomization consisted of choosing the serial number of the first card to be checked from a table of random numbers. Counting from this serial number, every tenth card through the entire data collection was then checked. It was decided in advance that if the number of cards with errors in the sample exceeded two percent, the entire data collection would have to be checked. As it turned out, there were 15 errors on ten of the 804 cards checked. This means that 1.24 percent of the cards checked contained errors. Put in a different way, 0.01 percent of *all punches* checked were erroneous. *Not a single one of these errors, however, concerned data which were actually used for the study*, i.e., dates, actor code, target code, or action code. I consider this to be well within normal safety margins for a study based on as large a number of cases as this is.

The sample on which the interaction analysis is based consists of 8035 interstate actions pertaining directly to shipping. It could possibly be argued that this is the universe of cases and that no sampling has taken place. In actuality, however, there has been a sampling process, although it has not been performed by the author, but rather by the newspapers used as sources.

Therefore, the possibility of sampling bias is related to the ways in which reporters, editors, and news services do their work. Many of the resultant bias possibilities are elusive and hard to pinpoint, usually because they occur in some way at random or due to special circumstances. There is one source of bias, however, that is systematic and impossible to avoid completely by any newspaper. This is the possibility of national bias—of selecting certain items for inclusion in the newspaper because they concern persons and events located within the nation. Such bias is not necessarily irrational; indeed, since any newspaper usually serves at the most a national constituency (and probably less, in the majority of cases), it is entirely rational for them to be more concerned with events close at hand than with those far away, other things being equal. This is what makes newspapers a source whose reliability in studies of international politics is quite often debatable.

Certain facts about the two sources selected here—the *New York Times Index* and the *Norges Handels og Sjøfartstidende*—give me reason to believe that national bias here is not quite as serious as it might be in other cases.

First, there is the entire attitude or philosophy of the *New York Times* as regards the reporting of events. "All the news that's fit to print" may be just a slogan, and an equivocal one at that. But the sheer volume of news reported in the *Times* indicates that the slogan becomes in practice an encyclopedic way of reporting events.

Secondly, there is the subject matter itself. Ocean shipping is a subject about as international in nature as they come. Of necessity, then, the reporting of maritime affairs can rarely avoid discussing events taking place abroad, and in most cases it is exactly the counterpositioning of different nationalities that makes shipping issues interesting to newspapers.

Thirdly, the *Norges Handels og Sjøfartstidende* serves a very special community in which shipping interests dominate. It is doubtful whether this Norwegian-language newspaper (containing some regular features in English) is much read outside Scandinavia. What makes its reporting on shipping so excellent, however, is that it is an important source of information for a shipping community whose interests cover perhaps more parts of the globe than any other. This means that Norwegian shipowners and the people working for them have to have a reliable source of information on what takes place in shipping affairs all around the world.

Fourthly, using newspapers from two different countries may be expected to cancel out at least some of the national bias.

One precaution had to be introduced in the coding of material from the *"NHS."* Since the newspaper is characterized by a considerable disparity between reporting facilities in Norway and those it has abroad, the "foreign" events reported tend to come from the various news services and specialized newspapers abroad, while events reported in Norway usually were covered by the newspaper's own staff. Due to the specialized character of the subject matter and the smallness of the national environment, it was quite easy for the *NHS* repeatedly to seek, and obtain, news items which it had no chance to acquire in comparable ways from abroad. For example, quite often when something happened abroad that affected the Norwegian merchant fleet, an *NHS* staffer apparently would call up the appropriate official at the foreign ministry and say "What's your view on this?" To avoid the obvious overload of Norwegian items that this would produce, any item which seemed to have been solicited in this way by the *NHS* was therefore excluded from the data collection.

A more accurate estimate of national bias in the sources can only be made on the basis of a test on the data, to see whether the United States or Norway were mentioned more often than would be desirable. Such a test was actually performed on two samples of 100 randomly selected items, one from each newspaper. (See Table A.1., below.)

Table A-1

National Bias in the Sources Used for the Interaction Analysis (100 Randomly Selected Action Items from Each Newspaper.)

Country mentioned as actor	Source		Total
	The New York Times Index	Norges Handels og Sjøfarts- tidende	
USA	20	13	33
Norway	1	10	11
Others	79	77	156
Total	100	100	200

It should be noted that the number of third-countries mentioned shows very little variation from one source to the other.

Beyond that, however, both newspapers show considerable national bias, judging from the way the *Index* reports on Norway and the way the *NHS* reports on the US, compared to how each reports on its own country. Actually, the *NHS* seems to be somewhat more subject to national bias than the *Index*. Therefore, national bias cannot be excluded as a source of skew in the data.

In sum, then, at least two potentially relevant sources of error have been indicated in the interaction analysis. One is the exclusion of the situational feedback variable acting upon the interaction process, and the other is the national bias built into the main sources used. I do not believe these are crippling sources of error, but their existence demands further verification of the findings of this study before they can be removed from the "tentative" category.

Interview-Questionnaire Data

The interview data embrace considerably more than has been presented above. Owing to necessary restrictions in the scope of the study, however, much of this material had to be left out. It still seems important to give a full account of the methodological procedures and problems involved.

Planning the data gathering involved a series of methodological decisions. The most important of these decisions were related to the choice of respondents, the construction of the interview schedule-questionnaire, the choice of method in obtaining responses, (whether by interviews or questionnaires), and the practical problems involved in actually doing the work.

The choice of respondents was crucial, and three considerations played a central role in this decision. First of all, the respondents had to be accessible. Secondly, they had to be knowledgeable insiders in intergovernmental shipping affairs. Thirdly, they had to be able to speak with some authority regarding governmental views on various issues.

In planning a study of international politics that has a global scope, the question of accessibility must perforce be rather decisive, if only because of the limited time and resources available. Some sort of international gathering of the right persons in one place at the same time seemed to be the best answer to this problem. More specifically, a meeting of diplomatic representatives who were also experts on matters of shipping appeared to be ideal. Intergovernmental shipping organizations regularly arrange meetings of this kind, and the real question was then only: which one?

Three intergovernmental organizations are especially active in this field: the Intergovernmental Maritime Consultative Organization (IMCO), the UNCTAD Committee on Shipping, and the OECD Maritime Transport Committee. The last is a regional organization and therefore disqualified here. In choosing between the other two, the decisive factor was the strongly technical character of the IMCO, in contrast to the highlighting of political aspects which is typical of the UNCTAD Committee on Shipping. Politics being the focus of attention, the Committee on Shipping was the body selected.

In constructing the schedule of questions, three considerations determined the choice of the structured over the unstructured form: (a) there was no need for in depth probing; (b) processing of responses must be relatively simple; and (c) it was assumed that personal access to the delegates would be problematic and that mailed questionnaires would have to be used. (More on this below.) The common pattern adopted calls for a few peripheral questions at the beginning to let the respondent adjust to the situation. (This practice does not always serve its intended purpose: one respondent became very impatient with this part of the interview, which probably reduced his usefulness in answering several of the subsequent questions.) Then followed the more substantive second part of the questionnaire, which covered the views of the respondent's government on selected crucial issues. This part was also designed to raise the respondent's interest in the interview, in that the questions were closely tuned in to problems likely to be uppermost in the minds of most delegates. The issues had been selected on the basis of careful reading of the documents from the preceding sessions, and included as the main headings: liner conference problems, flag discrimination, and the situation of developing countries in regard to shipping. The question on flag discrimination offered a special problem, since "flag discrimination" is an objectionable term to a number of countries while, on the other hand, identically worded questions clearly had to be put to all respondents. A solution, which turned out to be quite satisfactory, was found in the phrasing "preferential treatment of national-flag ships."

The third, and most sensitive, part of the interview raised questions concerning interstate influence in shipping and the sources of this influence. This part of the interview had to be left out here.

I noted above that the physical gathering of respondents in one location was a precondition for the success of the interviewing. Finding them all in Geneva in April 1969 did not, however, of itself answer the question "interview or mailed questionnaire?" Recent and similarly designed studies of UN organs (such as those of Robert Keohane and Gary Best)[20] had pointed out the crowded schedule of UN delegates as an important complicating factor in this regard. It weighted the author's thinking strongly in favor of questionnaires mailed to the delegates in Geneva, at their hotel addresses or in care of their permanent missions. (This in spite of a warning from my advisor, Professor Miles, then in Geneva, that delegates have a habit of dropping questionnaires in waste baskets—a warning that was justified by my subsequent experiences.) The schedule of questions was thus prepared with mail distribution in mind.

A combination of circumstances served, in time, to reverse this decision. First, an approach to the UNCTAD Secretariat to obtain the names of the delegates in advance met with the reply that any plans for distributing questionnaires among the delegates must be strongly discouraged. Secondly, upon arriving in Geneva I found that not only were the various permanent missions quite often ignorant (or claimed they were) of their delegates' hotel addresses, but several also said their delegates rarely, if ever, visited the mission when in town. In part, this may reflect a desire to protect the delegates from bothersome approaches. But I also believe the specialized nature of shipping affairs is related to this. A considerable number of delegation heads were experts working in government departments in their home countries. Their contacts with their countries' permanent missions in Geneva were therefore often only intermittent. They would come to Geneva to do a job with which the permanent missions usually had little association because of its highly specialized character. Thus, many delegates apparently spent their time either at the Palais des Nations, or somewhere in town with other nations' delegates, or in their hotel rooms.

For these reasons the idea of a mailed questionnaire was dropped in favor of interviews. In all, twenty-four interviews were undertaken in Geneva in the time period April 11 to April 30, 1969, of which twenty-two were satisfactory. In additon, two West-European delegates were interviewed in their home countries shortly after their Geneva trips, yielding a total of twenty-four satisfactory interviews. To supplement these interviews, an abbreviated version of the interview schedule was mailed as questionnaires to twenty-seven countries' delegates who had not been reached while the Committee on Shipping was in session in April. (The questionnaires were mailed in the last week of May and the first week of June, 1969. A follow-up letter was mailed to countries which had not responded by late October, 1969.) Ultimately, ten satisfactory responses were received—a fact which serves to underline the inadequacy of mailed questionnaires in surveys of diplomats. The final number of responses to the interviews-questionnaires was thus thirty-four.

Have the different situations facing respondents to the questionnaire and respondents to the interview had any effect on the results? Tables A-2, A-3, and A-4 show how the two subgroups responded to the questions discussed in

Table A-2
Governmental Views on Unfair or Discriminatory Practices by Liner Conferences

	Interview	Questionnaire (observed)	Questionnaire (expected)
Very rare	2	1	0.9
Some	9	5	3.9
Widespread	10	3	4.3
Don't know	2	1	0.9
Total	23	10	10.0

Table A-3
Governmental Views on Desirable Forms of Regulation of Liner Conferences

	Interview	Questionnaire (observed)	Questionnaire (expected)
Voluntary	8	6	3.5
Governmental	13	2	5.7
International	1	1	0.4
Don't know	1	1	0.4
Total	23	10	10.0

Table A-4
Governmental Views on Flag-Discrimination Policies

	Interview	Questionnaire (observed)	Questionnaire (expected)
Desirable	8	3	3.3
Undesirable but necessary	2	1	0.8
Undesirable and unnecessary	10	5	4.2
Don't know	4	1	1.7
Total	24	10	10.0

Chapter 4. Due to the small expected frequencies the chi square has not been computed, but a comparison of each observed with each expected frequency may still be useful. Ideally there should be no difference between the two.

The responses shown in Table A-4 come closest to the ideal. Table A-2 shows a small difference, while Table A-3 reveals a substantial difference from expected frequencies, amounting to a complete reversal of the trend of responses from the interview.

The problem with the questionnaires seems to be that governments with a particular constellation of attitudes on shipping politics—namely moderate or conservative—are more likely to return the questionnaire than other governments. This moderate-conservative bias is seen in all three tables: in Table A-2 there is a greater reluctance to say that "unfair practices" are widespread among liner conferences; in Table A-3 there is a much greater tendency to prefer no regulation of conferences; and in Table A-4 there is a slightly greater tendency to regard flag discrimination as undesirable and unnecessary.

These findings seem to detract from the value of the table in Chapter 4 which corresponds to Table A-3 here. One should keep in mind, however, that the key conclusions in Chapter 4 concerned (1) the polarization of views on the question of discriminatory practices, and (2) the great number of respondents that regarded flag discrimination as desirable. Neither conclusion is affected by the bias.

The views on regulation of liner conferences (Table A-3) were also found to be polarized, like the views on "unfair practices." It is mainly this reading of the responses that is placed in doubt here.

The difference between questionnaire and interview data may have a greater significance beyond the scope of this study. If it is true that governments with moderate or conservative views are always more prone to return questionnaires, this method of gathering data in international studies rests on shaky foundations and should probably be avoided if possible. Note also that the label "moderate-conservative" does not refer to an overweight of Western governments, since the proportion of developing countries is exactly the same (50 percent) among the interview respondents and among the questionnaire respondents. The underlying attitude dimension is more fundamental than that, in other words.

Among the practical problems of interviewing, none surpassed that of getting in touch with potential respondents. The author relied in the main on telephone calls to the permanent missions, in the first couple of days before a list of delegates was made available, asking for "the official in charge of the delegation to the UNCTAD Committee on Shipping." Due to problems already outlined, this procedure had quickly to be supplemented by contacts at the Palais, either before or after meetings. This worked fairly well, but depended both on the availability of the list of delegates and on learning to know my "victims" on sight by attending the plenary meetings.

Finding a place where the interview could proceed relatively undistributed was no real problem, since there were always plenty of empty meeting rooms at the Palais. Several interviews were also undertaken in various permanent missions, or in delegates' hotel rooms, and a few had to take place in less ideal settings. On balance, however, the kind of location seemed to make very little difference. Once the interview situation was established, the work tended to go rather smoothly. Actually, one of the most satisfactory interviews was conducted in a corner of the delegates' restaurant at dinner time.

All interviewing was done in English. Only two delegates offered some language difficulty, which was resolved by a few explanatory comments on the part of the author, taking pains to avoid leading the respondent.

On the whole, the respondents appeared to be interested and favorably disposed. Only one respondent actually refused to answer a question once the interview had started, although two others (the two "unsatisfactory" ones just referred to) initially agreed to an interview but turned around and refused when the appointment came up.

Finally, it should appropriately be pointed out that all interviews were conducted by the author alone.

The Liner Conference Data

The data were presented in Chapter 3 and provided the empirical foundations for the analysis of transaction patterns in the liner sector.

In compiling the data, the author relied mainly on the following source: *Croner's World Directory of Freight Conferences*, New Malden, Surrey, England: Croner Publications limited, 4th edition, monthly amendment service updated to June 1968. *Lloyd's Directory of Shipowners* was used as a supplementary source.

To recapitulate, the data presented in Chapter 3 showed the number of shipowners (i.e., liner companies) in each country that were members of one or more liner conferences in June 1968, as well as the countries they served as conference members. The numerical basis of the tables was referred to as *number of calls*, a concept introduced by the author and defined as follows: one call means *one shipowner serving (one or more ports in) one country other than his country of registry, as a member of one or more conferences.*

Since this information is not directly available in *Croner's*, my immediate purpose here is to show how the data were compiled and converted from their original source.

Croner's is a listing of liner conferences. As such it is probably the most complete source found anywhere, although the editor, Mr. Bridges, does not claim absolute completeness. Between 350 and 400 liner conferences are listed, giving in each case the following information:

1. conference title;
2. geographical area covered;
3. rebate information (whether rebates are given, in what form, and—in the case of deferred rebates—the length of rebate periods);
4. name and address of the secretary;
5. member lines.

The information culled for this study was that covered by points 2 and 5.

Compilation started with the member lines. Separate index cards were used for each member. The card showed the name of the line, and each different country served by the member was then taken down as the work proceeded. Thus, no country was listed more than once for each line, although the same line was often a member of several conferences serving the same country.[21]

Disregarding for the moment the question of geographical coverage, the file of conference member lines involved three problems: (1) the "home country" of the line was not shown in *Croner's*; (2) one shipping company may consist of several lines, and different lines from the same company are often given separate membership within the same conference; and (3) different lines often operate within conferences in "joint service" agreements.

Solving the first problem usually also gave the solution to the second. To find the country where a shipping line's main office was located, I relied primarily on *Lloyd's List of Shipowners*, which gives complete addresses for most of the world's shipping companies. *Lloyd's List* also gives the names of the various lines operated by each shipowner and a list of the vessels currently owned. Some lines could not be identified through *Lloyd's* or any other available shipowner directory. A list of these lines was therefore finally submitted to the Norwegian Shipowners' Association, which gave me valuable assistance in tracing their country of registry. Still, about 10 percent of the lines remain unidentified here.

The next step was then to reduce the file of member lines to a file of liner operators. Once the shipowner was identified, this simply meant combining the geographical coverage for the various lines so that each country was only listed once for the same shipowner. Note the remaining possibility that some of the shipping companies indexed may actually be lines within larger companies. This stems mainly from the rather inconsistent naming of lines in *Croner's*; thus, the same line was often referred to under different conferences by its full name, by an abbreviation of its full name, by a common nickname (e.g., "French Line" for Compagnie Generale Transatlantique), and by a "stripped" abbreviation consisting of initials only (e.g., "C.G.T.," "N.Y.K.," etc.). Also, *Croner's* does not consistently list lines only, but switches readily from the names of the lines to the names of shipowners operating several lines, and back again.

The third problem, "joint service," was solved by always listing the cooperating parties as if they were separate members; provided, of course, that they did not belong to the same shipping company.

The question of geographical coverage was also complicated by inconsistencies in *Croner's*. At times, the countries and/or the specific ports served were listed, and no problem existed. More frequently, however, regional designations that are part of the jargon of shipping were employed. Naturally, no explanation were given, but after a period of trial-and-error I was able to reconstruct the system behind the confusion. (How can an outsider be expected to know that "continent" in shipping jargon refers exclusively to the continent of Europe?) My reconstruction of the regional definitions may not always be exact, but then neither is the usage, and the interpretations listed below have, at any rate, been scrupulously followed in compiling the data:

Designation in Croner's:	Interpreted here as including:
"Continent" or "Continental Europe"	W. Germany, Netherlands, Belgium, France, Spain, Portugal.
"Black Sea"	USSR, Bulgaria, Romania, Turkey.
"Baltic"	Sweden, Finland, USSR, Poland, East Germany.
"Mediterranean"	Spain, France, Italy, Yugoslavia,

Designation in Croner's	Interpreted here as including:
"Mediterranean" (cont.)	Greece, Turkey, Syria, Lebanon, Israel, Cyprus, UAR, Libya, Tunisia, Algeria, Malta.
"North Europe"	W. Germany, Netherlands, Belgium.
"North Continent"	W. Germany, Netherlands, Belgium.
"Scandinavia"	Denmark, Norway, Sweden.
"Europe"	"Continent" plus "Scandinavia," "Baltic," "Black Sea," and Iceland, U.K., Ireland, Italy, Yugoslavia, Greece.
"Levant"	Turkey, Cyprus, Lebanon, Syria, Israel.
"Non-European Mediterranean"	Cyprus, Malta, UAR, Libya, Tunisia, Algeria, Turkey, Syria, Lebanon, Israel.
"Levant and Near East" ("Eastern Mediterranean")	Cyprus, UAR, Libya, Turkey, Syria, Lebanon, Israel, Greece.
"North Africa"	Algeria, Tunisia, Libya, UAR.
"Red Sea"	UAR, Israel, Jordan, Saudi-Arabia, Sudan, Ethiopia, Yemen.
"Gulf of Aden"	South Yemen, Somalia.
"Red Sea Coast Suez-Assab"	UAR, Sudan, Ethiopia.
"Persian Gulf" or "Arabian Gulf"	Saudi-Arabia, Iraq, Iran, Kuwait.
"Middle East ports west of Karachi and northeast of Aden, but excluding Aden and Karachi"	Pakistan, Iran, Iraq, Kuwait, Saudi-Arabia, South Yemen.
"Straits" or "Straits of Malaya"	Malaysia, Singapore.
"West Africa"	Mauritania, Senegal, Gambia, Sierra Leone, Guinea, Liberia, Ivory Coast, Ghana, Togo, Dahomey, Nigeria, Cameroun, Gabon, Congo (Kinsh.), Congo (Brazz.).
"River Plate"	Argentina, Uruguay, Paraguay.
"Carribbean"	Cuba, Haiti, Dominican Republic, Jamaica.

Designation in Croner's	Interpreted here as including:
"West Indies"	Barbados, Trinidad and Tobago.
"Leeward and Windward Islands"	Barbados, Trinidad and Tobago.
"US Great Lakes and St. Lawrence Seaway Ports"	USA

This particular way of compiling the data rests on the important basic assumption that all conference members serve all the countries covered by the conference as a whole, unless exceptions are stated. In a few cases this may not be realistic, namely the conferences that specify their coverage as either "Levant," "Non-European Mediterranean," "Levant and Near East," "Eastern Mediterranean," "Mediterranean," or "Red Sea" without reference to the problem of simultaneous service to Israel and the Arab states. The author has not in any case sought to adjust for such inconsistencies, but has recorded them as stated by the conferences.

Finally, a note on non-selfgoverning territories. These are not included in the survey, but conferences serving such territories have been completely excluded only when they cover the trade between the territory and the mother country and no other countries. Such trades are, in other words, considered domestic. In trades between non-selfgoverning territories and other countries, the latter are counted as countries served, but not the former. Two exceptions have been made: Hawaii and Puerto Rico have been counted as "USA" throughout.

Tests of Statistical Significance[22]

Three kinds of hypotheses have been tested for statistical significance in this study: (1) the hypothesis that the frequencies obtained for a given category in two or more different samples are not significantly different from each other; (2) the hypothesis that a given correlation coefficient (product-moment) is not significantly different from zero; and (3) the hypothesis that two correlation coefficients are not significantly different from each other.

For the first kind of hypothesis, several different tests are available, notably the chi square test, the difference-of-proportions test, and Fisher's exact test. The latter two may be used only with dichotomized variables.

Fisher's exact test has its main advantage over the others where very small samples are involved. When N is moderately large, this test gives about the same results as the chi square test corrected for continuity. Also, ". . . if the smallest cell frequency is greater than 5, the computations involved will become quite tedious."[23]

The chi square test is less accurate than Fisher's exact test when expected cell frequencies are in the neighborhood of 5 or smaller. It is the most versatile of the three tests however, because it can be applied to more than two samples at a time. In addition, the fact that the chi square is easy to compute is an important reason why it was so frequently used here. A large number of tests had to be computed using a desk calculator. Another consideration was the need to use the same kind of test for connected series of tables like those in Chapter 6, since different tests may yield different results and thus make comparisons more difficult.

As mentioned earlier, the correction for continuity (Yates' correction) was employed whenever the chi square was computed. The correction should be used in the case of small samples, since the sampling distribution in the chi square table assumes a relatively large N.

On the other hand, the larger the sample, the easier it is to obtain significance. This means that for the rather small samples used here the chi square test is an insurance against rejecting the null hypothesis when it should not be rejected. There is actually some danger of committing the opposite error—failing to reject the null hypothesis when it should be rejected. However, since our interest has mostly been in rejecting the null hypothesis, avoiding the latter type of error seems less crucial than avoiding the first.

The difference-of-proportions test was used on two occasions in Chapter 5, simply as an alternative to the chi square. The basic requirement, as mentioned, is that the variables must be dichotomized, (i.e., two samples and a dichotomized variable). For the purposes to which it was applied in this study, it does not have any particular advantage over the chi square test.

For both the second and third kinds of hypotheses mentioned above, the F-test may be employed, and in addition, Student's t may be used for the third type. Here, the F-test was used for both purposes. There was a trivial reason for choosing the F-test over the t-test to evaluate the difference between two correlation coefficients in this case: it was built into the standard computer programs used for correlation and regression.

Measures of Degree and Association: Yule's Q and Goodman-Kruskal's Gamma[24]

A considerable number of measures of association are available for use with contingency tables or simple ordinal scales (e.g., "high-medium-low"), for example Q, gamma, phi, Kendall's tau, or percentage difference. All of them have weaknesses of one kind or another, and problems of interpretation are usually involved.

Essentially, gamma and Q are rather similar measures, and in the case of 2×2 tables, they are actually the same. The advantage of gamma is that it is a measure used for larger tables that is still comparable to Q. The main weakness of both gamma and Q is that they involve products of cell frequencies in such a way that any frequency of zero will have a strong effect on the resulting coefficient. In the case of Yule's Q, which can only be used for 2 × 2 tables, if one of the four cells is zero, Q automatically attains its maximum value of ± 1. (Zero frequencies did not occur in any of the tables where Q was used above.) Therefore, only quite cautious comparisons have been made of one Q or gamma figure with another, and such comparisons have been avoided if possible.

As noted in connection with the significance tests, a large number of tables were calculated by hand, which puts a premium on measures that are simple to compute. One should also keep in mind that social-science propositions are normally rather imprecise and simple statements for which simple measures may often be no less appropriate than the more refined.

Technical Aids in Data Processing

All the interaction data were transferred to punch cards and later to magnetic tape. Some of the analysis was done on an IBM counter-sorter, but for the more demanding tasks standard programs developed at the University of Oslo were employed, and the processing was performed on the university's CDC-3500 computer.

Much of the analysis in Chapter 6 was done without complex technical devices. When the samples were small and correlation analysis was not involved, the use of a desk calculator was preferred. Limited computer time was also a consideration, and both the rather frequent "down" periods of the computer and the possibility of simple errors in using standard programs involved the risk of considerable loss of time.

Panama and Egypt as Special
Cases in Seaborne Trade

In Chapter 6, both Panama and Egypt were treated as exceptional cases in measuring the variable *seaborne trade*. By using the volume of seaborne trade as the normal basis of measurement, the variable was intended to take in the importance of seaborne trade to each country.

To Panama and Egypt, however, seaborne trade is obviously vastly more important than indicated by the rather small volume of trade found in each case. The canals bring these countries into close contact with a very large volume of trade that is not their own, but that passes within their territorial boundaries, is subject to passage dues, and is guided through the canals by pilots locally employed.

Hence, for the analysis of frequency of participation and propensity to conflict in the 1960-68 period (Chapter 6), the seaborne trade of Panama and Egypt is considered to be the volume of cargo moving through the canals, averaged between the two sailing directions. It should be noted that this correction is used only when seaborne trade as such is the variable. The third-flag index is, in other words, not affected, since the intention behind the correction is to make the variable reflect the maritime contact with foreign countries that seaborne trade (used alone) normally reflects.

Notes

1. E.g., percentagizing UN data on seaborne trade.
2. See also Chapter 2.
3. The entire category system is reproduced above, Chapter 2, pp. 21-22.
4. An analysis of interaction sequences was part of the original design for the present study but had to be abandoned because of rather serious problems in defining the sequences operationally.
5. Except when otherwise indicated, the coding rules used here are those of January 1968, found in Wayne R. Martin and Robert A. Young, "World Event/Interaction Survey WEIS Program Rules and Instructions," Department of International Relations, University of Southern California, January 1968, pp. 2-5 and *passim*, supplemented by Charles A. McClelland, "Comments on Meanings and Rationales in the WEIS Category System," Department of International Relations, University of Southern California, mimeo., December 1967, *passim*.
6. For the WEIS project itself, the source is always the NEW YORK TIMES.
7. See Wayne R. Martin and Robert A. Young, "World Event Interaction Survey (WEIS) Program Rules and Instructions," op. cit., p. 14. The code "NSC" means that the action is not directed against any particular country, which may seem confusing in this case. It should be borne in mind, however, that a blockade is an attempt to secure compliance from all states having transactions with the state which is the "target" of the blockade.
8. See below for further discussion regarding selection of sources.
9. The exact figures are as follows: NEW YORK TIMES, 5154 items; NORGES HANDELS OG SJØFARTSTIDENDE, 2881 items.
10. In view of the fact that the NEW YORK TIMES INDEX, rather than the newspaper itself, was the other source.
11. Not infrequently, the items indexed were in some way ambiguous due to their abbreviated form. All such items were recorded and looked up later in their full version in THE TIMES itself.
12. For those familiar with the WEIS category system, it should be noted that the version used here is based on the instructions of January 1968, which have since been slightly revised on this point. For the final version, see "World Event/Interaction Survey Handbook and Codebook," January 1969.

13. Charles A. McClelland, "Comments on Meanings and Rationales," op. cit., p. 6.

14. Martin and Young, op. cit., p. 18.

15. "World Event/Interaction Survey Handbook and Codebook," op. cit., p. 18.

16. McClelland, "Comments . . . " p. 2.

17. Ibid., p. 7.

18. Ibid., p. 1.

19. On double-coding, see Martin and Young, op. cit., pp. 16-17.

20. Robert O. Keohane, "Political Practice in the United Nations General Assembly," unpublished in Ph.D. dissertation, Harvard University, 1965. Gary Best, "Diplomacy in the United Nations," unpublished Ph.D. dissertation, Northwestern University, 1960.

21. Thus, the cards do not show the liner conferences of which a given line is a member, only the geographical coverage.

22. This discussion is based mainly on Blalock, SOCIAL STATISTICS, op. cit.

23. Blalock, op. cit., p. 225.

24. On Goodman-Kruskal's gamma, see Johan Galtung, THEORY AND METHODS OF SOCIAL RESEARCH (Oslo: Universitetsforlaget, revised edition 1969).

Appendix B

Question no. 6

It is often claimed that liner conferences have a distinct tendency to engage in unfair or discriminatory business practices that place both shippers and non-conference shipowners in a disadvantageous position. *Which of the following statements agrees most closely with your Government's position on this question?*

A. Almost all conferences in all parts of the world engage in such practices.
B. Such practices are found among some conferences, but it is not a common characteristic of all conferences.
C. Very few liner conferences engage in such practices.

Question no. 7

Does your Government feel that liner conference activities should be placed under *governmental* supervision or regulation, or does it feel that liner conferences should adjust their activities by their own *voluntary action?*

A. Governmental supervision or regulation is preferable.
B. Voluntary adjustment by the conferences themselves is preferable.
C. Supervision or regulation is preferable, but it should be carried out by an international organization or agency.

Question no. 12

Does your Government consider *preferential treatment of national-flag ships* over foreign ships to be

A. a desirable policy?
B. an undesirable but necessary policy?
C. an undesirable and unnecessary policy?

Note

1. Only questions covered by the analysis above (see Chapter 4) are included here.

Appendix C

List of Hypotheses

The hypotheses are listed in roughly the same order as they are introduced in the analysis.

Central Hypothesis

If a skewed distribution of values persists or is reinforced over time, then the frequency of conflict in the respective interaction system will increase.

Other Hypotheses, Tested in Chapter 5

If the frequency of conflict in the international system increases, then the frequency of systemic shipping conflict will increase.

When the actor state and the target state belong to different main groups of states, the act performed by the actor state is more likely to be a conflict act than if they both belong to the same group.

Hypotheses Tested in Chapter 6

If a government has formulated a general national policy on shipping questions as part of its overall foreign policy, then it will be more likely to participate in interaction over shipping questions.

If a country's merchant fleet is engaged in considerable third-flag carriage, then that government is more likely to take part in interaction over shipping questions.

As size of merchant fleet increases, the frequency of participation will also increase.

As size of seaborne trade increases, the frequency of participation will also increase.

States with large shares of the international distribution of shipping values will tend to have a higher propensity to conflict than states with small shares of values.

States with small shares of the international distribution of shipping values will tend to have a higher propensity to conflict than states with larger shares of values.

Appendix D

Index of Third-Flag Carriage[a]

	1947	1952	1957	1962	1967
Albania			.00	−.01	
Algeria				−.12	
Argentina	−.23	.01	−.02	.02	.01
Australia	−.15	−.11	−.10	−.16	−.04
Belgium	−.33	−.25	−.21	−.19	−.11
Brazil	−.07	−.04	−.04	−.04	−.07
Bulgaria				−.03	−.01
Burma	−.03	−.02	−.02	−.02	−.01
Cambodia			.00	−.01	−.01
Cameroun				−.01	−.01
Canada	−.46	−.44	−.36	−.37	−.37
Ceylon	−.04	−.03	−.03	−.03	−.02
Chile	−.07	−.04	−.02	−.04	−.07
Colombia	−.07	−.07	−.04	−.03	−.03
Congo (Brazzaville)				.00	−.01
Congo (Kinshasa)				−.01	−.01
Costa Rica	−.01	.01	.04	−.01	−.01
Cuba	−.18				
Cyprus				−.01	.01
Dahomey				.00	.00
Denmark	.01	.03	.07	.09	.08
Dominican Republic	−.02	−.01	−.01	−.02	
Ecuador	−.01	−.01	−.01	−.01	−.01
El Salvador	.00	.00	.00	.00	−.01
Ethiopia	.00		.00	.00	−.01
Finland	−.07	−.03	−.01	−.02	−.01
France	−.17	−.13	.01	.04	−.15
Gabon				−.01	−.02
Gambia				.00	
Germany/East			−.02	.00	.01
Germany/West	−.12	−.16	.02	.04	.05
Ghana			−.02	−.02	−.01
Greece	.05	.07	.09	.48	.32
Guatemala	−.01	−.01	−.01	−.01	
Guinea				−.01	−.01
Haiti		.00	.00	−.01	
Honduras	.01		.03	.01	.00
Hong Kong	−.03	−.02	.00	.02	.01
Iceland			.00	.00	.00

193

Index of Third-Flag Carriage (cont.)

	1947	1952	1957	1962	1967
India	−.18	−.13	−.08	−.04	.00
Indonesia	−.04	−.16	−.14	−.07	−.05
Iran		−.01	−.14	−.35	−.63
Iraq	−.01	−.01	−.07	−.06	
Israel	−.02	.00	.00	.01	.02
Italy	−.12	.07	.10	.03	−.24
Ivory Coast				−.02	−.02
Jamaica				−.06	−.07
Japan	.03	.06	.04	.09	.09
Jordan			.00	.00	−.01
Kenya				−.02	−.03
Korea, South	.00	−.01	−.03	−.03	−.03
Kuwait			−.42	−.52	−.58
Lebanon	−.01	−.01	−.15	−.10	
Liberia	.00	.06	.62	.82	1.00
Libya		−.01	.00	−.05	−.58
Malagasy				.00	−.01
Malaysia			−.04	−.12	−.12
Malta			.00	.00	.00
Mauritania				.00	
Mexico	−.04	−.05	−.02	−.02	−.02
Morocco			−.07	−.08	−.07
Netherlands	.05	−.04	−.13	−.16	−.34
New Zealand	−.06	−.03	−.02	−.02	−.03
Nicaragua	.00		.00	.00	
Nigeria				−.05	−.09
Norway	.16	.32	.59	.85	.77
Panama				.29	.22
Pakistan		−.03	−.02	−.02	−.02
Peru	−.02	−.01	−.04	−.05	−.05
Philippines		−.05	−.05	−.03	−.04
Poland	−.15	−.11	−.06	−.05	−.02
Portugal	.02	.01	.03	.03	.02
Romania			.00	−.02	−.01
Saudi Arabia			−.15	−.22	
Senegal				−.02	−.02
Sierra Leone				−.02	−.02
Singapore			−.12	−.13	−.16
Somalia				.00	.00
South Africa, Rep. of	−.05	−.08	−.07	−.07	−.06
Spain	.03	.03	.03	.01	.01
Sudan			−.01	−.01	−.01

Index of Third-Flag Carriage (cont.)

	1947	1952	1957	1962	1967
Sweden	.00	.00	.07	.15	.08
Switzerland				−.02	
Syria			−.06	−.15	−.12
Taiwan		.03			.01
Tanzania				−.01	
Thailand		−.03	−.03	−.04	−.07
Togo				.00	−.01
Trinidad-Tobago				−.12	−.16
Tunisia			−.03	−.03	−.04
Turkey		.01	.03	.02	.01
UAR	−.10	−.06	−.03	−.07	−.04
United Kingdom	.61	.77	1.00	1.00	.61
USA	1.00	1.00	.60	.43	.00
USSR			.10	.08	.23
Venezuela	−1.00	−.100	−1.00	−1.00	−1.00
Viet Nam, South		−.03	−.01	−.02	−.04
Yugoslavia	.00	.00	.00	.04	.03

[a]Source: See Chapter 6.

Appendix E

Typology of Specific Shipping Issues

A. Contaminated Issues

10. Blockade or quarantine declared; halting and/or shelling of ships.
11. Exclusion of ships from ports; blacklisting.
12. Halting, searching, seizing, or shelling ships; no blockade or quarantine declared.
13. Charges of espionage, interference with ships; actual espionage or interference.
14. World War II defeated powers' merchant fleets.
15. Embargo.
16. Use of sea-mines.
17. International pooling of ships for defense.
18. Wartime restrictions on shipping.
19. Other wartime issues.

B. Pure Issues

00. Flag discrimination, unspecified.
01. Discriminatory port dues or practices.
02. Discriminatory pilotage dues or practices.
03. Discriminatory lighthouse dues.
04. Cargo reservation; differential duties on cargoes.
05. Discriminatory currency or foreign exchange regulations.
06. Discriminatory use of tonnage measurements.
07. Discriminatory consular fees.
08. Reservation of coastal shipping to national flag.
09. Shipping subsidies; tax concessions.
20. Liner conference practices, unspecified.
21. Conference rebate systems and tying arrangements.
22. Liner conference membership.
23. Liner conference rates; rates in general.
24. Creation of new liner conferences.
25. Governments' demands for information and documentation.
26. Government-backed pools.
27. Consultation in shipping, shipper representation.
30. Flags of convenience, unspecified.
31. Registration of ships, "genuine link."

41. Shipbuilding.
42. Credits for shipbuilding or secondhand purchase; both parties developed countries.
43. Commercial international pooling of ships.
44. Leasing arrangements.
45. Insurance.
46. Chartering arrangements.
47. Nuclear propulsion.
48. Ownership issues; public vs. private.
49. Container shipping.
50. Maritime international law, unspecified.
51. Unspecified international maritime convention, treaty, or agreement.
52. Unspecified conference on maritime affairs.
53. Safety at sea, legal issues.
54. Free passage in international straits and canals.
56. Documentation for ships.
58. "Freedom of the seas."
59. Water pollution.
60. Less developed countries' shipping problems in general.
62. Credits or grants to less developed countries for shipbuilding or second-hand purchase.
65. Port improvement in less developed countries.
70. General rights and duties of ships in territorial waters.
71. Free ports.
72. Harbor use; excluding the question of access and that of discrimination.
75. Weather forecasting and services; iceberg control.
76. Salvage.
77. Shipwrecks, accidents, collisions.
78. Rescue services, navigational aids.
79. Ship radio use.
81. Labor unions, unspecified.
82. Stateless seamen, nationality of seamen.
83. Seamen: safety and welfare.
84. Seamen: training and education.
91. Registration of ships, other than "genuine link."
95. Establishment of new liner routes or services.

Appendix F

Interstate Conflicts 1945-1968

Indonesian	November 10, 1945 to October 15, 1946.
Indochinese	December 1, 1945 to June 1, 1954.
Madagascan	March 29, 1947 to December 1, 1948.
First Kashmir	October 26, 1947 to January 1, 1949.
Palestine	May 15, 1948 to July 18, 1948 and
	October 22, 1948 to January 7, 1949.
Korean	June 24, 1950 to July 27, 1953.
Algerian	November 1, 1954 to March 17, 1962.
Tibetan	March 1, 1956 to March 22, 1959.
Russo-Hungarian	October 23, 1956 to November 14, 1956.
Sinai	October 31, 1956 to November 7, 1956.
Sino-Indian	October 20, 1962 to November 22, 1962.
Second Kashmir	August 4, 1965 to September 23, 1965.
Vietnam	February 1965 through 1968.
Arab-Israeli	June 5, 1967 to June 10, 1967.

Source: Data compiled by J. David Singer and supplied to Maurice A. East, who undertook further processing. Used here by permission of J. David Singer and Maurice A. East. (Vietnam War and Arab-Israeli War added to the data by the author.)

Appendix G

The UNCTAD Formal Grouping of States, As Adopted by the
UN General Assembly (RES. 1995-XIX) on December 30, 1964;
Used Here in Chapter 5 to Identify Main International
Lines of Rift

Group A

Afghanistan
Algeria
Burma
Burundi
Cambodia
Cameroun
Central African Rep.
Ceylon
Chad
China, Rep. of
Congo (Brazzaville)
Congo (Kinshasa)
Dahomey
Ethiopia
Gabon
Ghana
Guinea
India
Indonesia
Iran
Iraq
Israel (here in Group B)
Ivory Coast
Jordan
Kenya
Kuwait
Laos
Lebanon
Liberia
Libya
Malagasy

Malaysia
Mali
Mauritania
Mongolia
Morocco
Nepal
Niger
Nigeria
Pakistan
Philippines
Rep. of Korea
Rep. of Vietnam
Rwanda
Saudi Arabia
Senegal
Sierra Leone
Somalia
South Africa (here in Group B)
Sudan
Syria
Thailand
Togo
Tunisia
Uganda
UAR
United Rep. of Tanzania
Upper Volta
Western Samoa
Yemen
Yugoslavia (here in Group B)

Group B

Australia
Austria
Belgium
Canada
Cyprus (here in Group A)
Denmark
Finland
France
Germany/West
Greece
Holy See
Iceland
Ireland
Italy
Japan

Liechtenstein
Luxembourg
Monaco
Netherlands
New Zealand
Norway
Portugal
San Marino
Spain
Sweden
Switzerland
Turkey (here in Group A)
UK
USA

Group C

Argentina
Bolivia
Brazil
Chile
Colombia
Costa Rica
Cuba
Dominican Republic
Ecuador
El Salvador
Guatemala

Haiti
Honduras
Jamaica
Mexico
Nicaragua
Panama
Paraguay
Peru
Trinidad and Tobago
Uruguay
Venezuela

Group D

Albania
Bulgaria
Byelorussian S.S.R. (Not included)
Czechoslovakia
Hungary
Poland
Romania
Ukranian S.S.R. (Not included)
U.S.S.R.

Selected Bibliography

Selected Bibliography

A. Literature on Shipping
and International Economics

Alexandersson, Gunnar, and Nordström, Göran. WORLD SHIPPING: AN ECO-
NOMIC GEOGRAPHY OF PORTS AND SEABORNE TRADE. Stockholm:
Almquist & Wiksell, 1963.

Askvig, Kristen. "Oljeindustrien og den 'døde kanal.' " NORGES HANDELS OG
SJØFARTSTIDENDE: Årsnummer, 1968.

Boczek, Boleslaw A. FLAGS OF CONVENIENCE IN THE LIGHT OF INTER-
NATIONAL LAW. Cambridge, Mass.: Harvard University Press, 1962.

Budde, Egil. "From Dakotas to Jumbo Jets in the Service of Air Freight."
NORWEGIAN SHIPPING NEWS, no. 10 c, 1970.

"Diplomatic Adjustment by the Maritime Nations." DEPARTMENT OF STATE
BULLETIN, January 17, 1966, 54, pp. 78-85.

Economist Intelligence Unit, Ltd. OCEAN SHIPPING AND FREIGHT RATES,
AND DEVELOPING COUNTRIES. Geneva: United Nations. Conference on
Trade and Development (E/CONF. 46/27), January 28, 1964.

Frihagen, Arvid. LINJEKONFERANSER OG KARTELLOVGIVNING. Oslo:
Universitetsforlaget, 1963.

Henell, Olof. FLAG DISCRIMINATION: PURPOSES, MOTIVES AND ECO-
NOMIC CONSEQUENCES. Skrifter utgivna av Svenska Handelshögskolan, nr.
3. Helsinki: Söderström, 1956.

Høegh, Leif. I SKIPSFARTENS TJENESTE. Oslo: Gyldendal Norsk Forlag A/S,
1970.

Kindleberger, Charles P. FOREIGN TRADE AND THE NATIONAL ECON-
OMY. New Haven: Yale University Press, 1962.

Lawrence, Samuel A. UNITED STATES MERCHANT SHIPPING POLICIES
AND POLITICS. Washington, D.C.: The Brookings Institution, 1966

Marx, Daniel, Jr. INTERNATIONAL SHIPPING CARTELS. Princeton, N.J.:
Princeton University Press, 1953.

Nøgård, Leif. LINJEFARTEN OG DENS PROBLEMER. Bergen: Skipsfartsøkonomisk Institutt, 1965.

Patton, J.R., Jr., and Schornhorst, F.T. "Cargo Preference and Flag Discrimination in International Shipping—Actions and Reactions." GEORGE WASH-
INGTON LAW REVIEW, December 1965, pp. 257-287.

Peterson, Kaare. "Trends in Shipping 1945-1970." NORWEGIAN SHIPPING
NEWS, no. 10 c, 1970.

R.S. Platou A/S. "A Survey of the Dry Cargo Market 1945-1970." NOR-
WEGIAN SHIPPING NEWS, no. 10 c, 1970.

Sarangan, T.K. LINER SHIPPING IN INDIA'S OVERSEAS TRADE. New York:

United Nations. Conference on Trade and Development. Trade and Development Board. Committee on Shipping (TD/B/C.4/31), 1967.

Snider, Delbert. INTRODUCTION TO INTERNATIONAL ECONOMICS. 3rd ed. Homewood, Ill.: Richard C. Irwin, Inc., 1963.

Sturmey, S.G. BRITISH SHIPPING AND WORLD COMPETITION. London: The Athlone Press, 1962.

_____. "National Shipping Policies." JOURNAL OF INDUSTRIAL ECONOMICS, November 1965.

Svendsen, Arnljot S. "Shipping in the Countries of the Eastern Bloc." NORWEGIAN SHIPPING NEWS, no. 2, 1962.

_____. LINER CONFERENCES AND FREIGHT RATES. Bergen: Skipsfartsøkonomisk Institutt, 1957.

_____. TRENDS IN WORLD SEABORNE SHIPPING. Bergen: Skipsfartsøkonomisk Institutt, 1967.

_____. SANS OG USANS I SKIPSFARTSPOLITIKKEN. Småskrifter, no. 20, Bergen: Skipsfartsøkonomisk Institutt 1967.

Tresselt, Dag. THE WEST AFRICAN SHIPPING RANGE. New York: United Nations. Conference on Trade and Development. Trade and Development Board. Committee on Shipping (TD/B/C. 4/32), 1967.

_____. SHIPPING AND SHIPPING POLICY IN LATIN AMERICA. Småskrifter, no. 21. Bergen: Skipsfartsøkonomisk Institutt, 1967.

United Nations. Conference on Trade and Development. Trade and Development Board. Committee on Shipping. SHIPPING AND THE WORLD ECONOMY (TD/14), 1967.

_____. CONSULTATION IN SHIPPING (TD/B/C. 4/20/Rev. 1), 1968.

_____. TERMS OF SHIPMENT. Report by the UNCTAD Secretariat (TD/B/C. 4/36), December 13, 1968.

_____. FREIGHT MARKETS AND THE LEVEL AND STRUCTURE OF FREIGHT RATES. Report by the UNCTAD Secretariat (TD/B/C. 4/38), December 16, 1968.

_____. INTERNATIONAL TRANSOCEANIC TRANSPORT AND ECONOMIC DEVELOPMENT. Report by the UNCTAD Secretariat in Connection with Economic and Social Council Resolution 1372 (XLV) Concerning Activities of the United Nations System of Organizations in the Transport Field (TD/B/C. 4/46), January 6, 1969.

B. Literature on Interaction Analysis and Issue-Areas in the Study of International Politics

Alger, Chadwick. "Interaction in a Committee of the UN General Assembly." QUANTITATIVE INTERNATIONAL POLITICS. Edited by J. David Singer. New York: Collier-Macmillan Free Press, 1968.

_____. "Interaction and Negotiation in a Committee of the UN General Assembly." INTERNATIONAL POLITICS AND FOREIGN POLICY. 2nd ed. Edited by James N. Rosenau. New York: Collier-Macmillan Free Press, 1969 (hereinafter referred to as Rosenau II).

Bales, Robert F. "A Set of Categories for the Analysis of Small Group Interaction." HUMAN BEHAVIOR AND INTERNATIONAL POLITICS. Edited by J. David Singer. Chicago: Rand McNally, 1965.

Dahl, Robert A. WHO GOVERNS? New Haven: Yale University Press, 1961.

Deutsch, Karl W., and Singer, J. David. "Multipolar Power Systems and International Stability." Rosenau II.

McClelland, Charles A. "The Accute International Crisis." THE INTERNATIONAL SYSTEM: THEORETICAL ESSAYS. Edited by Klaus Knorr and Sidney Verba. Princeton, N.J.: Princeton University Press, 1961.

_____. "Action Structures and Communication in Two International Crises." Rosenau II.

_____. THEORY AND THE INTERNATIONAL SYSTEM. New York: Macmillan, 1966.

_____. "Comments on Meanings and Rationales in the WEIS Category System." University of Southern California. Department of International Relations, December 1967. (Mimeographed.)

_____. "Access to Berlin: The Quantity and Variety of Events." QUANTITATIVE INTERNATIONAL POLITICS. Edited by J. David Singer. New York: Collier-Macmillan Free Press, 1968.

_____, and Hoggard, Gary D. "Conflict Patterns in the Interactions Among Nations." Rosenau II.

Martin, Wayne R., and Young, Robert A. "World Event/Interaction Survey (WEIS) Program Rules and Instructions." University of Southern California. Department of International Relations, January 1968. (Mimeographed.)

Pruitt, Dean G. "Stability and Sudden Change in Interpersonal and International Affairs." Rosenau II.

Rosenau, James N. "The Functioning of International Systems," BACKGROUND, November 1963.

_____. "Pre-Theories and Theories of Foreign Policy." APPROACHES TO COMPARATIVE AND INTERNATIONAL POLITICS. Edited by R. Barry Farrell. Evanston, Ill.: Northwestern University Press, 1966.

_____. "Foreign Policy as an Issue-Area." DOMESTIC SOURCES OF FOREIGN POLICY. Edited by James N. Rosenau. New York: Collier-Macmillan Free Press 1967.

Singer, J. David. "The Level-of-Analysis Problem in International Relations." THE INTERNATIONAL SYSTEM: THEORETICAL ESSAYS. Edited by Klaus Knorr and Sidney Verba. Princeton, N.J.: Princeton University Press, 1961.

_____, and Small, Melvin. "Alliance Aggregation and the Onset of War,

1815-1945." QUANTITATIVE INTERNATIONAL POLITICS. Edited by J. David Singer. New York: Collier-Macmillan Free Press, 1968.

University of Southern California. Department of International Relations. "World Event/Interaction Survey Handbook and Codebook." Technical Report no. 1. World Event/Interaction Survey. University of Southern California, January 1969. (Mimeographed.)

C. General Methodological References

Alker, Hayward R. MATHEMATICS AND POLITICS. New York: Macmillan, 1965.

Benson, Oliver. POLITICAL SCIENCE LABORATORY. Columbus, Ohio: Charles E. Merrill Publishing Co., 1969.

Blalock, Hubert M. SOCIAL STATISTICS. New York: McGraw-Hill, 1960.

Hellevik, Ottar. FORSKNINGSMETODE I SOSIOLOGI OG STATSVITENS-KAP. Oslo: Universitetsforlaget, 1971.

Jacobson, Harold K. "Deriving Data from Delegates to International Assemblies." INTERNATIONAL ORGANIZATION, vol. 21, 1967, pp. 592-613.

Janda, Kenneth. DATA PROCESSING. APPLICATIONS TO POLITICAL RESEARCH. Evanston, Ill.: Northwestern University Press, 1965.

Johnston, J. ECONOMETRIC METHODS. New York: McGraw-Hill, 1963.

Lininger, Charles, and Warwick, Donald. "Introduction to Survey Research." University of Michigan. Survey Research Center. No date. (Mimeographed.)

Miles, Edward. "The Logistics of Interviewing in International Organizations." INTERNATIONAL ORGANIZATION, vol. 24, 1970, pp. 361-370.

Selltiz, Claire; Jahoda, Marie; Deutsch, Morton; and Cook, Stuart W. RESEARCH METHODS IN SOCIAL RELATIONS. Revised one-volume edition. New York: Holt, Rinehart and Winston, 1959.

Zetterberg, Hans L. ON THEORY AND VERIFICATION IN SOCIOLOGY. 3rd ed. Totowa, N.J.: The Bedminster Press, 1965.

D. Sources of Quantified Data

Bridges, Roland, ed. CRONER'S WORLD DIRECTORY OF FREIGHT CONFERENCES; A GUIDE TO FREIGHT CONFERENCES THROUGHOUT THE WORLD, WITH AREAS, FREIGHT TERMS, REBATE PERIODS, SECRETARIES AND MEMBERS. 4th ed. New Malden, England: Croner Publications, 1965, monthly amendment service updated to June 1968.

East, Maurice A. "Stratification and International Politics: An Empirical Study Employing the International Systems Approach." Unpublished Ph.D. dissertation, Princeton University, 1969.

Fearnley & Egers Chartering Co. Ltd. TRADES OF WORLD BULK CARRIERS. Oslo: Fearnley & Egers Chartering Co. Ltd., 1961-1969.

Lloyd's Register of Shipping. LIST OF SHIPOWNERS. London: Lloyd's Register of Shipping, selected years.

NEW YORK TIMES INDEX, 1946-1968.

NORGES HANDELS OG SJØFARTSTIDENDE, January 1, 1946 to December 31, 1968.

Singer, J. David, and Small, Melvin. "Formal Alliances 1815-1965: An Extension of the Basic Data." JOURNAL OF PEACE RESEARCH, no. 3, 1969.

United Nations. Conference on Trade and Development. Trade and Development Board. TERMS OF REFERENCE AND RULES OF PROCEDURE OF THE COMMITTEE ON SHIPPING (TD/B/64/Rev. 1), 1965.

_____. Committee on Shipping. PROVISIONAL LIST OF PARTICIPANTS. (TD/B/C. 4 (III9/Misc. 1/Rev. 1), April 14, 1969.

_____. SUMMARY RECORDS (TD/B/C. 4/SR. 1-55), 1965-1969.

_____. General Assembly Resolution 1995-XIX, December 30, 1964.

_____. Statistical Office. Department of Economic and Social Affairs. STATISTICAL YEARBOOK. New York: United Nations, 1948-. (Selected years.)

YEARBOOK OF SCANDINAVIAN SHIPOWNERS. Oslo: Selvig's Publishing House, 1969.

Index

Index

Actor states, 100, Tables 5-5, 5-6, 5-7, 5-8, Chap. 5, n. 19; Table 7-1
Africa, 31, 33, 79, 80, 126, 130: rift group, 101; region, 30, Chap. 3, n. 1
Albania, 30
Alexandersson, Gunnar, 33
Alger, Chadwick, 11
Algeria, 45, 77
Alker, Hayward R., 16
Allied Control Council, 113
Almond, Gabriel A., 110
Analysis levels, 23, Chap. 2, n. 51; 157, 159
Anglo-Iranian Oil Company, Chap. 3, n. 2
Antilles (Netherlands), 49
Arab-Israeli Six-Day War (1967), 45, 77, 82, 96, 126
Arab states, 79: and Israel, 45, 76, 77, 82; and oil, 31, 43, 46; region, Chap. 3, n. 1
Aramco tap-line, 45, Chap. 3, n. 29
Argentina, 50, 78, 110
Asia region, 30, Chap. 3, n. 1; and rift group, 101; and seaborne trade, 31, 33, 49, 50, Chap. 3, n. 2; and shipping issues, 79, 80
Australia, 34, 49, 50, 51, 119
Autocorrelation, 93
Azar, Edward, 10, 13

Balance of payments, 40, Chap. 3, n. 21
Balassa, Bela A., 40
Bales, Robert F., 11
Baltic Shipping Exchange (London), 3, 5, Chap. 1, n. 13
Barley, 50
Bauxite, 49
Berlin blockade (1948), 12, 13, 76
Biafra War (1967-68), 77, 130
Blockades and embargoes, 45, 46, 76-77, Chap. 4, n. 6; 114, 115, 118, 123, 130
Bolivia, 118
Brazil, 49, 50, 78, 79, 129
Bulgaria, 33
Bulk trades, 40-41, 46-51. *See also* Tramping

Burma, 50

CIF (cost, insurance, freight), 38-39
COPDAB. *See* Conflict and Peace Data Bank
CREON, 10, 13
Canada, 1, 30, 45, 49, 50, 51, 114, 119
Cape of Good Hope, 45
Cargo liners. *See* Liner services
Cargo-preference policy, 50, 55, Chap. 4, n. 9. *See also* Flag discrimination; Cargo reservation
Cargo reservation, 43, 51, 55, 63, Chap. 3, n. 64, 102; 118. *See also* Flag discrimination; Regional cargo reservation
Caribbean area, 30, 42, 43, 45, Chap. 3, n. 26, 28
Carrying capacity. *See* Seaborne trade, Tonnage
Cartels, 2, 79-80
Central America 30, 31, 41, Chap. 3, n. 1
Ceylon, 50
Charters, 3, 4. *See also* Tramping
Chile, 78, 118
China-Taiwan "cold war" (1949-68), 77
China-USSR "cold war" (1960-68), 77
Chinese Civil War (1946-49), 76
China, 30, 76, 77, 110, 114, 115, 118
China, Nationalist. *See* Taiwan
Civil war, 76, 114, 130
Coal, 47, 48-49, 50, 51
"Cold war," 16, 45, 77
Committee on Shipping (UNCTAD), 73, 79, 80-81, 129, 133
"Common carriers," 62-64
Communist countries, 30, 50, Chap. 3, n. 39; 62, 77, 101, 114, 115
Conferences, 81, 83
Conflict and Peace Data Bank (COPDAB), 10, 13
Conflict, nonviolent, 159-60
Conflict patterns, classification of, 158-59, Table 7-1

213

About the Author

Olav Knudsen is assistant professor of International Relations at the Institute of Political Science, University of Oslo. He did undergraduate studies at the University of Oslo and the University of Denver, receiving the M.A. and Ph.D. from the University of Denver in 1969 and 1972. Dr. Knudsen has held teaching positions at Temple Buell College in Denver as well as the University of Oslo and was a Woodrow Wilson Dissertation Fellow in 1969–1970. Dr. Knudsen is currently continuing research on the political aspects of international shipping.